LUSITANIA

Tragedy or War Crime?

By the same author

Illiam Done: Patriot or Traitor?
The Life, Death and Legacy of William Christian

The Liberation of Sylvia Plath's Ariel:
Psychosemantics and a Glass Sarcophagus

Practical Manx: A Grammar of Manx Gaelic

LUSITANIA

Tragedy or War Crime?

JENNIFER KEWLEY DRASKAU

PETER OWEN
LONDON AND CHICAGO

PETER OWEN PUBLISHERS
81 Ridge Road, London N8 9NP

Peter Owen books are distributed in the USA and Canada by
Independent Publishers Group/Trafalgar Square
814 North Franklin Street, Chicago, IL 60610, USA

First published in Great Britain 2015 by Peter Owen Publishers

PAPERBACK ISBN 978-0-7206-1428-2
EPUB ISBN 978-0-7206-1739-9
MOBIPOCKET ISBN 978-0-7206-1740-5
PDF ISBN 978-0-7206-1741-2

A catalogue record for this book is available
from the British Library

Printed and bound in the UK by
CPI Group (UK) Ltd, Croydon, CR0 4YY

Contents

List of Illustrations 7

Introduction 9

ONE: The Greyhound of the Seas 13

TWO: The Arms Race and the War at Sea 21

THREE: In the USA: Sabotage, Espionage and Propaganda 39

FOUR: Sailing 63

FIVE: *U-20* 93

SIX: Friday, 7 May 1915 109

SEVEN: Disaster 123

EIGHT: Rescue 161

NINE: 'A Damned Dirty Business' 171

TEN: Causes and Conspiracy 185

Epilogue 205

Notes 219

Bibliography 227

Index 231

Illustrations

Between pages 128 and 129

The *Lusitania* being launched at Clydebank on 7 June 1906 (© *Crown Copyright. IWM.*)

A postcard showing the *Lusitania*, when launched the largest ocean liner in existence

A poster created by the Cunard Line proudly advertising the *Lusitania* and her sister ship the *Mauretania*, 'the largest, finest and fastest ships in the world'

The 32,000-ton *Lusitania* at sea (*George Grantham Bain Collection, US Library of Congress*)

The *Lusitania*'s captain, William Turner

The warning notice inserted by the Imperial German Embassy in US newspapers before the last sailing of the *Lusitania* (© *Crown Copyright. IWM.*)

An artist's impression of the sinking of the *Lusitania* on 7 May 1915 off the coast of Ireland

A lifebelt salvaged from the floating remains of the liner (© *Crown Copyright. IWM.*)

The eighteen-ton Manx fishing-boat the *Wanderer*; its crew saved 160 lives after the *Lusitania* sank (*Courtesy of Manx National Heritage*)

The *Wanderer* and its crew at its mooring, Peel, Isle of Man (*Courtesy of The Leece Museum, Peel, Isle of Man*)

The crew of the *Wanderer*, including its skipper, William Ball, wearing the medals they received for the rescue of the *Lusitania*'s passengers (*Courtesy of The Leece Museum, Peel, Isle of Man*)

One of the medals received by the *Wanderer*'s seven-man crew for their role in saving lives, presented on the Isle of Man's national day in July 1915 (*Courtesy of Manx National Heritage*)

Two British recruitment posters inspired by the torpedoing of the *Lusitania* (© *Crown Copyright. IWM.*)

An unofficial postage stamp commemorating the sinking of the ship

A poster published by the Central Council for the Organisation of Recruiting in Ireland that urged Irishmen to avenge the sinking of the *Lusitania* by joining up to fight (© *Crown Copyright. IWM.*)

Introduction

On 21 September 1914 Winston Churchill, First Lord of the Admiralty, in Liverpool on a recruiting drive, was said to have visited the *Lusitania* where she lay in dry dock undergoing modifications to equip her for wartime service. Accompanying him was Cunard's naval architect, Leonard Peskett. The two men discussed the ship's bulkhead arrangements. Peskett said, 'The Navy has nothing like her!' to which Churchill replied, 'We have. To me she is just another 45,000 tons of livebait!'[1]

The term 'livebait' was in the Zeitgeist. It was the nickname given to the big, old and obsolescent warships, 'the Live Bait Squadron', which found themselves in a new kind of warfare, waged by small, deadly underwater vessels whose stealthy attack would claim many lives. The armoured cruisers had little defence against these vessels, and the passenger liner *Lusitania* had none at all. In the space of little over an hour on the morning of 22 September 1914 the Royal Navy suffered one of the worst disasters in its history. Three armoured cruisers, HMS *Aboukir*, HMS *Cressy* and HMS *Hogue*, were sunk with the loss of more than 1,450 lives. Their nemesis, *U-9*, a small German submarine with a crew of fewer than thirty men, slipped away without a scratch. The cruisers were just ten years old but, because of the rapid pace of technological advances, were already outdated, slow and inadequately armed. Their task was to patrol the dangerous southern part of the North Sea. On 18 September Churchill had ordered that the ships 'ought not to continue on this beat. The risks to such ships is not justified by any service they can render.' For reasons of internal Admiralty politics this order was never enacted.[2] The disaster revolutionized maritime warfare and prepared the way for maritime conflict over the next four years. It also explains, to some extent, why the RMS *Lusitania*'s designated naval escort, another ancient warship, HMS *Juno*, was withdrawn by the Admiralty when submarine activity off the coast of Ireland intensified on 6 May 1915.

Was the *Lusitania* being converted for war work in September? The log of her commander at the time, Captain Dow, indicates that the ship was in Liverpool for routine maintenance. A refit would have taken a considerable time and was unlikely to have been undertaken in Liverpool. If Churchill did make the remark, it was probably out of a simple concern for the ship's safety. The grandson of Captain Dow, Michael Dow, adds that both his grandfather's brothers attended the subsequent official inquiry conducted by Lord Mersey into the loss of the liner and found nothing sinister or questionable at that time. 'It was wartime and, to those of us who are now accustomed to negligence claims in the law courts, would not seem unusual. Yet there are those who still believe there was a government-led cover-up when there was really nothing to cover up.'[3]

Was the *Lusitania* in Liverpool at all on that date? Jim Kalafus, researcher and authority on the ship, comments that she had been out of service for over a month prior to that date, having experienced problems with her turbines on her crossing from New York on 4 August, which took eight full days, making it her slowest crossing ever. Subsequent repairs were probably undertaken in order to restore the vessel's normal speed. The ship sailed for New York again on 12 September, arriving on schedule on the 18th. She sailed again from New York on 23 September. If these details are correct, it is impossible that the ship was in dry dock in Liverpool on the 21st, the date on which Churchill ostensibly made his 'livebait' comment.[4]

Kalafus quotes an article from a New York newspaper confirming these dates, saying, 'The war at sea affected the lives of all the maritime nations, even the smallest.'

B.E. Sargeaunt, Secretary-General and Treasurer of the Isle of Man, has written:

> There are not many parts of the British Isles in which the reality of the war was more vividly reflected than in the Isle of Man. The frequent interruption of the steamer communication with the Mainland in consequence of enemy submarine activity, the sound of guns at sea, the darkness of the streets as a result of the Extinction of Lights Order, the frequent landing in the Island of the crews of torpedoed vessels, and the recovery from the sea of bodies washed up around the coast, all helped to bring home to the residents of the Isle of Man the awfulness of the war. Coupled with these conditions, the continuous movement of prisoners of

> war and troops to and from the Island, the disappearance of the travelling public, who feared to make the sea passage in face of mines and submarines, and the numerous burials of sailors, soldiers, and prisoners of war in the graveyards of the Island, assisted in impressing the Manx public with the reality of the war. The crew of the first vessel to be sunk by a submarine in the Irish Sea was brought into Douglas on 30th January, 1915.The Harbour Master at Douglas was always most energetic in providing for the comfort of shipwrecked crews brought into Douglas.[5]

On the weatherbeaten north-west coast of the Isle of Man, on Monday 15 March 1915 twenty-year-old Stanley Ball and his father set off on foot from their cottage carrying everything they would need for the next fifteen weeks at sea. At the neighbouring village of Ballaugh they would board the steam train for the western port of Peel where they would meet up with the rest of the crew – William Gell from Ramsey, and the four Peel men, Thomas Woods, Robert Watterson, Harry Costain and John MacDonald – the last two mere teenagers. Together they made up the crew of Mr Charles Morrison's eighteen-ton lugger *Wanderer,* an ordinary Manx fishing boat soon to take her place in history.

Wealthy Charles Morrison had had *Wanderer* built in 1881 at the shipyard of Henry Graves in Peel, on the mouth of the River Neb; 55 feet long, with a beam of over 15 feet, she carried a full set of sails for a lugger – jib sail, foresail, mainsail, topsail and mizzen sail. A steam capstan winch sat on the foredeck to starboard. This was fed by a coal-fired boiler in the crew's after-cabin, which also had bunks for eight men and a cook stove. The *Wanderer* was steered by rudder-tiller but had no engine. The cabin, warmed by the steam pipes connecting the boiler to the winch, was a cosy refuge after a cold night's fishing. Each fishing operation involved shooting and hauling in over three miles' length of net. Stanley knew no other life than mackerel fishing, waiting each evening for the shoals to rise, then toiling through the night, shooting and hauling nets till break of day.

When Stanley and his father, Skipper William Ball, reached Ballaugh, the elder man exclaimed that they appeared to have reached the station at the same time as they had left the cottage. His wife had set the clock an hour fast to ensure the men would not miss their train.[6]

At Peel harbour the crew assembled and loaded the *Wanderer* with nets, 'mollags' (inflated sheepskins used as floats), the first-aid chest and a precious bottle of spirits for medicinal purposes. These last two items would prove unexpectedly useful.

Slipping out with the tide beneath the crumbling red sandstone walls of the ancient castle, they set sail for the fishing grounds off Kinsale in southern Ireland; just one nickey with her seven-man crew among the 1,700 Manxmen and boys whose lives were bound to the sea. But these men would return as heroes. A few weeks later their largely unsung deeds would affect the lives of hundreds of strangers in a maritime disaster that would shake the world and change the path of history, although its mysterious circumstances still form the basis of impassioned debate after a century.

The sinking of the RMS *Lusitania* off the Old Head of Kinsale on Friday 7 May 1915 was the single greatest shipwreck tragedy in Irish waters. Over 1,200 men, women and children died, including three German stowaways who had been discovered and locked up as suspected spies and whose names did not appear on any list.

The attack was both an international disaster and an outrage. When the suspicion began to arise that the Admiralty's mismanagement and possible negligence bore some responsibility for the disaster, there was an indecent scurry for a cover-up. This was far from successful. Conspiracy theories continued to flourish. Many reputations were tainted; some, such as those of the *Lusitania*'s commander, Captain Turner, deliberately. This murky shadow-play stood out in stark contrast to the heroism of the rescuers and to the fate of many of those unfortunates on board the stricken liner.

ONE

The Greyhound of the Seas

The *Lusitania*, famed for her speed, was known as the 'Greyhound of the Seas'. She was the jewel in the crown of the Cunard shipping line. Not only, albeit for a short time, the world's largest vessel, the *Lusitania* was more than just a ship; she was a challenging workplace, a floating five-star hotel catering to the world's most demanding and pampered travelling public. She was a vehicle for dreams – the dreams of the emigrant, the homesick, the ambitious, the world-weary. And yet she was more: she was the repository of British national pride, a highly politicized international symbol.

When news of her tragic loss struck a horrified world, conspiracy theorists claimed a more sinister significance for the great ship. They declared that she was a pawn, deliberately sacrificed in the brutal strategies of conflict, her loss and the attendant human tragedy collateral damage, her crew and passengers a human shield in the desperate game plan of ruthless warmongers. Their cynical suspicions were generated by an awareness of the 'special relationship' that existed between the *Lusitania*'s owners, Cunard, and the British government. This association dated from 1839 and had begun as a mutually beneficial business relationship, although, ultimately, Cunard would find the tentacles of officialdom increasingly invasive. The company owed its original success to the British Admiralty's decision to hand over the vital Atlantic mail service to a private steamship company. An announcement appeared in *The Times* of London: 'Steam vessels required for conveying Her Majesty's Mails and Dispatches between England and Halifax, Nova Scotia, and also between England, Halifax and New York.'

This issue of *The Times* did not reach Halifax, Nova Scotia, until two weeks after the time limit for tender had passed. None the less, as soon as it arrived it immediately attracted the attention of one canny Nova Scotian: Sam Cunard, the son of a Halifax carpenter, who was an ambitious young man with stellar aspirations. Cunard knew an opportunity when he smelled one. He left for England at once, hell-bent on winning the lucrative contract, even though the date had passed and, as his unsuccessful competitors would point out with chagrin, he was as yet not in possession of a single vessel.

Cunard was well aware that his pitch would not be easy. He knew he needed to convince the British authorities of his ability to provide a reliable, regular, year-round service. Two rival companies had already submitted their tenders. Despite these obstacles, Cunard forged ahead undeterred. His first step was to seek out and enlist the services of a shipbuilder of genius, Robert Napier, the great Scottish expert in marine steam engines. By 18 March 1839 Cunard had signed a contract with Napier for three large steamships.

Napier had recognized that the building of these great Atlantic steamers potentially represented his own big break. The Cunard Line's distinctive vermilion funnels banded with black were his design; it had already been used in other ships powered by his engines, including the PS *Menai* in 1830.

On 4 May 1839, Cunard's arguments having convinced the Admiralty, the mail contract was signed and sealed; now all Cunard needed was the necessary injection of capital in order to fulfil it. The British and North American Royal Mail Steam Packet Company was formed; the name was soon shortened to 'Mr Cunard's Company' or 'Cunard's'. Originally, the western destination for the sailings was to have been Halifax, Nova Scotia, but the contract was amended, making Boston, Massachusetts, the North American base. By 1848, in the era that saw the end of the great sailing ships and the new dominance of steam, Cunard's vessels were sailing to New York.

Cunard's contract with the Admiralty proved as profitable as he had hoped, and his fleet expanded and prospered as the government subsidies rolled in, but the relationship began to suffer as the arrangement became increasingly restrictive. The official contract had, predictably, been awarded on certain conditions that grew increasingly irksome as time went on. Among the terms stipulated in the contract, Cunard's ships were to be made available for use by the Admiralty for the purposes of training naval personnel. Moreover, the Admiralty insisted that a naval officer must always be aboard on every sailing in order to 'safeguard the mails'. Furthermore, not only must all Cunard vessels be built to Admiralty specifications, they must also be equipped to mount guns in the event of war or national emergency. Accordingly, when the Crimean War broke out in 1854, Cunard fulfilled his contractual obligation, turning over his steamships, fully equipped, to transport troops to the front. His valuable contribution to the war was duly noted, and in March 1859 he was knighted.

After Sam Cunard's death in 1865 the Admiralty subsidies continued to pour in and the company continued to expand. But on the international political scene great changes were afoot; they would impact on the Cunard Line and ultimately decide the fate of the *Lusitania*.

The 'Blue Riband' prize was an unofficial accolade awarded to the passenger liner crossing the Atlantic on regular service with the fastest average speed. Its prestige value was enormous. It was also profitable, since it led to increased passenger bookings.

Historically, British shipping lines, notably Cunard, had dominated the transatlantic race. Their first serious rival was the American-owned Collins Line, which was heavily subsidized by the US government, but after Collins suffered various setbacks and a series of catastrophes Cunard was in a position to regain the ascendancy.

Then, in the 1890s, a new threat to British dominance arose from an unexpected quarter. Up to this point the recently unified Germany, whose shipbuilding industry was in its infancy, had hardly been a serious contender in terms of international maritime competition. Hence, the British shipping industry was rocked to its foundations when Germany seemed to threaten British interests with an unforeseen leap forward – namely, the building of four fast new state-of-the-art luxury liners, nicknamed the 'four flyers'. Since the mid-1850s the German companies Hamburg-Amerika and Norddeutscher Lloyd had been running a conservative and respectable packet-and-passenger service to New York catering to the increasing numbers of immigrants from Europe to the USA. But leading lights in German shipbuilding, men such as Robert Zimmermann, had – in common with students of the industry from many other countries – spent years sitting at the feet of British masters, absorbing skills and expertise at the shipyards of Jarrow, Belfast, Tyneside and the Clyde.

Few outside Germany had seen it coming. At the time, neither Germany nor her workmanlike but essentially modest Atlantic service were taken seriously as a threat or rival by the great shipping lines of the Atlantic. But after the Franco-Prussian War the ambitions of the emerging Germany, which prior to the efforts of Wilhelm I of Prussia and Otto von

Bismarck had been a jumble of warring sub-states, were beginning to take wing. The new managing director at Norddeutscher Lloyd, Johann Lohmann, realized that the shipping line's policy needed rethinking and updating. Aware of the promotional value of the coveted and prestigious Blue Riband award, he was determined to win it and receive the kudos and the resultant improved business he anticipated that this would bring in its train. In 1880 he ordered twelve new ships. They were all to be built at British yards, as Germany still lacked the capacity. The emphasis was to be on comfort and elegance. The new liners would offer not only speed and safety but extraordinary comfort and luxury in a bid to attract passengers, especially wealthy 'cabin-class' ones. To this end Lohmann engaged the services of Germany's foremost interior designer, Johannes Poppe.

Poppe seized the opportunity to create an ostentatious baroque revival in keeping with Wilhelmine pretensions: the spirit of Germany, flexing her muscles on the international scene, fuelled by the monstrous ambitions of her Kaiser, found reflection in Poppe's overwrought interiors featuring pillars, balustrades, cherubs, statuary, tapestries, gilding and a rash of flattering portraits of the Imperial Family.

Wilhelm II, haunted by his own antithetical attitude towards his mother's country, had specifically tasked Norddeutscher Lloyd with building up a maritime power that would surpass Britain's own. Initially the contest focused on merchant vessels; however, on the advice of the Kaiser's newly appointed Secretary of the Navy, the redoubtable Admiral Alfred von Tirpitz, the intense shipbuilding rivalry would soon apply, with heavy consequences, to the war fleet as well.

In 1897, the *Kaiser Wilhelm der Grosse*, owned and operated by Norddeutscher Lloyd, snatched the coveted Blue Riband; she was the first liner to have four funnels. After the resounding success of her maiden voyage she attracted large numbers of passengers dazzled by her triumph and reassured by her impressive size. People began to refuse to sail in vessels that did not have four funnels. A few years later Hamburg-Amerika's slightly larger *Deutschland* pushed the record speed up to 24 knots. If Britain was to succeed wresting back dominance of the Atlantic crossing from Germany and America, clearly the acquisition of new steamers was essential.

By the mid nineteenth century, and especially after the establishment of the German Empire in 1871, the other European powers, including flourishing Victorian Britain, found themselves obliged to confront the rising challenge from Germany. She had become a populous polity whose industrialization of her coal, steel, iron and textile industries was gaining ground both economically and politically. At her head was the King of Prussia, Wilhelm II, who became Kaiser in 1888. The devastation that would afflict Europe in the years after 1914 was in no small way attributable to the conflicting strands of Kaiser Wilhelm II's complex personality.

Wilhelm combined a huge but vulnerable ego with exaggerated sensitivity where his own person was concerned. He once complained to King Victor-Emmanuel of Italy, 'In all the long years of my reign my colleagues, the Monarchs of Europe, have paid no attention to what I have to say.'

Unstable, desperate for respect, erratic and hysterical, with flashes of brilliance and longer periods of depression, Wilhelm would ensure that the situation would change. He would have the attention he craved. His aggressive pursuit of aggrandizement brought him into conflict with Otto von Bismarck, Minister President of Prussia, who, after the harsh process of German unification, had brought stability to the international scene by maintaining the balance of power. For historian Eric Hobsbawm, Bismarck 'remained undisputed world champion at the game of multilateral diplomatic chess for almost twenty years after 1871', devoting himself exclusively, and successfully, to maintaining peace between the powers.[1] In 1890 Wilhelm dismissed Bismarck and dismantled the Bismarckian alliance system that had helped to maintain peace.

Besides Germany, British shipping lines had another dangerous rival. In 1901 the American financier J. Pierpoint Morgan formed the International Mercantile Marine Company (IMM) with the express aim of creating a monopoly on the North Atlantic passenger route. He had already acquired a consortium that included the America Line, Dominion Line, Red Star Line and Holland-Amerika Line. In 1902 Morgan managed to acquire the famous White Star Line, too. White Star ships still flew the Union Jack, but they were US-owned, and the American magnate's voracious gaze would soon turn to Cunard. Lord Inverclyde, grandson of Samuel Cunard's original partner George Burns, was said to demonstrate astute business acumen and a strong character; he was, in the face of this challenge, credited with saving Cunard from absorption and obscurity.[2]

The British government watched the rise of the IMM mega-consortium with ill-concealed dismay. When the IMM made an offer for Cunard, it was declined, but Cunard still lacked the resources to finance the building of new ships. If Cunard was to see off the opposition from both Germany and America, it desperately needed to expand and modernize its fleet. Lord Inverclyde, the Chairman of Cunard, applied to the British government for financial assistance. The government was reluctant to see the British shipping industry collapse and to suffer the attendant loss of prestige. Conscious of growing international tensions, it was only too aware, moreover, that it needed a reserve of vessels it could call upon for a variety of maritime services in the event of war. The government's response to Cunard's application was sufficient funding to enable the shipping company to commission two new ships. These great liners would dazzle the world and re-establish British maritime supremacy. They would be larger, faster and more outrageously luxurious than any vessels the world had ever seen.

The terms of the agreement between Cunard and the British government were said to be as onerous for both parties as they were prolix. For Cunard, the contract meant increased subsidies and a loan from the government of the £2,600,000 needed to build the two new ships at the favourable rate of only 2.75 per cent, to be repaid over twenty years. The giant steamships would receive an annual operating subsidy of £75,000 each, plus a mail contract of £68,000.

A public copy of the agreement is open to inspection in the Cunard archives at the Sydney Jones Library within Liverpool University. The company's obligations were detailed and manifold, including stipulations that the vessels were to be built 'with all dispatch', and were to be capable of speeds of 24–25 knots an hour in moderate weather.

Cunard also prepared a lengthy memorandum for the company, which included the following clauses and stipulations.

All plans and specifications were to be submitted to the Admiralty before any building work commenced and were to be modified if the Admiralty so requested within one month. The construction was to be approved by an inspector whose appointment was to be agreed upon by the Admiralty and the company, at their joint expense. During the term of the agreement the entire Cunard fleet was always to be at the disposal of the Admiralty for hire or purchase. The Admiralty was to be afforded every facility for placing fittings in the event that the vessels were to be taken up as armed cruisers.[3] And the company was to remain British.

Swan Hunter and Wigham Richardson would build the *Mauretania*. The Clydebank shipyard of John Brown and Company would build the

Mauretania's sister ship. Two years were spent in perfecting the design of the two monster liners. The basic requirement was their ability to maintain an average speed of 25 knots. It was estimated that this would require a daily coal consumption of 1,000 tons at full power. This meant that there would have to be coal bunkers holding 6,000 tons or more.

On 7 June 1906, at John Brown's shipyard on the Clyde, Lord Inverclyde laid the first rivet on the keel plates of the *Lusitania*. At 12.30 in the afternoon Lady Inverclyde named the new vessel 'Lusitania', the name given by the Romans to their province now known as Portugal. The launch of the *Lusitania* was attended by 600 guests, with thousands more turning up uninvited to watch the ceremony. The huge ship was then moved to the fitting-out berth, where she would spend the next year, being completed.

Her design included, in accordance with the Admiralty contract, a secret compartment for guns and ammunition so that she could become an armed cruiser if required in the event of war. It should have been clear from the outset that, in the case of the handful of ocean-going monster vessels like the *Lusitania*, this scheme was over-ambitious and ill-thought-out and would be difficult to put into practice. These enormous ships were quite unsuited to the task, by virtue of their sheer size, their prohibitive fuel consumption – 910 tons daily or 37.6 tons an hour – and the fact that few ports were logistically capable of catering to their requirements in respect of supplying and refuelling. A further argument against their potential effectiveness in the event of war was the ease with which their towering silhouettes and four funnels could be recognized by an enemy. Moreover, their lack of defensive armour left them, like other surface vessels, fatally vulnerable to attack by the latest development in maritime weaponry, the submarine.

As it transpired, the *Lusitania* was never pressed into military service, although the other two members of the grand ocean-going trio, *Mauretania* and *Aquitania*, were. The *Lusitania* spent the whole of August 1906 in John Brown's shipyard undergoing modification. Her two-day formal shakedown trials had revealed a violent twofold vibration problem: the outer propellers were affected by the wake of the inner ones, and the unprecedented high speed at which her propellers rotated caused unacceptable levels of resonance of her framework. Extensive bracing and additional supporting structures needed to be installed, and the whole of the second-class section required refitting. In order to complete these improvements, all the second-class accommodation in the stern had to be gutted. When these complex modifications had been completed, Cunard then accepted the *Lusitania*.

At the ship's launch, the Chairman of John Brown and Company declared, 'There is not a Briton anywhere who ought not to feel proud that this launch has placed Great Britain firmly at the forefront of marine architecture.' The conditions that governed the signing of the substantial financial agreement that had permitted the *Lusitania* and the *Mauretania* to be built in the first place had effectively placed the company at the disposition of the Admiralty. Consequently, the company was now under the control of the British government.

British policy, stated in the Naval Defence Act of 1889, was to maintain a navy superior to Britain's two largest rivals combined. The Admiralty had estimated that by 1906 the rapidly expanding German navy would be the world's second largest, and its prophecy was fulfilled. It was concluded in 1906 that Germany was now Britain's one possible naval rival and potential adversary. Germany had been slow to embrace the latest weapon in the maritime armoury, but in December 1906 the Imperial Naval Command took delivery, from Krupp's Germania yard in Kiel, of *U-1*, Germany's very first submarine.

TWO

The Arms Race and the War at Sea

The *Lusitania* could not have been built without the substantial financial support of the British authorities. Such assistance did not come without strings attached. The *Lusitania* and *Mauretania* had been commissioned and designed specifically as armed auxiliary cruisers, the entire cost being met by the Admiralty, who also provided Cunard with an annual operating subsidy of £75,000 per ship. Consequently, when war broke out in 1914 the *Lusitania* was automatically placed on the acquisitions list as an armed merchant cruiser.

Her bulkhead design followed that of warships, with longitudinal bulkheads creating coal bunkers along the sides of the ship. Modern analysis has identified this as a weakness, because the construction compromised the *Lusitania*'s buoyancy and stability. It made the ship prone to the rapid development of a list when it suffered underwater damage. The problem was exacerbated by the decision to build a superstructure nine decks high when the ship's beam was comparatively narrow at 87 feet. The Royal Navy itself had recognized the vulnerability of the longitudinal bulkhead design in the construction of warships; for this reason a general order was issued forbidding cruisers to enter danger zones unescorted. In the merchant fleet, as hostilities intensified the number of fare-paying passengers declined, and the cost of running the giant ships began to prove crippling.

In the course of the winter of 1914–15 many ocean-going liners were mothballed. The *Lusitania* did remain in commercial service, but Cunard was obliged to introduce economy measures in a bid to curb outgoings on manpower and fuel. Of the ship's twenty-five boilers only nineteen would be functioning. Her Number 4 boiler room would be put out of operation. The effect was to reduce the ship's top speed from 25 knots (46 km/h) to 21 knots (39 km/h). Even so, the *Lusitania* remained the fastest commercial liner still in operation, capable of outrunning any submarine.

She was also adequately manned, although William Turner, her captain at the time of her sinking, wistfully commented that seamanship was not what it had been in his young days. At the same time, in his first newspaper interview after the disaster, given to the *New York Times*, Turner denied allegations that the crew aboard the *Lusitania* had been inexperienced or that they had not known their duty. The regular crew, he said, like those of other big British liners, were all naval reservists; when the war started they had all been called up, together with the reserve officers, to serve their country.

> I had a scratch crew to take their places, but they were about as good as most sailors that go to sea nowadays. The old-fashioned able-seaman, who could reef, knot, splice or steer, disappeared with the sailing ships. What green hands there on board were among the coal trimmers in the stokehole, as it does not require nautical training to push a barrow of coal along a deck. All hands were well drilled in their duties regarding the lifeboats in case of accidents and knew their stations.[1]

The captain praised the steward teams, the firemen and the sailors. He added that if any portholes were open, the passengers had opened them themselves. (One problem was that the staff did not have the right to inspect the state of portholes, even in the third-class cabins.)

Official concern for the *Lusitania*'s safety fluctuated widely as the elaborate strategies and successive events of a world at war unfolded. Initially, every precaution was taken. Before her first voyage eastbound after war was declared, the liner's distinctive Cunard livery was disguised with a coat of grey paint, ostensibly to make her less conspicuous – although her massive silhouette could never be concealed.

However, it was not long before there was a temporary easing of hostilities, and Britain breathed again, lulled into a false sense of security through the erroneous belief that the Royal Navy was having no problem containing the German maritime threat. Confidence restored, the *Lusitania* was repainted in her original colours, her name emblazoned in gilt letters, her funnels gleaming once more in the traditional Cunard vermilion banded with black; her superstructure was repainted a dazzling white, and a band of gold-bronze was added just above the black paint.

The relief was short-lived. Soon the greatest military threat to surface vessels ever devised would burst upon the maritime scene. The emergence of the submarine as the supreme weapon of naval attack revolutionized naval warfare. Its runaway success gave the lie to the chorus of traditionalist naysayers on both sides who had previously scoffed at the notion that submarines would ever play a decisive part in naval engagements. Hitherto, submarines had played only a minor role, their operations being restricted to coastal defence. The few far-sighted people who understood their lethal potential, and were convinced that their contribution in future maritime conflicts would be crucial, had never been taken seriously by fleet commanders. There had been a tendency to dismiss the submarine as merely the latest technological gadget that had captured the imagination of younger officers. Submarines were in many quarters widely resented as a fanciful and ephemeral notion, a new-fangled craze that diverted funds and resources from more worthwhile traditional seafaring vessels and armaments.

Yet submarines also had their passionate defenders in both the British and the German high commands, voices crying in the wilderness at a crucial point in military history. Two of the loudest voices extolling the military virtue of the submarine belonged to a pair of admirals, one German, one British, whose attitudes and personalities displayed an uncanny parallel: these men were Admiral Alfred von Tirpitz and Admiral John 'Jackie' Arbuthnot Fisher. Stubborn, uncompromising and ruthless in their policies and their ambitions to attain and maintain naval supremacy, both men had encountered energetic opposition as they pressed for a larger and more efficient fleet of warships. Had their masters listened to these implacable old warriors the outcome of the First World War might have been very different.

A brief consideration of the two men's careers is revealing. Originally, Admiral Alfred von Tirpitz, Kaiser Wilhelm's Secretary of State for the Navy, had joined in the general derision when the development of the submarine as a naval vessel was discussed. In 1901, when the issue was raised in the Reichstag, Tirpitz announced dismissively, 'We have no money to waste on experimental vessels. We must leave such luxuries to wealthier states such as France and England.'[2]

However, by 1911 Tirpitz's initial enthusiasm for great dreadnought battleships had been replaced by a passionate advocacy for submarines; he was now convinced that the only means by which Germany could wage a successful maritime campaign would be through unrestricted submarine warfare. He would eventually come into conflict with the vacillating Kaiser over this, and, like his English counterpart, Fisher, would eventually make good his threat to resign his post at a crucial stage in the war.

The distinguished career of Admiral Alfred von Tirpitz was characterized by irony. In the first place, Tirpitz, by his own admission an indifferent student, had been at a loose end as a teenager, with no fixed idea of pursuing a career at sea. But when a friend joined the Prussian Navy, a modest force at the time, sixteen-year-old Alfred was captivated by the idea. In 1865, with his parents' blessing, he became a naval cadet. Nobody could have imagined at that point that the undistinguished youngster would become the architect of the mighty German Imperial Navy, building it up from a motley and unimpressive collection of vessels into the dangerous international force it was to become.

During the early years of young Alfred's career at sea, the Prussian Navy and the British Royal Navy enjoyed a cordial relationship; the Germans respected the Royal Navy's professionalism and looked to them for advice on how best to develop their own service. The ships and men of the Prussian Navy enjoyed much time in British ports; Tirpitz himself, who spoke fluent English, commended the English port of Plymouth, claiming it showed greater hospitality to German sailors than Kiel did, and that it was also easier to obtain quality supplies and equipment there than at home. (Such was his affection for England that in the 1890s he would send his daughters to be educated in England at the famous Cheltenham Ladies' College.)

After the unification of Germany in 1871 the Prussian Navy became the German Imperial Navy, with a corresponding increase in scope and aspiration. Over the next decade or so, Tirpitz moved steadily up the ranks. He was chiefly employed in the development of torpedoes and torpedo boats and would later describe these as the happiest years of his life.

In 1887, when the torpedo boats escorted Prince Wilhelm, soon to become Kaiser, to England to attend the Golden Jubilee of his grandmother Queen Victoria, Tirpitz and the future Kaiser met for the first time. A few years later, at a dinner with senior naval officers at Kiel, Wilhelm, now Kaiser of the unified German Empire, solicited the views of his dining companions as to the best way forward for the Imperial Navy. Now conscious that his beloved torpedo boats had had their day, Tirpitz vigorously argued the case for building up the Imperial fleet with battleships, of which he had now become a keen advocate. The notion of a fleet of mighty dreadnoughts immediately caught the volatile Kaiser's imagination and fired his expansionist ambition.

He did not forget the dinner-party conversation with Tirpitz, and nine months later Tirpitz found himself transferred to Berlin with a brief to develop the fighting force of the German High Seas Fleet. The solution he proposed called for identical battleships in flotillas of eight, rather than groupings of mixed vessels as advocated by the German Navy State Secretary Friedrich von Hollmann. The two men clashed, and in 1895, frustrated that his suggestions were being sidelined, Tirpitz demanded to be replaced.

Hollmann won that battle, but his triumph was short-lived: his own plans for a shipbuilding programme were derailed in turn when the Reichstag dug its heels in and opposed funding. When Admiral von Senden-Bibran, chief of the Naval Cabinet, advised the Kaiser that it was time to replace Hollmann and that the ideal candidate was Tirpitz, the impulsive Wilhelm immediately appointed him. Nine days after taking up office Tirpitz visited the Kaiser in Potsdam and presented him with a Very Secret Memorandum that would alter the course of European history.

Tirpitz was conscious of the Kaiser's close family ties with the British Royal Family, especially with his grandmother Queen Victoria who, it was claimed, died in his arms. His adored mother, Queen Victoria's eldest daughter Vicky, had always striven to engineer an even greater rapprochement between Germany and Britain. Despite this knowledge, Tirpitz's Anglophile tendencies and the previous cordial relations enjoyed by the British and German navies, Tirpitz's Memorandum identified England as Germany's most dangerous naval enemy. He argued that while a war against France and Russia would be waged on land, if Britain were the enemy the war would be fought at sea. If Germany intended to engage the Royal Navy, the greatest possible number of battleships would be needed. Commerce raiding, using cruisers, would not be successful as Germany lacked sufficient bases, whereas England had many.

Tirpitz made no secret of the fact that he scorned the philosophy of his predecessor Hollmann. Hollmann had favoured a mixed fleet, acquired piecemeal as funding was forthcoming. Tirpitz felt the navy he had taken over as State Secretary was hardly fit for purpose. A major overhaul of the shipbuilding programme was called for. He dismissed the German Navy as a collection of experiments in shipbuilding whose exoticism was surpassed only by the Russian Navy of Nicholas II.

The unpredictable Kaiser was impressed by Tirpitz, especially when it appeared that Tirpitz had convinced the Reichstag to allocate funds for a continued expansion of the Imperial Navy where others, including Hollmann, had failed. Tirpitz eventually succeeded in obtaining the Reichstag's agreement to pledge a seven-year programme of financial support for the development of the German war fleet.

Enthralled by the glorious prospect of supremacy at sea, and gripped by enthusiasm for every new technological detail that caught his attention, the Kaiser now spent much of his time sketching ships and devising improvements, regularly distributing copies of his latest brainwave. Although the Kaiser's keen interest in the enterprise was invaluable, it was also tricky: diplomatically deflecting his Imperial master's whimsical schemes caused Tirpitz many headaches.

Notwithstanding, with the funding in place and fuelled by the Kaiser's passionate enthusiasm, the German shipbuilding programme progressed relentlessly, implemented with Teutonic system, until at last the bubble of British complacency was punctured and alarm bells began to sound in London. On 15 November 1901, Lord Selborne, First Lord of the Admiralty, brought it to the attention of the Cabinet and the Prime Minister, Lord Salisbury, and the Cabinet that Germany's determined and aggressive naval policy was becoming clear. It was apparent that the Kaiser intended to promote a programme that would expand German trade, possessions and interests worldwide and that, in order to achieve this ambition, Germany would need a naval force sufficiently powerful and effective to compete with the Royal Navy. In his Cabinet Paper eleven months later Lord Selborne identified the target of German naval expansion: it was obviously designed not for a possible land-based campaign against France and Russia but against Britain, the world's leading naval power. It was also possible to pinpoint accurately the designated theatre of war: this would be the North Sea, because German battleships, with their cramped crew quarters and limited cruising range, would be ill-suited to commit to a campaign in any other area.

By 1905 the strength of the German Navy exceeded that of both France and Russia. It had a long way to go before it would rival the British Navy, but it was making giant strides in that direction. One person who was keenly aware of the potential threat was another indomitable old warhorse, the British counterpart to the bombastic and aggressive Tirpitz,

Admiral 'Jacky' Fisher, the First Sea Lord. Fisher had been appointed Commander-in-Chief of the Mediterranean Fleet in 1899, a post he held until 1902. In this position, he is widely credited with having dragged the Royal Navy out of the eighteenth century, democratically overhauling the process of recruiting officers exclusively from the ranks of the gentry. He equipped the service for modern naval battles by ruthlessly scrapping obsolete and unsuitable vessels, which he dismissed as too weak to fight and too slow to run away, likening them to a miser's hoard of useless junk. He also revolutionized naval training techniques and tactics.

Fisher was astute and determined, with a great aptitude for self-publicity. Like Tirpitz, he had become acquainted with the Royal Family; in 1882, while escorting Queen Victoria on a visit to the French Riviera, he had become a friend of the future King Edward VII.

Fisher is often described as the greatest British admiral since Nelson, but his abrasive personality was his downfall (the King, although he counted Fisher a friend, once asked him to stop shaking his fist in his face).[3] He achieved rapid promotion, and his success was not always popular with his naval colleagues. In 1903 he was promoted to the position of First Sea Lord. Like his German counterpart Tirpitz, Fisher had first espoused the cause of the mighty dreadnoughts with which his name was to become all but synonymous. Believing that they offered the best option for the Navy as the arms race against Germany intensified, Fisher was instrumental in promoting a programme of battleship building. In 1906 he presided over the launch of the immense and innovative HMS *Dreadnought,* the prototype of the 'all-big-gun ship'; with its ten twelve-inch guns *Dreadnought* immediately rendered all existing battleships obsolete. The ship revolutionized naval construction and was immediately copied by Germany; she would become the symbol of the escalating arms race between the two powers.

Again in common with Tirpitz, by 1904 the prescient Fisher had abandoned his former dismissive stance on the submarine and had already foreseen the immense revolutionizing effect that it would have as an offensive weapon. Marvelling that others were too obtuse to perceive its potential, he wrote, 'The submarine will prevent any fleet remaining at sea continuously . . . it is astounding to me how the very best amongst us fail to recognize the vast impending revolution in naval warfare and naval strategy that the submarine will accomplish.'

Fisher's enthusiasm for submarines encountered little resonance among his colleagues. The Royal Navy's greatest icon, Admiral Lord Nelson, had described them as 'sneaky dodges down below', and many in the Admiralty maintained that view, continuing to regard submarines as underhand and distinctly un-British. Indeed Fisher's critics dismissed submarines as the weapons of weaker nations. But, in the face of considerable opposition from conservative elements, Fisher, as First Sea Lord, doggedly proceeded with his plan to develop the Submarine Service.

Although the British were the first to power a submarine on the surface with a diesel engine, some French submarines were steam-powered. Fisher, who had already urged the move towards oil and away from coal-powered vessels, went so far as to state that in future all military engagements at sea would be dominated by the submarine. Because Britain lagged behind Germany in the development of the oil-powered submarine engine, she was keen to develop her own steam-powered submarines.

In 1908 Fisher, still wary of Germany's intentions, predicted with uncanny accuracy that war would break out in October 1914. He based his calculation on the time it would take Germany to complete the Kiel canal, enabling her to move her war fleet from the Baltic to the North Sea.

Having been promoted to Admiral of the Fleet in 1905, he was made Baron Fisher of Kilverstone in December 1909. Although largely supported by the government, both Fisher's reforms and his aggressive and flamboyant character brought him into conflict with older traditionalists within the Royal Navy, such as Admiral Lord Charles Beresford, Commander-in-Chief of the Channel Squadron. Fisher was his own worst enemy: despite his brilliance, he had a propensity to antagonize people, both in the Navy and during his political career, and his relations with Beresford eventually degenerated into a destructive feud.

Still resisting Fisher's reforms, Beresford generated sufficient support for an inquiry to be opened into the First Sea Lord's actions at the Admiralty. Although Fisher's name was cleared, he felt that his reputation had been tarnished and that consequently he was somewhat isolated within the naval hierarchy. On 25 January 1911, his seventieth birthday, Fisher retired. Over the next three years, he served on commissions that investigated transitioning the British fleet from coal to oil, a move he had always supported.

As for Tirpitz, in the same year that Fisher retired he was promoted to Grand Admiral of the German Imperial Fleet. The outbreak of war would bring new opportunities and challenges for both men. Tirpitz was given the command of the whole of the German Imperial Navy, which, despite its ambitious building plan, still counted only eighteen battleships and battle cruisers, whereas the British possessed twenty-nine. It was this discrepancy that finally convinced Tirpitz that the future lay with U-boats.

Tirpitz developed his 'risk theory', which has been described by historians as ill-founded and riddled with inconsistencies: he claimed that by building a powerful war fleet and positioning it in the North Sea, it would be possible to coerce a Britain reluctant to seek confrontation into major colonial and other concessions that would pave the way for German expansionism overseas. In the event, the awareness of Germany's intentions merely spurred Britain on in her shipbuilding programme.

By 1909, naval authorities in Germany were at last ready to concede that submarines constituted the best possible offensive weapon against the fast battleship. With the development of more dependable diesel engines and of the gyrocompass, they could no longer be dismissed as unreliable. But controversy still reigned about their appropriate strategic use. Tirpitz argued that they should be used for economic warfare; recognizing that Britain intended to interrupt supply lines and starve Germany into submission, Tirpitz hoped to turn the tables on the enemy and achieve the same effect. Fisher foresaw this intention, and warned that, if it came to war, the German Imperial Navy would dispatch submarines to attack and sink merchantmen. Yet again, he remained a voice crying in the wilderness as far as the Royal Navy was concerned. Fisher's warning was disregarded, and his counsel went unheeded even as late as 1912. By this time, he had become a vociferous champion of submarines.

Abandoning his erstwhile advocacy of the great dreadnoughts, Fisher asserted that submarines would spell the end for large battleships. This prophecy was incorrect, but Fisher was one of the few in the Royal Navy and elsewhere to recognize the crucial role that submarines would play in the Great War. Even the growing number of members of the Royal Naval hierarchy who shared Fisher's prediction that submarines would assume paramount importance had difficulty convincing politicians and the media.

The most effective weapon against submarines, the depth charge Type D, would not become available until January 1916, while Ernest

Rutherford's pioneering piezoelectric hydrophones (acousto-electric transducers for in-water use) would come into use late in the First World War. Both submarines and surface vessels would use piezoelectric hydrophone technology to detect the presence of enemy vessels. For submerged submarines travelling blind, hydrophones would be the sole means of ascertaining enemy presence. Before the war no such means of detection had been developed.

In October 1914, with the outbreak of war, Fisher was persuaded by Winston Churchill, First Lord of the Admiralty, to abandon retirement and take up the appointment of First Sea Lord. He replaced Prince Louis of Battenberg, a man whom Fisher admired but who had been hounded out of office on account of his German name and background, largely as a result of mischievous campaigns in the media. During the events leading up to the outbreak of hostilities, there had been meetings and a lively correspondence between Churchill and Fisher. Fisher's attitude towards war had not softened with age. He believed that military supremacy was Britain's best guarantee of security and also offered the sole potential source of world peace, declaring:

> If you rub it in, both at home and abroad, that you are ready for instant war, with every unit of your strength in the first line and waiting to be first in, and hit your enemy in the belly and kick him when he is down . . . then people will keep clear of you.[4]

With two such vast egos and irascible temperaments as those of Fisher and Churchill, a clash was inevitable. Their complex and turbulent alliance finally crashed upon the rock of Churchill's disastrous Gallipoli campaign. Fisher, never enthusiastic about Churchill's planned invasion of the Dardanelles with the intention of capturing the Turkish capital, had, none the less, uncharacteristically gone along with the plan for a while. However, once it became clear that the campaign was doomed to failure, and would continue to consume resources, especially naval resources, at an alarming rate, Fisher denied that he had ever supported it, and urged that it be abandoned forthwith. In its place, he urged an attack on Germany through the Baltic. When his advice was again ignored, he threatened several times to resign. Finally, on 15 May 1915, in protest over Churchill's misuse of 'spare' Admiralty vessels in the ill-fated Gallipoli campaign, which depleted Fisher's cherished Grand Fleet and diminished the Royal Navy's dominance of the

Mediterranean, Fisher made good his threat and dramatically tendered his resignation. Despite Churchill's pleas to reconsider the decision, and appeals from the media and the public, Fisher remained adamant. Furious with Churchill, he contacted Bonar Law, leader of the opposition, indicating that he considered Churchill a menace who ought to be removed.

With Fisher's petulant resignation, Churchill's position had quickly became untenable; it triggered a series of events leading to Churchill's replacement by Arthur J. Balfour (whom Fisher opposed) in a reconstituted Cabinet. Churchill subsequently resigned and spent a period serving on the Western Front.

However, if Fisher had secretly hoped to be recalled when he recovered from his pout, any chance of this was eliminated by an ill-advised memorandum he sent to the Prime Minister setting out his conditions for returning to office, winning the war and eradicating the submarine menace. Admiral Sir Henry B. Jackson was appointed as First Sea Lord. The curtain had finally rung down on Jacky Fisher's extraordinary naval career. Balfour wrote to the Earl of Selborne on 20 May, 'I am afraid Jacky is really a little mad.'[5]

In June 1915 Fisher was named chairman of the Board of Invention and Research, an entity tasked with promoting scientific work for the Navy. The board earned the unenviable nickname of the 'Board of Intrigue and Revenge' before it was dissolved in December 1918.

Its activities appear to have concentrated on anti-submarine warfare, and considerable progress was made towards developing the ultrasonic detection system later known as ASDIC (sonar). The system was in use but still in its rudimentary stages towards the end of the war.

Fisher and Churchill eventually managed to reconcile their differences. The relationship between these two brilliant men of vision, courage and large egos, had always been complicated, despite their mutual respect and admiration. In March 1916 Churchill recommended to an astonished House of Commons that Fisher should be recalled. However, there was no possibility of this happening.

Fisher's resignation came only three months after his warning about German intentions had proved accurate: in February 1915, on the recommendation of Admiral Tirpitz, Kaiser Wilhelm announced an aggressive policy of unrestricted submarine warfare. The Kaiser and his Chancellor had long vacillated about the principles regarding the deployment of U-boats. Tirpitz alone had a clear vision and a well-thought-out naval strategy, which mirrored British aims and tactics – namely, the interruption of the enemy's supply lines. While reasonable respect was to be shown to neutral countries and consideration given to humanitarian issues, neutral ships as well as enemy craft would be fair game for attack if they entered the war zone of the North Sea between Britain and Germany.

The *Lusitania*'s fate would be sealed because the definition of vessels that might be legitimately labelled 'fair game' resided in a vexed grey area. International law governing the actions of surface warships had been drawn up in the days of sailing ships, long before the invention of submarines. These rules had subsequently been supplemented before the First World War by various international agreements, including the Declaration of Paris (1856) and the Hague Conventions (1899 and 1907), and certain other naval agreements established during the twentieth century. (These same conventions were also in effect during the First World War.) Advances in technology, such as radio and the submarine, meant that by the First World War the time-honoured 'Cruiser Rules' or 'Prize Rules' were outdated and their practical relevance was questionable. Although in wartime enemy warships were regarded as legitimate targets for surprise attacks, the position with regard to enemy merchant shipping was murkier and more ambivalent. The submarine still occupied an anomalous position in international law, which lagged behind technological development.

Under the Cruiser Rules, which governed commerce raiding in war, a commerce raider encountering an enemy ship would order it to halt – if necessary by putting a shot across its bows – and inspect its papers. If it proved to be an enemy-flagged vessel, its crew and passengers would be allowed to gather possessions and provisions and abandon ship, escaping in the lifeboats. The U-boat commander might also make other provision for their safety before destroying the vessel or sailing it into port as a prize of war. To follow this procedure (as most U-boat captains did at the start of the war) was to throw away a U-boat's main advantage: surprise. Surface warships had great difficulty in detecting the presence of submarines and little retaliation against them. One well-aimed torpedo from a submarine could sink an armoured warship. But torpedoes were accurate at only about 1,000 metres; the submarine had to be manoeuvred into position so as to achieve the deadly strike. Potentially lethal invisible menaces submarines might be, but they were sluggish, especially when submerged and blind at depth. At this time submarines were not robust. They had limited endurance, were structurally quite fragile, their targeting devices were crude and unreliable, and their performance was rudimentary. When surfaced and at a standstill they were highly vulnerable to attack. They could be rammed and sunk or shelled and fatally damaged. At a conference in London in 1912, after losing several merchantmen to submarine attack, the decision was taken that Britain would begin arming cargo ships and liners.

Surface vessels, the rules stated, were required to fly their own flag; stop when confronted, allow themselves to be boarded and searched and refrain from hostile or evasive action. But by early 1915 orders had been issued to British merchantmen to run down and ram any submarine that surfaced and attempted to implement Cruiser Rules. Several U-boats were dispatched by ramming or fell victim to sudden attack by nearby cruisers while surfaced. The German High Command's response was 'unrestricted submarine warfare' – torpedo attacks achieved by stealth, without warning.

Fisher, as usual, had foreseen it all: in 1912 he presented a paper to the Cabinet in which he argued that submarines would find adherence to Prize Rules impossible, for practical reasons. He pointed out that ordering a submarine to capture a merchant ship was delusional; a submarine could not capture a prize. It could not tow, nor would it have the extra hands needed to deliver a captured prize to a neutral port. Space restrictions would preclude a submarine from taking aboard survivors or prisoners. Submarines were a functional and basic construction; they had exposed piping, and they were crammed chock-full of machinery and men. Submarines had only one option in conflict: to sink her capture. If a merchant ship were armed, as the new rules now permitted, a submarine would be put in a position of kill or be killed.

Fisher asked what would happen if the Germans were to use submarines against commercial vessels without restriction? This prophetic query was disregarded by most who heard it as a flight of malicious fantasy on the part of Fisher, in some quarters now regarded as demented. Winston Churchill, First Lord of the Admiralty and political head of the Royal Navy, dismissed the notion as inconceivable. Such behaviour, he stated, would never be countenanced by a civilized power. His view that naval warfare would remain a gentlemanly affair, governed by the rules of the tournament, was supported by senior naval opinion. But Fisher knew that as the conflict intensified, attitudes would grow more ruthless. There would be less room for sentiment, morality or traditionalist scruple. Each would have to commit every last resource, and eventually, with the bloody escalation into total war, the distinction between combatants and civilians would be blurred. This would be no medieval joust: it would be war with no holds barred. Fisher's horrific vision was indeed prophetic: in the same spring that the *Lusitania* was sunk Germany introduced poison gas into the Western Front and with a solitary zeppelin launched the first air raid on the civilian population of London.

The British nation, with its overwhelming sea power, had implemented a naval blockade of Germany on the outbreak of war in August 1914. In doing so it revived a strategy that had proved a crucial coercive instrument in the maintenance of British maritime supremacy for hundreds of years. All the belligerents were deeply dependent upon imports, principally from the Americas, to feed their populations, and provide supplies and armaments to their military machines. Cutting off these lines of supply now became the priority for Britain. The drawing-up of a list of 'contraband' elements, including foodstuffs, created a stranglehold on US trade with the Central powers. In early November 1914 Britain went further, declaring the North Sea a war zone, with any ships entering the area doing so at their own risk. The measure was unusually restrictive and highly effective; it would become known as the Hunger Blockade.

The Northern Patrol and Dover Patrol closed off access to the North Sea and the English Channel respectively. The Germans, decrying these measures as a blatant attempt to starve the German people into submission, were determined to retaliate in kind. German High Command, abandoning all pretence of following Cruiser Rules and arguing that its actions were retaliation for the British Navy's blockade of German ports, resorted to unrestricted submarine warfare as the way to turn the tables on Britain by imposing its own blockade.

By the end of 1914 Kaiser Wilhelm had decided that his High Command and the Reichstag were right and acquiesced. It was a high-risk strategy certain to evoke international outrage and a course of action born of desperation. In Germany there were fears that the sinking of neutral vessels, especially American ships bound for Britain, would provoke hostile reactions and even a declaration of war.

The German Chancellor, Theobald von Bethmann-Hollweg, rightly feared that unrestricted submarine warfare, based on a policy of 'shoot first and ask questions afterwards', would antagonize the USA and other neutrals. However, the pressure from Britain was simply too great. In response to the British declaration in November 1914 that the entire North Sea was now a war zone, on 4 February 1915 Admiral Hugo von Pohl, commander of the German High Seas Fleet, published a warning in the *Deutscher Reichsanzeiger* (*Imperial German Gazette*):

> *German Admiralty Declaration Regarding Unrestricted U-boat Warfare*
>
> (1) The waters around Great Britain and Ireland, including the whole of the English Channel, are hereby declared to be a War Zone. From 18 February onwards every enemy merchant vessel encountered in this zone will be destroyed, nor will it always be possible to avert the danger thereby threatened to the crew and passengers.
>
> (2) Neutral vessels also will run a risk in the War Zone, because in view of the hazards of sea warfare and the British authorization of 31 January of the misuse of neutral flags, it may not always be possible to prevent attacks on enemy ships from harming neutral ships.[6]

In time, this declaration and its consequences would bring non-European nations (such as Brazil and the USA) into the war. It was pointed out to the Germans, particularly forcibly by the Americans, that such arbitrary action constituted a war crime. Inevitably, neutral shipping would be inadvertently sunk.

While surface warships were expected to follow the rules of 'visit and search', 'unrestricted submarine warfare' meant that merchantmen could be sunk without warning in a declared blockade zone, whether they were belligerent or neutral, armed or unarmed. This was clearly illegal and infringed the rights of neutral shipping to freedom of the seas.

Although in the USA there was some sympathy for the German point of view that the British blockade was excessively harsh and contravened maritime agreements, little attempt was made by US authorities to convince Britain to release her iron grip on maritime trade. At the same time, the USA steadfastly refused to give credence to the notion that Germany's policy of unrestricted submarine warfare was a legitimate counter-measure.

Germany was gambling that the short sharp shock effected by a ruthless and efficient submarine campaign would bring about a swift victory in the war at sea. Thus, ignoring international protestations – US appeals to the Kaiser having brought about only a brief delay – on 4 February 1915, the seas around Great Britain and Ireland having been classified as a war zone, Germany's U-boat commanders were officially given carte blanche to ignore the antiquated Prize or Cruiser Rules and sink Allied shipping as the opportunity arose. As for neutral shipping, it would just have to take its chances. Thus began a trial of strength between the U-boats and the Allied navies in what was to be the first of three episodes of unrestricted submarine warfare, each one bloodier and more vicious than the last. In March 1915 a rotating operational force of six U-boats sank 85,000 tons of Allied shipping. In each of the months of May, June and July 1915 over 100,000 tons of Allied cargo ships were lost. Eventually Allied tonnage lost to U-boats in the First World War would count some 5,000 freighters, tankers and sailing ships – 11 million tons of shipping. More than 15,000 British civilians would lose their lives.

While the lethal toll taken by U-boats escalated rapidly, the U-boats themselves did not escape unscathed: four U-boats were lost in April 1915 and another three in the period May to July 1915. In the German submarine service, 4,849 men lost their lives, a mortality figure representing 40 per cent of personnel.

However, the impact of Allied commercial shipping losses almost paled into insignificance in the international consciousness alongside the sinking of the passenger liner *Lusitania* in May 1915 and the White Star liner *Arabic* in August 1915, with great loss of life, including that of many Americans. Both vessels were lost off Kinsale on the coast of Ireland. These two events resulted in claims – which subsequently appeared to have been at least partly justified – that the vessels were transporting supplies of material to support the Allied war effort. None the less, the international uproar occasioned by these atrocities panicked the Kaiser and the German establishment, and on 1 September 1915 the first bloody chapter of unrestricted submarine warfare was suspended.

On 25 November 1915 the German Navy issued a secret order stipulating the restrictions that applied to U-boat attacks on passenger liners. Nevertheless, by the end of 1915 the total of British shipping sunk had risen to 4 per cent of the total British mercantile tonnage. For the Germans, this was not perhaps the devastating tally for which they had hoped, but it gave Britain cause for grave concern. (In 1917 Germany once more declared unrestricted submarine warfare. Later on, in the

Second World War, events would follow the same model: in 1939 Germany adhered to the Prize Rules for the first two months of the conflict, before throwing caution to the wind and once more wholeheartedly embracing the policy of unrestricted submarine warfare.)

In spring 1915 a handful of far-sighted people of German origin, now settled in the USA and watching international developments with increasing horror, foresaw the damaging political effects a German submarine attack on a passenger liner carrying civilians, including women and children would have, especially if the victims were American. Such carnage would not go unpunished: it would present Germany's enemies with a heaven-sent propaganda opportunity and stir up hatred in the powerful lobbies of the USA, with severe consequences. There would be an international outcry, and Germans would be regarded as moral outcasts. Consequently, on 17 April 1915, when the *Lusitania* left Liverpool on her 201st transatlantic voyage, due to arrive in New York on 24 April, a group of German-born Americans voiced their concerns to a representative of the German Embassy. The embassy took them seriously and decided to issue a warning to people intending to travel on the liner on her return voyage. The warning took the form of a paid advertisement placed in fifty US newspapers, many of them based in New York. Over breakfast on the morning of 1 May 1915 some of those about to embark on their fairy-tale voyage aboard the world's most luxurious liner glanced at the headlines in their newspapers. Their attention was caught by an unusual message, both stark and unequivocal:

> Travelers intending to embark on the Atlantic voyage are reminded that a state of war exists between Germany and her allies and Great Britain and her allies; that the zone of war includes the waters adjacent to the British Isles; that, in accordance with formal notice given by the Imperial German Government, vessels flying the flag of Great Britain, or of any of her allies, are liable to destruction in those waters and that travelers sailing in the war zone on ships of Great Britain or her allies do so at their own risk.

THREE

In the USA: Sabotage, Espionage and Propaganda

The German–American community could not fail to notice that the USA under President Woodrow Wilson, while ostensibly maintaining her time-honoured policy of neutrality, had nevertheless shown greater tolerance towards the British naval blockade than towards the German submarine campaign. From a British point of view, the blockade of neutral ports, which in effect severed Germany's lines of communication and cut off Germany's supply lines for foodstuff imports as well as materiel and other goods, was simply the most logical and efficient way of exploiting Britain's maritime dominance. The unrestricted submarine campaign ordered, with the active encouragement of Admiral Tirpitz, by the Imperial German authorities – despite misgivings on the part of some including the Kaiser – was a desperate ploy to break free of Britain's stranglehold. In theory, both Britain's seizure of neutral ships bound for neutral ports and Germany's unrestricted submarine warfare were in contravention of the outdated maritime laws still in force at the time; in the global context, both strategies bordered on the illegal. Maritime neutrality was a vexed question with many grey areas.

More crucially, the emergence of the latest and most deadly weapon in the arsenal of maritime warfare, the submarine, created a critical complication for which international maritime law simply lacked precedents.

The US government had already expressed its concern over Germany's ratcheting-up of submarine warfare, yet its comments on the British blockade had been comparatively restrained, exciting charges of partiality from some observers. The stance adopted by President Wilson was viewed by some as favouring Britain, whether or not the President himself was conscious of it. Certainly it was true that US foreign policy was traditionally dictated to a high degree by the President's character and personal inclination.

Before entering office in 1913 President Wilson, nicknamed 'the schoolmaster in politics', had largely focused his attention on domestic matters – the economy, jurisprudence, education – rather than foreign affairs. High-minded, intelligent and idealistic, he would be credited with many progressive reforms. Wilson was a thoughtful person with noble intentions, but his devotion to democracy and his apparent self-imposed mission to save the world caused irritation in some quarters. He was sometimes accused of adopting a Messianic stance, 'notably by the equally brilliant, influential but curmudgeonly H.L. Mencken . . . Mencken called him Archangel Woodrow. The term, used by Mencken to deride other people including Wilson's Secretary of State William Jennings Bryan, was not one of approbation.'[1]

Whatever his personal sentiments, Wilson made sterling efforts to maintain the USA's neutrality. (When he was re-elected by a narrow margin in 1916 the main pillar of his platform would be 'He kept us out of the war.') While Wilson's critics recognized his bias, in his own mind the President firmly believed himself to be ideologically neutral. Contemporary documentation indicates the depths of Wilson's self-deception. His emotional, cultural and intellectual predisposition to favour Britain was perhaps inevitable in one raised as a Presbyterian and born of an English mother. Before becoming President, Wilson had enjoyed many holidays spent in Britain. Intellectually he was an admirer of British political institutions. As the war progressed, despite his growing impatience with Britain's repeated violations of US neutrality, Wilson persisted in interpreting events in a manner favourable to British interests. When he insisted on assurances that would guarantee the safety of all American lives from submarine attack, no matter on which ships they travelled, the effect of this policy was to make the USA the *de facto* protector of all Allied shipping. In essence, it meant that if any US citizens happened to be travelling aboard a vessel that came under attack, this constituted an act of war against a neutral power. [2]

With the outbreak of war in 1914 the USA had proclaimed its neutrality and continued the endeavours towards brokering peace. The nation's insistence on her neutral rights included allowing private corporations and banks to sell or loan money to either side. However, the British blockade meant that in reality only the Allies were in a position to benefit from this ruling and to receive US money.

This evident partiality sat ill with Wilson's Secretary of State, William Jennings Bryan. Bryan unsuccessfully attempted to stem the flow of US credit, describing money as the worst kind of contraband in the world, since it governed all other transactions. Wilson adhered to traditional concepts governing the recognition of blockades, the neutral transporting of 'contraband' goods and the travelling of civilians on ships belonging to the combatant nations. Bryan correctly pointed out that technological innovations such as the submarine had radically transformed the nature of international law, rendering it impossible to protect American citizens travelling into a war zone. Bryan sought to persuade the President to prohibit such travel by pointing out the potential political consequences. He argued that Americans who recklessly courted danger by travelling on a British vessel were placing business interests ahead of the risk of embroiling their country in a disastrous international situation.

Despite Bryan's foreboding, and even in the face of the outpouring of fury kindled in America when the torpedoing of the *Lusitania* resulted in US deaths in 1941, the atrocity would not set in train the consequences triggered by later events affecting the nation, such as the December attack on Pearl Harbor and that on New York's Twin Towers of 2001, largely because President Wilson refused to be provoked into allowing the disaster to result in immediate military retaliation. He also succeeded in averting violent political reaction in the USA.

None the less, it is possible to trace back to this single act of aggression many subsequent events of the First World War, especially with respect to US involvement. The sense of outrage and disgust provoked in American hearts by the apparent assault on decency and the breach of the moral code governing even hostile actions fed into a growing desire for vengeance. The brutality of the attack, and repugnance for the minds that conceived it, took hold and burned deep within the national psyche. With the sinking of the *Lusitania* a line had been crossed; it appeared to increasing numbers of people that the hounds of hell had begun to slip their chains. The doomsayers recognized that horror of unimaginable proportions was about to be unleashed upon the world. Bryan, a man committed to the cause of peace, wrote with chilling foresight:

> It is not likely that either side will win so complete a victory as to be able to dictate terms, and if either side does win such a victory it will probably mean preparation for another war. It would seem better to look for a more rational basis for peace.[3]

His appointment as Secretary of State had been William Jennings Bryan's reward for his backing of Wilson's 1912 presidential campaign. While he supported Wilson's decision to allow US military intervention in the Mexican Civil War in 1914, Bryan remained a staunch and successful advocate of peaceful diplomacy. He succeeded in persuading some thirty nations to sign treaties committing each to arbitration of international disputes. He also made less successful attempts to negotiate a treaty with Germany; these 'Treaties for the Advancement of Peace' established procedures for conciliation rather than for arbitration. In September 1914 Bryan wrote to President Wilson urging mediation by the USA, the largest and most powerful neutral power, in the conflict that had just broken out in Europe. Bryan regarded the US partiality towards Britain with considerable apprehension.

In November 1914, Sir Cecil Spring-Rice, the British ambassador in Washington, wrote to Sir Arthur Nicolson, British Permanent Secretary for Foreign Affairs, concerning William Jennings Bryan's views about the Great War.

> Bryan spoke to me about peace as he always does. He sighs for the Nobel Prize, and besides that he is a really convinced peaceman. He has just given me a sword beaten into a ploughshare six inches long to serve as a paperweight. It is adorned with quotations from Isaiah and himself. No one doubts his sincerity, but that is rather embarrassing for us at the present moment, because he is always at us with peace propositions. This time, he said he could not understand why we could not say what we were fighting for. The nation which continued war had as much responsibility as the country which began it. The United States was the one great Power which was outside the struggle, and it was their duty to do what they could to put an end to it. I felt rather cross and said that the United States were signatories to the Hague Convention, which had been grossly violated again and again without one word from the principal neutral nation. They were now out of court. They had done nothing to prevent the crime, and now they must not prevent the punishment.
>
> He said that all the Powers concerned had been disappointed in their ambitions. Germany had not taken Paris. France had not retaken Alsace, England had not cleared the seas of the German navy. The last month had made no appreciable difference in the

> relative positions of the armies, and there was now no prospect of an issue satisfactory to any Power. Why should they not make peace now, if they had to make peace a year hence after another year's fruitless struggle. It would be far wiser if each said what it was fighting for and asked the United States to help them in arriving at a peaceful conclusion.
>
> I asked him if he thought that under present circumstances Germany would give up Belgium and compensate her for her suffering. If not, how could the United States Government go on record as condoning a peace which would put the seal on the most disgraceful act of tyranny and oppression committed in modern times? I didn't believe there was a man in the country not a German or a Jew who could advocate such a cause.
>
> He got rather angry and said that if that was what we wanted, why did we not say so. He added, 'Who can tell who was really responsible for what had happened in Belgium or whether the treaty wasn't only a pretext?' I reminded him that he was a great admirer of Gladstone, who was like him, a great lover of peace, and that Gladstone had always maintained that if we had gone to war for Belgium in 1870, we should have gone to war for freedom and for public right and to save human happiness from being invaded by a tyrannous and lawless power, and that in such a war as that while the breath continued in his body he was ready to engage. This rather surprised him as he had read in the newspapers that Gladstone had always maintained that the Belgian Treaty was not binding.[4]

Despite their differences, Bryan campaigned as a private citizen for Wilson's re-election in 1916. When the USA finally declared war in April 1917 Bryan, aged fifty-seven, would write to Wilson:

> Believing it to be the duty of the citizen to bear his part of the burden of war and his share of the peril, I hereby tender my services to the Government. Please enrol me as a private whenever I am needed and assign me to any work that I can do.[5]

Wilson did not allow him to rejoin the military, nor did he offer him any wartime role. In 1914, as the storm clouds gathered over Europe, although Bryan was Secretary of State, President Wilson's chief adviser on foreign policy was his close friend and confidant the self-styled 'Colonel' Edward House, whom he had entrusted with a series of important assignments, even though House held no official office. House, a wealthy Texan, eschewed the limelight, preferring to operate behind the scenes. He shared Wilson's vision of the USA as the saviour of the world. In this regard House would embark on what he would call in his diary 'the great adventure', the most momentous mission of his unofficial diplomatic career. In 1914, Wilson confided to his friend House his view that the Kaiser had built a war machine and then lit the fuse. He referred to the Germans as 'selfish and unspiritual' in their conversations.[6]

In his wartime political balancing act, at times the President's standpoint appeared vacillating. He seemed to entertain notions that were apparently contradictory, yet he always maintained that he was acting on the basis of a single immutable principle. Reluctant to declare war, Wilson intended to find some manner of intervention that would allow the USA to bring a peaceful ('spiritual' was the term Wilson preferred) mediation of the conflict.[7]

However, a new factor added another dimension to the military conflict, causing it to intensify still further. The runaway success of the German U-boat campaign astonished even those who had masterminded it. In part owing to the official scepticism that had greeted the emergence of the submarine as an effective maritime weapon, and also because of the rapid explosion of submarine technology, surface vessels had developed no effective defences against underwater attack.

Initially the USA had continued to conduct business as usual, trading merchandise such as food, clothing, medicines, equipment and even arms to the aggressors on both sides. US ports were open to all powers on condition that they were used for non-military purposes. At the start of the war both sides had agreed to refrain from interference with neutral shipping. Occasionally US merchant ships were seized, but both sides paid for any cargo they appropriated, and there were few major issues.

However, Germany's new aggressive U-boat strategy changed matters. When Germany announced that she could no longer guarantee the safety of neutral ships, President Wilson realized that this new threat would revolutionize warfare. This consciousness inspired him to redouble his endeavours to bring about mediation and achieve a peaceful settlement. The USA was rapidly emerging as the superpower of the future. Now Wilson offered his services as arbiter between Europe's warring nations.

In a last-ditch attempt at pre-emptive reconciliation in 1915 he dispatched his trusted adviser House on a visit to Germany, France and England in the hopes of brokering peace. Wilson also warned Germany that if American lives were lost through illegal German submarine operations the consequences would be serious.

Edward House set off for Europe, hoping to forge a diplomatic alliance between Germany, Britain and the USA and to establish a kind of international supervisory council that would be able to cooperate in the interests of preserving world peace. Over the previous decade, the European powers had amassed arsenals of alarming military and naval capacity. House, somewhat optimistically, hoped to persuade them to abandon the escalation of the arms race, the expectation being that conflict might be averted if the balance of power were to be maintained between the two great European power blocs: France, Britain and Russia on the one hand and Germany and Austro-Hungary, and possibly Italy, on the other.

But the attitudes House encountered on his peace-brokering mission in Europe dented his optimism. He wrote to Wilson from Berlin on 29 May:

> The situation is extraordinary. It is militarism run stark mad. Unless someone acting for you can bring about a different understanding, there is some day to be an awful cataclysm. No one in Europe can do it. There is too much hatred, too many jealousies.[8]

House had already spent several weeks in London when on 27 June 1914 he lunched in London with Edward Grey, the British Foreign Secretary. This meeting had been arranged by Walter Hines Page, the US Ambassador to Britain. House had both good news and bad news for Grey. In Berlin on 1 June he had been granted a private audience with Kaiser Wilhelm II. House recorded in his diary that they discussed 'the European situation as it affected the Anglo-Saxon race'; the Kaiser had expressed the view that Britain, Germany and the USA – as the best representatives of 'Christian civilization' – were natural allies against the barely civilized Latin and Slavic nations (this category included France and Russia). The Kaiser urged that all Europeans should rally to defend Western civilization against 'the Oriental races'. House assured the Kaiser that Britain would not contract any military alliance with Russia and France as long as Germany agreed not to pursue her ambitious plan to destroy Britain's domination of the seas.

Wilhelm, for his part, appeared willing to entertain the idea that the USA, whether represented by the President or by House himself, might usefully act as moderator in the attempt to achieve a rapprochement between the rival European powers. House had left Germany after assuring the Kaiser that he would endeavour to obtain British agreement to such an American initiative. He had then written to President Wilson from Paris on 3 June, advising the President that one emotion shared by both England and Germany was a fear of one another.

House entered his discussions with Grey buoyed by a spirit of optimism that war could be averted, even though both men were keenly aware of the current tensions in Europe: the French were still nursing their grievances over Germany's annexation of Alsace and Lorraine in 1871, while Britain was desperate to maintain cordial relations with Russia. Moreover, Germany's aggressive naval programme remained a major concern. Churchill, as the civilian head of Britain's Royal Navy, was painfully aware of the dangers and had several times proposed a 'holiday' from warship-building in an attempt to relieve the constant retaliative dynamic between Germany and Britain, termed by politicians 'the sea war waged in the dockyards'. But Churchill's proposal was rejected by Germany and attracted criticism at home.[9]

Any suggestion of a British overture, whether prompted by Churchill or anyone else, was dismissed out of hand by the Kaiser's implacable Admiral Tirpitz. When House encountered the Admiral in Berlin it was apparent that the old warrior's former Anglophilia had been replaced by 'a decided dislike . . . that amounted almost to hatred'.[10] Neither Tirpitz nor the Imperial Navy Office appeared willing to contemplate curtailing the process of building up their mighty war fleet. Indeed, Tirpitz had on several occasions threatened his resignation if his life-long ambition to establish Imperial Germany as master of the seas were to be placed at stake.

House's positivity was tempered by misgivings. During his visit to Germany, he had noted the bellicose spirit and martial posturing that appeared to prevail there. He warned Grey that, although he had concluded in Berlin that neither the Kaiser nor the majority of his closest advisers wanted war, their prime aim being Germany's commercial and economic expansion, the mood in the army was aggressive and poised for combat. House had registered with alarm the militant spirit abroad in Germany, both in the armed forces and among the population.

Nevertheless, by the time their meeting came to a close, House and Grey had succeeded in reassuring one another that, when it came to it, none of the Great Powers, England, Germany, Russia nor France, truly desired war.

They parted in hope but were overtaken by events the next day. On 28 June 1914 Archduke Franz Ferdinand of Austria, heir to the throne of Austria-Hungary, was assassinated in Sarajevo by Serbian nationalist Gavrilo Princip. This triggered a diplomatic crisis. Austro-Hungary delivered an ultimatum to Serbia. International alliances forged over the previous decades were invoked. On 28 July Austro-Hungary fired the first shots in its campaign to invade Serbia. Russia mobilized, Germany invaded neutral Belgium and Luxembourg and marched on towards France, while Britain declared war on Germany.The conflagration that would engulf the world broke out.

Although in his 1925 memoirs Sir Edward Grey claimed to be unable to remember saying it, this famous remark has been attributed to him, apparently uttered to a friend as he gazed out from his office and watched dusk fall over Saint James's Park on 3 August 1914: 'The lamps are going out all over Europe. We shall not see them lit again in our time.'[11]

When the German practice of unrestricted submarine warfare, which President Wilson perceived as a violation of the rights of neutrals, resulted in May 1915 in the sinking of the *Lusitania* and the deaths of 128 US citizens, Wilson declared that the USA would not seek retaliation: peace was in the world's best interests. Instead, he sent the German government the first of three strongly worded protests in which he asserted the right of citizens from neutral countries to travel unmolested on the high seas and urged Germany to cease attacks on non-belligerent shipping, appealing to her sense of morality.

William Jennings Bryan was alarmed by the President's terse demands for 'strict accountability for any infringement of [American] rights, intentional or incidental'. He urged Wilson to send a similar protest to Britain about her blockade, which could also be construed as a flagrant violation of neutral rights, but Wilson refused. Despite the outrage over the *Lusitania* atrocity, US citizens, members of Congress and President Wilson were still resolved to avoid becoming involved in the conflict.

In defiance of the increasingly strong protests from the USA, in August 1915 the British liner *Arabic* was sunk by the German submarine *U-24*. Wilson again sent a sharp note demanding an immediate cessation of German submarine warfare. Again, the protest received the most cursory of acknowledgements from the Imperial government.

Bryan's apprehensions deepened; it appeared to him that the tone of the Presidential communiqués was dangerously antagonistic and risked dragging the USA into war with Germany. Rather than append his signature to Wilson's latest note, Bryan chose to resign his position as Secretary of State.

Bryan's replacement as Secretary of State in 1915 was Robert Lansing, a lawyer and politician who had been appointed as legal adviser to the State Department at the outbreak of war in Europe. Lansing's position was clear from the outset. A champion of the cause of freedom of the seas and the rights of neutral nations, he vehemently denounced the attack on the *Lusitania* and the loss of American lives. In his memoirs he would reveal that he had always been convinced that the USA and Britain were ultimately destined to become allies, thus openly echoing the often unspoken sentiments of President Wilson. In reality, Lansing's influence on foreign policy would be negligible. Foreign policy was conducted by the President himself, with the advice of his friend, Edward House. In Washington, there was a new joke doing the rounds:

> Question: How do you spell Lansing?
> Answer: H- O- U- S- E !

Although House persisted in his efforts to bring the warring parties to a truce, he also began to recommend that the USA should prepare for war by building up military power. Early in 1916 he admitted that despite his endeavours a break with Germany was inevitable. It could not be averted but only deferred.

Although a study of US diplomacy under President Wilson reveals his pro-British bias (there was, for example, a House–Grey memorandum, never a House–Zimmerman memorandum[12]), for a long time the President's genuine desire for peace kept his personal partiality in check. Moreover, Wilson was disinclined to embark on a European war. His personal life was also absorbing much of his attention. In early 1915, a mere six months after the death of Ellen Axson Wilson, his first wife, Wilson had met the much younger Edith Bolling Galt. Wilson was immediately smitten and initiated a charm offensive to woo Edith, even to the extent of sharing state secrets with her. The couple became secretly engaged. Wilson's political advisers feared that his remarriage less than a year after the death of Ellen Wilson would offend the sensibilities of the American public and prove detrimental to his re-election prospects. They schemed to prevent the marriage, but, despite their machinations, the President and Edith Galt married in December 1915.

Since the outbreak of war in 1914 Germany's principal aims concerning the USA had been twofold. The first was to ensure that America remained neutral. The second was to cut off the supplies of food and armaments streaming from the USA to the Allies. In pursuit of these two aims, Germany employed diplomacy, espionage and sabotage, her agents often engaging in a series of surreal antics that rivalled the most outlandish genre fiction.

Until the outbreak of war in 1914, during an uneventful and superficially cordial period in German–American relations, Germany's Ambassador to Washington, an experienced diplomat named Count Johann Heinrich von Bernstorff had performed his largely ceremonial role unexceptionably. But the outbreak of hostilities, followed by the German decision to launch an unrestricted submarine campaign, changed things. In the USA an upsurge of feeling against Germany was gathering momentum, despite the heterogeneous character of the population of the USA (at the outbreak of the First World War one-third of the population had been born abroad) and despite the presence of the large German–American community. The latter had been targeted by German propagandists but with little success.

Several factors, both emotional and economic, fuelled this rising tide of ill feeling towards Germany. Furnishing the belligerents with merchandise had been profitable for the USA, as the war gradually undermined Europe's industrial and agricultural base. The difficulty of exporting supplies to Germany and her Allies because of the British blockade meant that financial interests connected with the economic upswing were more closely aligned with the Allies.

Moreover, the Allies possessed a much more efficient propaganda machine. According to one journalist, the British censors eliminated three-quarters of the dispatches from American correspondents in Central Europe. The British, unconsciously echoing Wilson's Messianic vision, portrayed themselves as saviours of the world from the depredations of the Teuton savages, while the French lost no opportunity to remind the USA of France's contributions to US independence.

Ambassador Bernstorff was informed by Berlin that his duties would now extend beyond the formal and ceremonial. His new role would include responsibility for Germany's espionage and sabotage activities in the Western Hemisphere, specifically, those directed against the USA. He was informed that he would be assisted in this endeavour by the future Chancellor of Germany, Captain Franz von Papen, currently military attaché in Mexico, due to be transferred to the USA. Also aiding him would be Captain Karl Boy-Ed, naval attaché, and Dr Heinrich Albert, a German lawyer already serving as commercial attaché to Ambassador Bernstorff, who would be the finance officer for the sabotage operations. With Bernstorff in Washington, the other three men established their operational base in New York City.

Albert opened an office at 45 Broadway; von Papen and Boy-Ed used an office in the Wall Street area. Furthermore, the aristocratic 38-year-old Captain Franz von Rintelen was dispatched to New York in April 1915, travelling on a false Swiss passport issued in the name of his brother-in-law, as 'Emil V. Gasche'. His mission was sabotage, both military and industrial. He claimed he was sent by the German Naval Ministry to replace Karl Boy-Ed, who was considered inefficient and unsatisfactory.

Germany's inept endeavours to subsidize the US press and influence American opinion had so far made little headway in the face of the well-oiled Allied propaganda machine. By 1915, the country had been utterly discredited. Franz von Rintelen wrote:

> Everybody in Germany was raging. Large packets of newspapers had been received from America, and there was not a word of truth in the reports that were being made about the military situation. We were particularly indignant at the numerous stories of atrocities, which had found their way into the American papers. With this kind of journalism it was inevitable that not only the mass of newspaper readers, but gradually also official circles in America, would assume an anti-German attitude.[13]

Having established an embryo German spy ring in the USA, the men's first assignment was to recruit potential agents for their sabotage and subversion operations. The group's early efforts were unimpressive, but von Rintelen possessed certain advantages: he was familiar with the Manhattan banking scene, he spoke fluent English, and his aristocratic birth ensured him an entrée in social circles. He compensated for his lack of specialist training as a spymaster with his energy and resourcefulness. Within weeks of his arrival in the USA he had managed to enlist the crews of some 80 German ships berthed in New York Harbor.

Upon his arrival in USA, von Rintelen had posed as a businessman under the pseudonym of Frederick Hansen and had set up a company, the Austrian- subsidized Transatlantic Trust Company, at 57 William Street in Manhattan, where he deposited a large sum of money. Although his activities were funded and directed from Berlin, he was given a relatively free hand. His mission was to sabotage US ships carrying munitions and supplies to the Allies. To that end, he formed a union to organize strikes and go-slows among munitions workers. From offices at 55 Liberty Street in New York City (around the corner from the Transatlantic Trust Company), together with the German spymaster, Heinrich Albert the lawyer, von Rintelen established a cover firm called the Bridgeport Projectile Company. The purpose of this dummy corporation was to purchase and destroy munitions, especially gunpowder, that would otherwise be shipped to the Allies, in an operation that would come to be known as the Great Phenol Plot. He spent $500,000 on all this. Most of the money was paid, probably on false pretences, to his American agent, David Lamar, the notorious financial conman known as the 'Wolf of Wall Street'.

Von Rintelen and Lamar conceived a plan to foment strikes in munitions factories and shipping agencies. Their goals were to force an embargo on munitions through Presidential or Congressional action, hinder the manufacture and shipping of munitions through attacks on financial institutions and litigation against pro-Allied business organizations, to create a craving for peace among the population and to promote and harness pro-German sentiment. They hired Frank Buchanan, former President of the International Union of Structural Workers, serving in Congress as the representative of the Seventh District (Northern Chicago area). Buchanan was expected to introduce and lead the battle in Congress for embargo legislation. He proved an efficient agent until the Germans made the mistake of paying him, after which he went on a prolonged drunken spree and was useless.

Von Rintelen turned the engine room of the SS *Friedrich der Grosse*, NGL Pier, in Hoboken into a bomb factory, and persuaded Walter Scheele, a German-born chemist based across the river in New Jersey, to create cigar-shaped incendiary devices. These comprised a tube in which two chambers were separated by a thin copper disk. One of these chambers contained sulphuric acid, while the other was filled with picric acid. The first endeavour was such a fiasco that the would-be bomb layer, Maurice Conners, ended up selling the firebombs to a junk dealer. Subsequent attempts possibly met with greater success: certainly, von Rintelen claimed to have recruited a number of Irishmen working on the docks and persuaded them to plant these firebombs on Allied shipping berthed in US ports. Indeed, the shipping news reported a series of mysterious incidents in which ships about to transport munitions from the USA were damaged and their cargoes ruined by fires.

Hitherto the US response to German secret activities had been equally amateurish. The USA possessed no national intelligence service *per se* but relied on diplomats and a handful of military and naval attachés for information. The country employed no expert code-breakers, and their communications security was rudimentary. Incredibly, there was no federal statute that forbade peacetime espionage and sabotage. Planting bombs and passport fraud – to name only two of the illegal activities already perpetrated by German agents – had to be investigated piecemeal by federal, state and local authorities. No federal agency had either the power or the resources to follow leads that hinted at a foreign-directed conspiracy to violate the laws of multiple jurisdictions. Things soon began to change, however.

During 1915 von Rintelen negotiated with Victoriano Huerta, the President of Mexico (disliked by many Mexicans, who nicknamed him 'El Chacal' or 'El Usurpador'), for money to purchase weapons and submarine bases. He hoped to persuade Mexico to declare war on the USA, with the knock-on effect of diverting US attention and resources and terminating the USA's export of munitions to the Allies. Their clandestine meetings, held in New York hotels were observed by the Secret Service, and von Rintelen's telephone conversations were routinely intercepted and recorded.

One of the spymasters' first recruits was Horst von der Goltz. Born Franz Wachendorf, he had adopted the name of this old aristocratic military family in order to impress the Mexicans while fighting in Pancho Villa's revolutionary forces.[14] Incarcerated in Chihuahua with other German mercenaries, he was approached by the German consul, Otto Kueck, himself on the run from Pancho Villa. Kueck recruited von der Goltz, who soon found himself with three other German would-be sabotage agents, armed with two suitcases of dynamite and orders to blow up the Welland Canal that linked Lake Ontario with Lake Erie. In the autumn of 1914 companies shipping commodities and raw material for US munitions regularly used the canal.

On the pretext of blasting tree stumps on a farm, Captain Hans Tauscher, the Krupp representative in New York, had obtained the dynamite from the Dupont Powder Company. Tauscher gave the dynamite to Goltz, who stored it at a German safe-house operated by Martha Held. Her terrace house at 123 West 15th Street in Manhattan was also the gathering place for German ship captains who docked in New York. To help him in his plan, von der Goltz – using the alias Bridgeman H. Taylor – engaged the services of several men. The small group of saboteurs left New York for Buffalo by train. Unbeknownst to them, they were being trailed by the American Secret Service. Upon their arrival at the canal they discovered that on the Canadian side it was heavily guarded. The saboteurs – notably Goltz – got cold feet and abandoned the plan. Returning to New York, he asked von Papen for money to enable him to return to Europe. Although Goltz wrote in his memoirs that he returned to Germany, where he was given a new mission and was travelling back to the USA to carry it out when he was picked up by the British, there has been speculation that in fact he never reached Germany but gave himself up to the British authorities at Falmouth. In 1916 Goltz figured as a major prosecution witness in the USA in the trial of von Papen and other German spies and saboteurs. Despite confessing to having himself been a sabotage agent, he avoided prison and appears to have spent the rest of his life in New York.

In 1917–18 the turncoat and resourceful Goltz published his autobiography, *My Adventures as a German Secret Agent.*[12] He played himself in the propaganda film *The Prussian Cur* (*Der preußische Hundesohn*).[13] The film's unflattering title referred to Kaiser Wilhelm II.

Heinrich Albert, in addition to his role as paymaster for German espionage and sabotage operations in the USA, was a fixer: he could arrange forged passports and documents. The next operational plan concocted by the spymasters von Papen and Albert was to obtain US passports for use by German army reservists residing in the USA who wished to return to Germany to fight. After the reservists reached Germany, military intelligence appropriated the passports, which they recycled, using them to send spies into Britain, France and Russia. However, this was no longer such an easy undertaking. The American State Department had tightened up on its lax passport regulations and required more extensive proof of US citizenship, as well as photographic identity of the applicant. To circumvent the new regulations, the Germans resorted to passport fraud.

To complement their sabotage operations the Germans had established their cover company, the Bridgeport Projectile Company, to conduct a covert operation to promote labour unrest and encourage strikes by labourers at US munitions factories. Under their three-pronged plan the cover company was to acquire vital raw materials, manufacturing equipment and tools to prevent them reaching legitimate companies; to win armaments and powder contracts that it would fail to honour; and to pay unrealistically high salaries, forcing rival companies to either follow suit or risk disruption in their workforces. This ambitious, bold plan was scuppered by the carelessness of its own agent, Heinrich Albert. Albert, despite his skill and intelligence, was slapdash. He was exposed as a spy because of his suspicious association with another colourful character, George Sylvester Viereck, poet, propagandist and editor of the pro-German publication *The Fatherland.* Viereck had been born in Germany to a German father and an American mother and was allegedly of Imperial blood; his father, Louis, had been born out of wedlock to the German actress Edwina Viereck and was reputed to be the son of Kaiser Wilhelm I, grandfather of the current Kaiser, Wilhelm II. Certainly, it was another member of the ruling Hohenzollern dynasty who assumed legal paternity of young Louis.

Between 1907 and 1912 George Viereck's fanatical Germanophile activities saw him expelled from various social clubs and fraternal organizations in the USA. So notorious did he become that in August 1918 a lynch mob would storm his house in Mount Vernon, forcing him to seek refuge in a hotel in New York City.

Before President Wilson signed an Executive Order on 14 May 1915, authorizing surveillance of German Embassy personnel in the USA, the Secret Service's operations had been limited to watching clerks, technicians and errand boys for the Germans. After Wilson's order, William J. Flynn, chief of the Secret Service, immediately assigned a ten-man squad to keep the Germans under surveillance. Frank Burke, a young agent, was appointed to head up this unit, which was based on the top floor of the Customs House at the Battery. Burke instigated surveillance of all individuals he knew to be involved in German activities, including Viereck, who was under investigation by the Secret Service for violations of America's neutrality laws. When Viereck started calling on Albert at the offices of the Hamburg-Amerika Line at 45 Broadway in Lower Manhattan, the association inevitably started alarm bells ringing.

It was further negligence on the part of Albert that led to the final devastating exposure of the German spy ring in the USA. Every day Albert travelled between his office at 45 Broadway and his Ritz-Carlton hotel room aboard the elevated train. On 27 July 1915 an advertisement appeared in the *New York Evening Telegram*. It read, 'Lost on Saturday. On 3:30 Harlem Elevated Train, at 50th St. Station, Brown Leather Bag, Containing Documents. Deliver to G.H. Hoffman, 5 E. 47th St., Against $20 Reward.'

The briefcase, carelessly left on the train by Albert, had been picked up by a counterintelligence officer. Albert, despite being relatively recognizable, a tall, heavy figure, his right cheek criss-crossed with sabre cuts, had hitherto been below the radar of US counterintelligence. None the less, he was being tailed by Burke, an officer of the Bureau of Investigation, on the orders of William Flynn. Albert had dozed off, and, waking with a start at his stop, had jumped off the train leaving his briefcase behind. Burke quickly seized the case, concealed it and got off himself. Albert, realizing at once what he had done, boarded again, searched desperately for the missing briefcase and, finding it gone, rightly assumed someone had taken it. He rushed out into the street in search of the culprit. Spotting Burke, Albert began to give chase. Burke hopped on a streetcar heading uptown, telling the conductor he was being pursued by a madman who had caused a scene on the elevated train.

The conductor, seeing Albert racing after the streetcar, arms flailing, told the motorman not to stop at the next corner. The streetcar hurried on, leaving Albert gesticulating helplessly in the street. Albert, in despair, hurried to the German Club on Central Park West, where he held an impromptu meeting with the military attaché, von Papen, and Captain Karl von Boy-Ed. They decided that a common thief must have snatched the case and would find nothing in it of value. They agreed that the best strategy to recover their vital documents would be to place an advertisement in the local newspapers offering a reward.

For the USA Albert's lost briefcase proved a revelation and a windfall: it contained Berlin telegrams, communications from German agents, financial records and reports and documents proving that Albert had spent $27 million on establishing an espionage network in the USA, using German money to fund dock strikes, attacks on shipping and bombs planted in munitions plants. The briefcase also contained papers with details about the 'Great Phenol Plot' and other covert activities intended to serve the German war effort. The 'Phenol Plot' was a conspiracy to divert American-produced phenol, or carbolic acid, away from the manufacture of high explosives and instead to use it to produce aspirin, profiting the German-owned Bayer Corporation.

When Burke opened the briefcase and saw the papers, he notified Flynn, who contacted Secretary of the Treasury William G. McAdoo at his summerhouse in North Haven, Maine. McAdoo decided that the contents proved beyond doubt that the German Embassy in the USA was violating the neutrality laws. He took the contents of the briefcase to President Wilson who told McAdoo to consult with Edward House and Secretary of State Robert Lansing.

The US government was in a quandary: if official use were to be made of the information gleaned from the incriminating documents this would prove that a government agency had stolen documents from a fully accredited diplomat. House suggested a solution: the contents of the papers would be given to a newspaper to publish. The obvious choice was the anti-German *New York World,* whose editor, Frank I. Cobb, agreed to publish the material without attribution in return for exclusive rights. The newspaper published the contents as front-page news on 15 August 1915. Albert was identified as the German spymaster, and it was alleged that the German government was financing Viereck's newspaper, *The Fatherland.* Letters between Viereck and Albert, published in the *New York World,* revealed that Albert, the espionage paymaster, was funding Viereck to the tune of $1,500 a month.

Other newspapers picked up the story and began bombarding Albert. In an attempt to restore calm, Albert provided the *New York World* with a 2,500-word statement in which he claimed that the press had misinterpreted his documents. His disclaimer was not believed. Henceforth, he would be mockingly referred to as 'the minister without portfolio'.

A further attempt to blow up the Welland Canal was made in September 1915 by Paul Koenig, head of a small detective agency that handled requests from the Atlas Line, a subsidiary of the German shipping company the Hamburg-Amerika Line. This bureau, operating from the offices of the steamship company at 45 Broadway, expanded after the war began and eventually became the most dangerous sub-centre of criminal intrigue maintained in the USA by the German government.[15]

On 22 August 1914 von Papen had instructed Koenig to recruit and supervise a gang of saboteurs. Koenig forbade his agents to meet with him at his office; instead, he used various locations, the identities of which were coded using a 'safety block system'. For example, a street indicated during a telephone conversation meant that the actual meeting would take place five blocks further away. Koenig's recruiting area was the docks. German steamship lines had attempted to send ships to sea under false cargo manifests in order to supply German naval raiders, and because of this violation of US neutrality German steamships were detained in Hoboken for the duration of the war. The crews loitering about the docks were a happy hunting ground for Koenig. His activities eventually aroused the suspicions of the Bomb Squad. Officers followed him to popular German hang-outs in the city, including the German Club in Central Park West, which was also frequented by his fellow conspirators, Albert, Boy-Ed and von Papen. The Bomb Squad placed a tap on Koenig's telephone with no result, until a few days later a man rang and delivered a torrent of foul-mouthed abuse. Officers identified the number as that of a public telephone in a bar, and checks in the neighbourhood and at the bar allowed them to identify the caller as George Fuchs, a distant cousin whom Koenig had recruited to spy on the Welland Canal. Later Fuchs had moved to New York City, where Koenig had hired him to work for $18 a week. The Bomb Squad lured Fuchs with a letter offering him a job. A meeting was arranged, with an undercover police officer posing as the company's representative. The undercover officer succeeded in gaining Fuchs's confidence. Fuchs revealed the secret plot concerning the Welland Canal and explained how he had come to New York to work for Koenig but had been dismissed for his disorderly antics, including fighting and drinking. A few hours later, Koenig was arrested. A search of his house produced his little black book in which he had meticulously recorded details about all his agents and their assignments.

Besides Walter Scheele, the enterprising von Rintelen had assembled a hand-picked gang that included Eno Bode, a German citizen and superintendent of the Hamburg-Amerika Line; Otto Wolpert, a German citizen and pier superintendent of the Atlas Line; and Erich von Steinmetz, a captain in the German Navy. Steinmetz claimed to have entered the USA disguised as a woman, smuggling dangerous pathogens, including cultures of the equine disease glanders with which it was proposed to inoculate warhorses intended for the Western Front. After a number of failed attempts, he succeeded in posing as a researcher and took the cultures to a laboratory where it was determined they were dead.

After the failure of his first sabotage attempts against shipping, von

Rintelen persuaded a German–American woman to write to the Russian military attaché in Paris, Count Alexis Ignatieff, offering the services of Rintelen's dummy import–export company, E.V. Gibbons, to supply goods to Russia. After winning a contract to supply munitions and tinned-meat products von Rintelen obtained a $3 million loan, which he deposited in a bank. He had a partial shipment loaded on the SS *Phoebus*. Unseen by the guards patrolling the decks armed with carbines, anti-British stevedores concealed several of Scheele's incendiary devices in the holds, now piled high with artillery shells for Russia. Later, *Shipping News* reported that there had been an accident in which the SS *Phoebus* from New York had caught fire at sea and been towed into the port of Liverpool by HMS *Ajax*. Von Rintelen then loaded two large cargo vessels with material. To divert suspicion he hired detectives to guard the vessels. After the ships left port they met the same fate as the *Phoebus*.

The unsuspecting Russians continued to deal with von Rintelen until several barges loaded with ammunition suddenly sank as they were being moved from the Black Tom Island terminal to ships waiting in the harbour. The Russians, their suspicions aroused, demanded immediate delivery of the rest of their large order. Rintelen quickly paid off his loan at the bank and liquidated his cover company. By the time the Russians obtained legal counsel the firm of E.V. Gibbons was no longer in existence.

The Bomb Squad was no closer to catching the saboteurs. It was decided to send several German-speaking officers into bars to strike up conversations with the customers. One officer struck it lucky when one of the patrons asked him whether he would like to be introduced to a man who was doing some work for the Germans. The officer, who used the cover story that he was a special agent for German Ambassador von Bernstorff, was subsequently presented to Captain Charles von Kleist. Von Kleist was completely taken in and became incautious. He proceeded to tell the officer about his work for a certain Dr Walter T. Scheele, who claimed to be a member of the German Secret Service. Although Scheele's Hoboken laboratory was ostensibly fabricating agricultural chemicals, von Kleist said its real purpose was the manufacture of fire bombs. A few days later, he led officers to the back yard of his house, where he dug up one of the empty bomb containers. Kleist was arrested and taken to headquarters. Thomas Tunney, the chief of the Bomb Squad, interviewed him and then stepped out of the room for several minutes. A workman was near by repairing a light fixture. Von Kleist, having heard the workman speak English with a German accent, asked if he would deliver notes for him. The workman agreed. In reality, the workman was an undercover police officer.

Scheele escaped and fled to Cuba but was later arrested by the Havana police. The other members of Scheele's operation and von Kleist were tried, convicted and sentenced to eighteen months in gaol. Von Rintelen, now at last under intense investigation by American authorities, left the USA on 3 August 1915 aboard the *Noordam*. When he arrived in Britain on 13 August British port-control officers arrested him, and he was interned until April 1917 when he was extradited to the USA to face trial.

For more than a year the German saboteurs, von Papen and Boy-Ed, focused on the critically important objective of Black Tom Island. Black Tom was a major munitions depot with several large 'powder piers', located in New York Harbor not far from the Statue of Liberty. Even after von Papen and Boy-Ed were recalled in 1915 the espionage and sabotage operation continued to target Black Tom. Months before his eventual capture von Rintelen had established a team of agents who would be responsible for the destruction of Black Tom Pier. He hired several agents to perform various tasks that ranged from smuggling explosive charges on to ships to bribing stevedores.

It remains unknown who lit the first fuse to cause the explosion at Black Tom. Police investigations pointed to a man named Michael Kristoff who was living at a boarding house in Bayonne, New Jersey, and who was reported by his landlady to keep odd hours and often return home smelling of fuel or with small soot stains on his hands or clothing.

All lay still and dark on Black Tom on the night of 30 July 1916 when small fires suddenly appeared, flickering in the blackness. Some guards on the island sent for the Jersey City Fire Department, but others fled as quickly as they could. That night, Johnson Barge No. 17 was packed with fifty tons of TNT, and sixty-nine railway freight cars were storing more than a thousand tons of ammunition, ready for shipment to Britain and France.

> Just after 2:00 a.m., an explosion lit the skies – the equivalent of an earthquake measuring up to 5.5 on the Richter scale, according to a recent study. A series of blasts were heard and felt some 90 miles in every direction, even as far as Philadelphia. Nearly everyone in

> Manhattan and Jersey City was jolted awake, and many were thrown from their beds. Even the heaviest plate-glass windows in Lower Manhattan and Brooklyn shattered, and falling shards of glass preceded a mist of ash from the fire that followed the explosion. Immigrants on nearby Ellis Island had to be evacuated.[16]

Several days after the explosion had destroyed the entire Black Tom facility, federal officials and the media attributed the massive blast to carelessness, not sabotage. In fact, the investigation by the police departments of New York and New Jersey and by federal authorities lasted many years but failed to determine the precise cause of the tremendous conflagration.

Both Boy-Ed and von Papen were expelled from the USA in 1915 amid allegations of espionage and sabotage of munitions industries in a country that at the time was still neutral. Before he left, Boy-Ed announced pompously that he would naturally refrain at this eleventh hour from yet again refuting the stories published about him in the US press; the majority of these, he claimed, were sheer fabrications, invented by members of the media.

The storm of international protest, especially in America, that greeted the sinking of the *Lusitania* caused the Kaiser and his government to lose their nerve and draw in their horns. To avoid further opprobrium and the antagonism of neutral countries the Kaiser ordered that submarine activity should be reined in. But in early 1916 Germany announced that she proposed to regard all ships, including merchant vessels, in the waters around Europe as legitimate targets that could be attacked without warning. After further admonitions from Wilson that this breached the international military code, Germany responded only by blowing up the cross-channel passenger ferry *Sussex* on 24 March 1916. Wilson threatened to break off diplomatic relations with Germany. The Kaiser, realizing that this would probably bring the USA into the war and that Germany would be unable to defeat the combined strength of the Entente powers and the USA, agreed to respect certain shipping lines. American involvement in the war had been averted once again, but the reprieve would be of brief duration.

In Germany, a disappointed Admiral Tirpitz tendered his resignation; this time, to his surprise, the Kaiser accepted it.

After the sinking of the *Lusitania*, the position of Wilson's Ambassador to Germany, James Gerard, became virtually untenable. In 1917 he was asked to leave. (President Wilson once referred to Gerard as 'an ass' in the margin of a dispatch passed on to his future wife Edith Galt.) After his recall, Gerard gave what has often been described as a 'notorious' speech in November 1917 to the Ladies Aid Society. Under the title 'Loyalty and German–Americans' Gerard was outspoken in demanding absolute commitment to the cause of crushing the German Army and with it the Kaiser. He effectively questioned the loyalty of German–Americans residing in the USA and suggested that firm action should be taken were they to in any way question the USA's commitment to beating Germany.

> Now that we are in the war there are only two sides, and the time has come when every citizen must declare himself American – or traitor!
>
> We must disappoint the Germans who have always believed that the German–Americans here would risk their property, their children's future, and their own neck, and take up arms for the Kaiser. The Foreign Minister of Germany once said to me 'your country does not dare do anything against Germany, because we have in your country 500,000 German reservists who will rise in arms against your government if you dare to make a move against Germany.
>
> Well, I told him that that might be so, but that we had 500,001 lamp posts in this country, and that that was where the reservists would be hanging the day after they tried to rise. And if there are any German–Americans here who are so ungrateful for all the benefits they have received that they are still for the Kaiser, there is only one thing to do with them. And that is to hog-tie them, give them back the wooden shoes and the rags they landed in, and ship them back to the Fatherland.
>
> I have travelled this year over all the United States. Through the Alleghenies, the White Mountains, and the Catskills, the Rockies and the Bitterroot Mountains, the Cascades, the Coast Range, and the Sierras. And in all these mountains, there is no animal that bites and kicks and squeals and scratches, that would bite and squeal and scratch equal to a fat German–American, if you commenced to tie him up and told him that he was on his way back to the Kaiser.[17]

When the USA finally declared war on Germany the German Ambassador, von Bernstorff, returned home. Three days later, on 17

February 1917, three Germans were arrested for attempting to sabotage the Black Tom Island facility, which had been rebuilt. In wartime the penalty for saboteurs caught in the act was death. With the ringleaders gone the other German saboteurs fled the USA.

By 1917 it was too late for Germany to seize the initiative. Germany had allowed the advantage to slip from her grasp. Had the Kaiser heeded Tirpitz's advice and resolutely embraced the ruthlessly effective strategy of unrestricted submarine warfare while Germany still held the upper hand, rather than allowing himself to be intimidated by the outpouring of international reproach, Germany might well have won the First World War – or at least have been in a position to undertake peace negotiations at an earlier stage.

FOUR

Sailing

On 30 April 1915 the *Lusitania* lay berthed at the New York docks, the hub of a bustling throng of boarding passengers, porters and dockers loading cargo of various kinds. The ship's manifest would show commodities such as meat, copper, medical supplies, furs, cheese, oil and machinery. But another cargo was being loaded, too, less openly. The quayside was crowded with relatives and friends of passengers and crew, sightseers attracted by the legendary splendour of the great ship, awed by her towering majestic presence, and a gaggle of newsmen and photographers on the scent of a headline.

For drama was in the air. This would be no ordinary crossing. The *Lusitania* would be sailing into the jaws of death. The German Embassy had issued a stark warning that any vessel sailing into the 'European War Zone' would henceforth be regarded as a legitimate target for German submarines. The warning stressed that passengers travelling on Allied vessels did so at their own risk. The Germans would later be able to claim, with some justification, that passengers had been given fair warning that they might be subjected to an attack.

NOTICE

> TRAVELLERS intending to embark on the Atlantic voyage are reminded that a state of war exists between Germany and her allies and Great Britain and her allies; that the zone of war includes the waters adjacent to the British Isles; that, in accordance with formal notice given by the Imperial German Government, vessels flying the flag of Great Britain, or of any of her allies, are liable to destruction in those waters and that travellers sailing in the war zone on ships of Great Britain or her allies do so at their own risk. *IMPERIAL GERMAN EMBASSY, WASHINGTON, D.C., APRIL 22, 1915*

The German Embassy's warning appeared in the newspapers on the morning the *Lusitania* was scheduled to leave New York. In some cases it was printed next to an advertisement for the ship. It created a flurry of excitement and some alarm, especially among those of a nervous disposition, because it seemed as though the *Lusitania* was being directly targeted. A few anxious people cancelled their voyage, but the reaction of others was more sanguine.

When the warning was read out over the telephone to Charles Sumner, Cunard's representative in New York, Sumner made light of it. He declared robustly that he found it hard to credit that the warning was genuine; he doubted that it had been issued by the German Embassy. It was not the first time, Sumner said, that people had tried to cause trouble for Cunard by spreading false alarm among prospective passengers. Why, only a few days previously someone had demanded payment of $15,000 to prevent the publication of an advertisement potentially detrimental to the shipping line. He himself, Sumner proclaimed, had not the slightest fear of submarines. The great liner's speed would prove a safeguard against attack.

Captain William Turner, Master of the *Lusitania*, echoed these sentiments, declaring stoutly that this talk of torpedoes was a great joke: the *Lusitania* was too fast to be caught by any submarine.

This cool dismissal was exactly what those acquainted with the character of the *Lusitania*'s experienced skipper would have expected. It was a character upon which much opprobrium would later be heaped when catastrophe struck; those at the highest level, in their desperation to evade any responsibility, would seek to cast suspicion on Turner's integrity. In view of later developments it is perhaps worth glancing at the career of the man who commanded the *Lusitania* on that last ill-fated voyage.

A gruff, gritty Scouser, Captain 'Bowler Bill' William Turner was a mariner's mariner. The sea was in his blood. Resilient, resourceful and courageous, his spirit had remained undaunted throughout the many perils and near-disasters he had survived during a long and distinguished career at sea. It would take unscrupulous political machinations and unworthy attempts at scapegoating by those in authority to break that spirit and tarnish that reputation.

William Turner was born in Everton near Liverpool in October 1856 to a sea captain and his wife, the daughter of a mill owner. The Turners hoped that their son William would embrace a respectable career in the

Church, but the boy declared he had no intention of becoming a 'devil dodger' and persuaded his parents to allow him to go to sea at an early age: some authorities claim he was thirteen when he embarked on this career, while others maintain that he was just eight years old. Certainly he was only a young lad when, on his first voyage as a cabin boy aboard the barque *Grasmere,* the vessel was shipwrecked off the coast of Northern Ireland. Refusing the offer of help from those with stronger arms, young Will swam to safety through the stormy seas by himself.

Nothing deterred young William Turner from pursuing his dream of a life at sea: not the battering he endured when rounding the Horn in the White Star clipper the *Queen of Nations*, under his father's command; not being swept overboard while serving as second mate of the *Thunderbolt*, bound for Calcutta, and spending eighty minutes in shark-infested waters; nor even his ill-fated voyage aboard the *War Spirit,* where yellow fever decimated his fellow crewmen as the waterlogged vessel drifted for four days until rescue came. He joined Cunard in 1878 as Third Officer of the *Cherbourg* and was soon playing a leading part in a series of heroic episodes. When leaving Liverpool's Huskisson Dock the *Cherbourg* collided with a barque, sinking her. The pilot and four members of the barque's crew drowned, but William leaped into a boat and managed to save two people who had clambered into the rigging of the sinking vessel.

In February 1885 Turner again revealed his mettle when he rescued a boy who had fallen into Alexandra Dock. For this courageous action he was awarded the Liverpool Shipwreck and Humane Society's silver medal. Further feats of daring would follow, each testifying to William Turner's courage and quick thinking. In 1897, while he was serving as Chief Officer aboard the Cunard steamer *Catalonia*, the ship's look-out sighted off the Grand Banks of Newfoundland a French schooner, the *Vagne*, dismasted and sinking fast in a gale. Turner immediately got up a volunteer rescue party, and despite the atrocious weather conditions they managed to save the schooner's entire crew. He was presented with an illuminated address in recognition of this exploit from the Liverpool Shipwreck and Humane Society in December 1897.

Turner possessed a quick, irreverent wit and was a born raconteur. He liked to boast that he was the quickest man on any sailing ship – except for a Greek he met once, who, Turner speculated wryly, had perhaps numbered a monkey among his ancestors. In one of his tales he recounted how as a cabin boy he had been scrubbing the decks in the captain's cabin and, overcome with pangs of hunger, had filched a slice of bread and butter that happened to be lying on the table. Hearing the captain's footsteps approaching, with great presence of mind Turner slapped the bread butter-side-up on the underside of the table, thus escaping detection.

Irrepressible as he was, young Turner entertained serious aspirations. In pursuit of his ambition to become a captain, when on leave and during shore duties he assiduously studied navigation. Sailing ships were his passion, but he soon realized that steam was the future. His aspiration was to serve as master of a Cunard vessel. When he discovered that it was company policy never to promote a man to the rank of Master unless he had already commanded a square-rigged sailing ship, Turner left the company to obtain this qualification. Having obtained his Captain's Certificate in 1886, in 1889 he sailed out of New York Harbor as master of a three-masted barque, the *Star of the East*, a clipper bound for Australia.

Just before leaving port Turner resurrected an old sailing-ship custom. Entering a gentlemen's outfitters, he purchased a bowler hat. For the rest of his life, whenever he went ashore he would wear his bowler, gaining the nickname 'Bowler Bill'.

The *Star of the East* made a successful round trip under Turner's command. Armed with a glowing reference from the ship's owner, he once more approached Cunard. After service on the *Umbria*, carrying troops during the Boer War, in 1903 Turner, now aged forty-seven, was given command of the Cunard ship *Aleppo* on the Mediterranean service.

The bosses at Cunard did not really know what to make of Turner, and their feelings were equivocal. On the one hand, they considered him the safest pair of hands on their payroll, capable of squeezing maximum knots out of a vessel and breaking speed records with apparent ease. When it came to the tricky operation of docking vessels his skill was unsurpassed. There was no doubt of his superb competence as a seaman, nor of his value to the company, and they eventually paid him £1,000 a year.

However, Cunard's milch-cow was her first-class service for the wealthiest and most exacting passengers, socialites, tycoons and celebrities for whom flattery and fawning flunkies were a prerequisite in a lifestyle of unremitting luxury. In addition to superb navigational skills the Master of a Cunard passenger liner was expected to display the social graces of an ambassador; he had to be a master of 'schmoozing'. Turner's brusque Scouse pragmatism and acerbic wit struck the wrong note. He was a seaman first and foremost, and he simply could not be bothered to pander to the pampered first-class passengers. Millionaires and celebrities expected not only to be transported efficiently, swiftly and in comfort; they expected invitations to dine at the Captain's table, to be amused and entertained and have their every whim indulged. Turner, unimpressed by their wealth and fame, dodged these unwelcome encounters as far as possible, deliberately taking his meals on the bridge to avoid those whom, privately, he likened to a pack of chattering bloody monkeys.

Curiously, human nature being perverse, Turner's reluctance to grovel to the customers had the reverse effect. His offhand manner imbued the elusive Captain with a kind of mystique. The more he shunned them, the more Cunard's first-class passengers were fascinated by him; he became the subject of animated and speculative conversation, and passengers began to ask Cunard's booking agents which ship Turner was commanding and whether there were still berths available.

Baffled, Cunard put him in command of the *Carpathia* for the whole of 1904. The same phenomenon occurred. When Turner was transferred to the *Ivernia* on the Boston run, passenger revenues for this service, too, improved. It was mystifying, but the money men at Cunard studied their bank balance and acknowledged that the lucrative bookings were far from unwelcome.

In 1907 Turner took command of the *Lusitania* on the recommendation of her retiring Master, Captain Jim Watt. He saw the ship through her early crossings to New York, taking the Blue Riband in the process with a record speed of 25.88 knots; under his command the great vessel acquired her nickname the 'Greyhound of the Seas'. Turner was promoted Commodore of the Cunard Line, and in November 1907 he was given command of the *Lusitania*'s sister ship, the slightly faster *Mauretania*, on her maiden voyage. Both vessels set new speed records on his watch, taking the Blue Riband several times. The *Mauretania*'s 1909 speed record of 26.06 knots would stand unchallenged for twenty years.

While captaining the *Mauretania* Turner had yet another opportunity to display heroism in a dramatic situation by saving the crew of the steamer *West Point*, which had caught fire. He was again awarded the Liverpool Shipwreck and Humane Society's Medal.

While Turner's professional career flourished, as was the case with many seafarers, his home life ashore hardly was on an even keel. In August 1883 he had married his cousin, Alice Hitching of Halifax, at the

Church of the Holy Innocents, Manchester. After their marriage William and Alice moved into their new home in Sale, near Manchester, where later two sons were born to them, Percy in 1885 and Norman in 1893. Soon after the birth of their second son, however, Alice left William and the family home, taking the children. By 1906 the couple were living apart, and William advertised for a housekeeper. In 1908 he met Mabel Every, a former nurse in her early twenties. With the appearance of Mabel on the scene, Turner's life ashore would take a more settled turn.

By 1914 Turner's older son, Percy, a tumultuous character described as happiest when involved in a fight, had abandoned his career in the Merchant Marine and become involved in Huerta's rebellion in Mexico, narrowly escaping being put up against a brick wall and shot. Norman, the younger son, was by then an officer serving in France with the Royal Artillery.

On 30 May 1914 William Turner commanded Cunard's newest and largest ship, RMS *Aquitania*, on her maiden voyage. By now one of the most famous skippers sailing the North Atlantic, Turner enjoyed the respect and affection of his crew, despite his reputation as a strict disciplinarian who did not suffer fools gladly. He was shortly to return to the command of the *Lusitania* again.

Turner was in his element: under his command the speed of crossings and the turnaround times improved, and the prestigious vessel was invariably impeccably presented.

Although passengers were fascinated by the curt Scouse skipper, the attraction was far from mutual. Cunard felt the need to employ a Staff Captain, John Anderson, purely to undertake the necessary socializing aboard their great *Lusitania*.

It was entirely in keeping with Turner's bold character to dismiss the warning printed in the US newspapers as scaremongering. He had also been assured by the Admiralty that the elderly Eclipse-class cruiser HMS *Juno* would be provided as an escort to the *Lusitania*. Personally he felt sure that his ship would hardly need to rely on the old *Juno*, with her unimpressive top speed of a mere 18 knots, slower than the *Lusitania* could achieve even though only three of her boilers were currently in operation because of the need for wartime economies. Turner's experience coincided with the perceived wisdom that it would be the *Lusitania*'s speed that would protect her from attack, rather than any naval escort.

Although the German warning caused a flutter of disquiet among some passengers, others experienced a frisson that only added to the thrill of their prospective voyage. Many more resolutely pooh-poohed the notion of danger, refusing to believe that a luxury ocean-going liner flying the US flag would be a military target. Displaying the star-spangled banner would surely guarantee her immunity. The passengers also seemed not to be alarmed if they noticed that the liner had been camouflaged, her distinctive scarlet funnels painted dark grey, almost black, her white lifeboats painted grey, too.

The staunch attitude of several of the most prominent passengers served as an example to others and strengthened their resolve. Some of these important figures had even received personal warning telegrams but had chosen to ignore them. Less famous passengers felt reassured, assuming that well-known men such as 37-year-old multimillionaire Alfred Vanderbilt and George 'Champagne King' Kessler, the wealthy wine merchant, would be well informed; surely they must have inside sources to notify them if there really were danger.

In September 1907 Vanderbilt and his friend Thomas Slidell had watched the *Lusitania* complete her maiden voyage to New York from the vantage point of Vanderbilt's yacht. Newsman Slidell would accompany Vanderbilt on the *Lusitania*'s fatal voyage.

Vanderbilt was a frequent traveller. Some years he crossed the Atlantic as many as seven times. In May 1915 he was travelling to chair a meeting of the International Horse Breeders' Association. The 1914 meeting had been cancelled because of the outbreak of war, but it was decided that the meeting in 1915 would go ahead. Slidell was aware that Vanderbilt had a more serious reason for travelling. A concerned and generous philanthropist, he intended to return to England in order to offer a fleet of wagons to the Red Cross. He himself intended to volunteer and offer his services as a driver. Slidell said Vanderbilt 'felt every day that he was not doing enough'. His wife Margaret and their two children would remain behind in New York, staying in the Vanderbilt Hotel on Park Avenue.

The heroic manner in which the multi-millionaire would spend his last hours a few days later was in keeping with the nobility of his character, giving lie to his playboy image. The night before Alfred was due to embark in the *Lusitania* the Vanderbilts spent the evening at the theatre, watching the Broadway play *A Celebrated Case*, co-produced by David Belasco and Charles Frohman. Coincidentally Frohman was also due to sail aboard the *Lusitania* the next day. The next morning, when they opened their newspapers and saw the warning, Alfred and Margaret Vanderbilt laughed it off. A little later Alfred received a telegram that read, 'THE LUSITANIA IS DOOMED. DO NOT SAIL ON HER'. It was ominously signed 'MORTE'. Alfred made light of this warning, too.

Vanderbilt family legend contends that Alfred had previously booked passage on the maiden voyage of the White Star Line's *Titanic* and that he had cancelled his booking because his mother had had a premonition of disaster. His Uncle George had booked the same voyage, and he, too, cancelled his reservation. But his luggage was loaded on the *Titanic* and ended up at the bottom of the ocean.

Charles Frohman, the renowned theatrical impresario, whose play the Vanderbilts had just enjoyed on Broadway, also received personal warnings about sailing aboard the *Lusitania*. One warning was mysterious and anonymous; the other was a telegram from his friend John Drew that read, 'I'll never forgive you if you get blown up by a submarine.'[1]

The 58-year-old Frohman was bound for the London theatre scene with the intention of assessing the latest West End productions as potential Broadway hits. He usually visited London a couple of times a year, often in the autumn. When Frohman received the warnings he pretended to ignore them and responded with his customary dry quips: after managing so many stars, he said, mere submarines held no terrors for him. When asked if he was afraid of submarines he joked that the only thing that frightened him were IOUs. Nevertheless he took the unusual precaution of dictating his whole programme for the next season's productions, something he had never done before.

Frohman's main worry was not U-boats but his articular rheumatism; this painful condition had been triggered by a bad fall a few years back, and the sea air seemed to aggravate the symptoms. He had even considered bowing out of the trip and sending someone else in his place, but he had little faith in anyone else's judgement. Besides, no other impresario carried his cachet. He compromised by booking passage for himself and his valet William Stanton on the fastest ship currently on the Atlantic run. The *Mauretania* had already been drafted for war duty; this left the *Lusitania*.

The writer Justus Miles Forman also received warnings. Besides his respected novels, Forman wrote what he called 'little fluffy things', popular magazine stories that earned him reams of fan mail from ladies. He quipped that women always wanted to know whether he was as handsome as his heroes always were, but he refrained from telling them. Forman's butler would later relate that shortly before he left home on that last morning his master received a phone call from an unidentified man with a thick German accent who warned that if he sailed on the *Lusitania* he would be blown up. The German promptly hung up, and Forman dismissed the call as a prank by one of his high-spirited friends. As they drove to the quayside, Forman's chauffeur was concerned for his employer's safety. He suggested that his employer was running a risk: a pack of Germans were lying in wait to destroy the ship. Forman pooh-poohed the notion, asking what chance the Germans would have of catching Justus Miles Forman.

When he reached the pier on that warm, damp Saturday Forman discovered that Charles Frohman and several others had received similar warnings that they, too, had shrugged off. As they glanced round the crowded Pier 54 on the North River and saw the constant stream of taxis and limousines sweeping up, conveying the 1,200 passengers, it did not seem that many had been deterred. The liner's six decks of passenger accommodation towered over the bustling quay, where a band was playing in the drizzle. Hundreds of crewmen and dockers were completing preparations for departure. Once on board, first- and second-class passengers strolled about the deck, surveying the crowded waterfront below. The scene was unusually busy, the German warning having attracted a horde of reporters and photographers to the quayside. When the paparazzi spotted Frohman and Vanderbilt they asked the millionaires to pose on deck for a picture with the *Lusitania*'s Captain, William Turner. Frohman was asked why he was not travelling with Ellen Terry on the *New York*, due to sail later the same day, at noon; Frohman replied that his protégée, the glamorous actress Rita Jolivet, was sailing on the *Lusitania*. That was explanation enough.

Newly-wed Albert Bestic was delighted with his appointment as the *Lusitania's* new Third Officer. He had always thought of the *Lusitania* as his dream ship. He was quickly introduced to his fellow officers and formed his first impressions. He found Staff Captain 'Jock' Anderson friendly and felt at ease. First Officer Arthur Rowland Jones, from Flintshire, looked a little dour. Bestic would later learn that the First Officer's idea of relaxation was sitting in his cabin perusing the collected works of Conrad.

Second Officer Percy Hefford, like Bestic, was recently married. Bestic's new colleagues warned him to avoid socializing too much with the passengers, especially the ladies.

The embarkation process was slower than usual, because of the extra safety procedures that had been put in place. And there was another complication: the *Lusitania* was originally scheduled to leave New York at 10 a.m., but her sailing was delayed by two and a half hours while forty-one passengers and crew were transferred to her from the passenger ship SS *Cameronia.* It is often claimed that the *Cameronia* had been suddenly requisitioned by the Admiralty. However, both the Cunard Line official website and Arnold Kludas, maritime historian and former director of the scientific library of the German Maritime Museum in Bremerhaven, state that the *Cameronia* was not requisitioned for troop transport until January 1917. Contemporary accounts suggested that the *Cameronia* was on her way to Halifax, Canada, to collect supplies and Canadian troops.

Whatever the reason for the delay, the *Lusitania*'s passengers had not been informed. Consequently, in the heightened tension, speculation and frustration were rife. Saloon passenger Dr Howard Fisher was travelling to Europe to help his brother-in-law establish a hospital in France; he was accompanied by his sister-in-law, Dorothy Conner, a Red Cross volunteer nurse. They wondered whether perhaps sailing had been delayed because the threat of submarines had caused Captain Turner to lose his nerve.

At last, just as the gangplank was finally being raised Senior Third Officer John Idwal Lewis noticed a woman running along the dock shrieking entreaties to wait for her. The gangplank was lowered again so that the woman could board. Lewis later learned that the woman was second-cabin passenger Alice Middleton.

The loading over, the great ship began to ease gently out of harbour to the strains of the band and the last cries of farewell. A lone movie cameraman stood at the entrance to Pier 54 filming the great ship's departure.The celebrated American author Elbert Hubbard spotted the cameraman from the *Lusitania*'s deck and gave him a cheery wave. Hubbard, the colourful founder of the Roycroft Artisan community, hailed as a prophet by some and condemned as a charlatan by others, was travelling to Europe with Alice, his second wife, with the intention of obtaining an interview with the Kaiser, about whom he had been very rude. The cameraman went on filming from high on the pier catwalk as tugs backed the mighty *Lusitania* into the Hudson River. Her passengers watched the New York skyline recede into the distance. As the faces on the dock merged into a distant blur along the waterfront, the *Lusitania* steamed past the rising metropolis and its landmarks for the last time.

As she passed the Battery the drizzle stopped and the sun broke through the clouds. To many it seemed a good omen. One female passenger is said to have remarked, 'I don't think we thought of war. It was too beautiful a passage to think of anything like war.' First-time passengers excitedly explored the splendours of the floating luxury hotel where they would spend almost a week. The size, speed and construction of the great liner were reassuring. Even though the 1912 sinking of the White Star Line's *Titanic* a mere three years before had shaken the shipping industry to its core and exposed deficient safety standards, the *Lusitania* seemed as impregnable as a seaborne castle.

Her size alone not only contributed to the sense that she was invincible; it meant that in order to function efficiently a major logistical operation was required. The ship carried between 800 and 900 crew members, some to attend to navigational matters and a whole team to shovel coal into the furnaces that pressurized the boilers. The vessel consumed 1,000 tons of coal a day. This was delivered to the docks aboard twenty-two coal trains, each comprising thirty trucks. Each coal truck weighed approximately 10 tons. On the dockside the coal was loaded into the ship's bunkers through hatches in the hull, a filthy process that spread a thick coating of coal dust over the deck, often penetrating to other areas. The black dust then had to be hosed off before passengers boarded. Meanwhile cooling the liner's massive steam turbines required 65,000 gallons of water a minute.

Other staff attended to every need and catered to every whim of the 1,200 passengers: some 400 stewards, fifty cooks and an assortment of other staff – musicians in the ship's orchestra, telegraph operators, lift attendants, printers, bell-hops. There were also seventy crew involved in sailing the ship and an additional 390 engineers. Everything about the vessel inspired confidence. The *Lusitania*'s speed was legendary. She also seemed rock-solid in her immensity and design. Her hull was divided into thirty-four watertight compartments. Surely if the worst came to the worst, people reasoned, the great floating city was designed to withstand multiple torpedo strikes and still remain afloat.

Concerns about safety receded as the opulence of the surroundings dazzled the first-time passengers. The *Lusitania*'s towering six-deck silhouette and gold décor redefined luxury on the high seas. The luxury of the first-class accommodation was breathtaking. Money appeared to have been no object, neither for the designers nor for those who paid the price to enjoy its splendours: regal suites in first class cost $4,000 for a one-way trip at a time when the average working man earned $20 a week. First-class passengers could enjoy a post-prandial stroll along a promenade walk, covered to protect their cosseted forms from the onslaught of the elements. In first class, amid a décor incorporating Corinthian columns and potted palms, the élite could enjoy gourmet dining in an ambience of elegance and refinement. The first-class dining-room, two decks high and surmounted by an ornate dome, was the grandest room afloat, the jewel in the crown of James Millar's architecture.

The neo-classical Louis XVI mahogany-panelled first-class saloon, occupied two levels, Shelter Deck C and Salon Deck D. Its ornate circular central well was topped by a dome measuring 29 feet by 23 feet, lavishly decorated with frescos in the style of Francis Boucher that featured chubby *putti* and depictions of the four seasons. The upper area, 65 feet by 65 feet, bounded on each side by promenades, could seat 147. The lower level, 85 feet by 81 feet, seated 325. Celebrating the best of European and British design, the craftsmen had used the finest oak and cedar wood from ancient forests, intricate wrought iron and bronzes, blending styles from French Renaissance to English manor-house. No expense had been spared to give passengers the illusion that they were in a luxury hotel rather than in the middle of the Atlantic Ocean: the sole ominous note was the fact that the brocaded shield-back swivel chairs, like the tables, were bolted to the floor as a precaution against rough seas.

Even in wartime the ornately decorated menu remained lavish: a choice of soups, followed by fish, ham, beef, vegetables, a choice of desserts, ices and coffee. Consumption was conspicuous. The volume of resources required for one Atlantic crossing was awe-inspiring: 130 pigs, 40 oxen, 10 calves, 80 sheep, 60 lambs, 150 turkeys, 350 ducks, 90 geese, 200 pheasants, 400 pigeons; while some 4,000 other fowls were consumed.

The first-class lounge and music room on A Deck exuded a similar opulence, with inlaid Georgian mahogany panelling and stucco, two high fireplaces of green marble beneath a barrel-vaulted skylight with stained-glass windows representing the months of the year. The reading and writing room featured another glass-domed ceiling and functioned essentially as a ladies' lounge. Its walls were tastefully panelled in grey and cream silk, interspersed with carved pilasters and mouldings. The chairs and writing desks were of the finest mahogany. The rose-coloured carpet was complemented by Rose du Barry silk curtains and upholstery. If the writing room was the preserve of the female passengers, gentlemen could repair to the smoking-room, aft of the lounge and music room on Boat Deck A. Here the décor was Queen Anne, with Italian walnut panelling and red furnishings. The Verandah Café, aft of the saloon accommodations on Boat Deck A, behind the smoking-room, had been a new departure for Cunard. When first introduced it had not found favour with Cunard's over-indulged clientele, but it had now been refurbished with palms, trellises and wicker garden furniture to create a more welcoming ambience. An innovative if ambitious feature was that the wall could be opened up on to the promenade, with the aim of giving patrons the impression that they were seated in a Parisian sidewalk café. However, the uncooperative weather conditions of the North Atlantic meant that this was a rather underused feature. It would nevertheless be a forerunner of the design elements observable today in modern cruise ships, which are intended to create a 'resort' atmosphere on board.

Saloon cabins on Decks A through E ranged from one shared room to various en-suite accommodations in different decorative styles. The largest of these were the two regal suites on Promenade Deck B, forward of the grand staircase and between the first and second funnels. Each regal suite boasted two bedrooms, a personal dining-room and pantry for private dining, a parlour and a bathroom. The portside regal suite was decorated in the style of the Petit Trianon at Versailles.

Charles Frohman, the so-called 'star-maker', credited with creating the 'star' system in theatre and film, had seen it all before. After watching New York slide into the distance, he went down to his stateroom, B-75, to browse through his first batch of playscripts, munching candy and fruit from the 'bon voyage basket' sent him by his protégée, the actress Maude Adams, to whom it was rumoured he was secretly married.

His other protégée, the stunning French-born actress Rita Jolivet, who had been described by W. Stephen Bush in his review of *The Unafraid* in the *Moving Picture World*, 10 April 1915, as 'a Frenchwoman of striking beauty and of some histrionic talent, a more typically French woman could not be imagined', found herself far from satisfied with her accommodation. She knew it was her own fault. She had impulsively decided to book the quickest passage available out of a sudden burning desire to see her brother Alfred before he left for the front line; her last-minute reservation meant that she had ended up with a disagreeably cramped inside cabin on D Deck. Her friend Ellen Terry had suggested she join her and travel aboard the *New York*, but the ship was slower than the *Lusitania*, and Jolivet, having made her decision, could brook no delays. Besides, she did not intend to spend much time in her cabin. The sumptuous public rooms and the beautiful palm court were her natural environment, and they drew her like a magnet. There she would meet up with her mentor, Frohman, the young Romanian-born opera singer Josephine Brandell and other friends including her brother-in-law, and they would find plenty to amuse them during the voyage. Jolivet had been surprised to discover that her brother-in-law George Ley Pearce Butler was also on board. Butler had abandoned his career as a banker to become a respected singer under his stage name George Vernon. After another career change, he was now earning a fortune in the import business. Employed as an agent of the Russian government, he was bound for London to secure an arms deal for Russia. He also intended to bring his young wife, Jolivet's sister Inez, the violinist, back to the USA with him. Jolivet and Brandell, their admirer Wallace Phillips and Vernon (formerly Butler), together with Forman, Frohman and the playwright Charles Klein, formed a little theatrical clique that naturally gravitated together on board. Klein and Forman often tried to persuade Frohman to leave his room, without much success.

Frohman was a shy man, and constant pain made him reluctant to leave his stateroom, even taking many of his meals there; but he did present the men with a bottle of champagne to show friendship. He also reassured Forman about the failure of his topical play *The Hyphen,* about Irish–Americans and German–Americans. He promised that their fellow passenger Charles Klein, the British-born actor and playwright who had had a narrow escape when he cancelled his booking aboard the *Titanic* at the last moment because of a business appointment, would introduce Forman to the most influential theatre people in London. Klein had just finished work on a new play that he had given Frohman to read.

Brandell had many international engagements and had already crossed the Atlantic several times aboard the *Lusitania*, but this time it was different. The talk of war and submarines had set her panicking. Her friend Mabel Crichton, with whom she was travelling, spent much time attempting to allay her terror. Brandell kept saying she worried that the liner would not, after all, be able to outrun a submarine; later she confessed that she had spent much of the journey 'in a state'. Her cabin, like Jolivet's, was down on D Deck. All the bathroom fittings were silver-plated; but what use was opulence, she reasoned, if she would not have time to escape from her cabin if the liner were to sink after an attack by a submarine? Her anxiety did not abate, and she expressed her fears to her dining companions. Despite the splendour of her surroundings, the white Corinthian-style pillars crowned with gold leaf, the potted palms, the buffet heaped with delicacies, Brandell was tormented by her terror of submarines. Such was her state of anxiety that her dining companions, her friend Mabel and two interesting and successful gentlemen, the Hungarian-born fashion designer Max Schwarcz and Francis Bertram Jenkins, the New York manager of Holland and Sherry wool importers, were concerned for her. Jenkins hardly allayed Brandell's fears by wondering aloud if the ship carried enough lifebelts, but her friend Mabel thought the provision was adequate. She often went round the tables at mealtimes collecting tips for the orchestra.

One other passenger who found herself dissatisfied with her cabin was Theodate Pope, who was travelling to England with her maid Emily Robinson and Edwin Friend to seek support to found a society for psychical research. Pope found to her horror that she had been allocated a cabin close to the three cabins occupied by the noisy Crompton family. Paul Crompton was shipping accoutrements made from sheepskin for the British Amy. He and his wife Gladys occupied cabin D-56, three of their children were in D-58 and the other three and their nursemaid were in D-60. Pope found the noise created by the excited children intolerable and demanded to change cabins. She was moved to A-10. After this move she relaxed enough to conclude that her fellow travellers were 'a quiet shipload of passengers'. She remained convinced throughout the voyage that the Germans 'intend to get us . . . but we would surely be convoyed when we reached the war zone'.[2]

Another first-class passenger, the attractive young Margaret Mackworth, watched the New York skyline retreat with a heavy heart. Intelligent and forthright, blonde and blue-eyed Margaret had other matters on her mind besides submarines and seasickness. She had been in the USA accompanying her father, the industrialist and Liberal MP David Alfred Thomas, whom David Lloyd George – recently appointed as Britain's First Minister of Munitions – had entrusted with the mission of arranging a supply of armaments for British forces. Mackworth, like her fellow passengers, had been impressed by the size and elegance of the liner, but she was reluctant to leave the glamour of New York City and return to Britain, which was embroiled in war. She was also depressed by her awareness that her marriage of seven years to the coal baron and keen fox-hunter Sir Humphrey Mackworth was foundering. Margaret had drifted into her alliance with the much older Humphrey after enduring several 'seasons' of the 'marriage-market' socializing expected of débutantes after they had 'come out' and been presented to the monarch at Queen Charlotte's Ball. The London débutante scene had not really been to her taste. Before she embraced her feminist cause she had been considered shy, a serious young woman with neither the liking nor the gift for inconsequential small talk.

While Margaret was tired of her marriage, she was keenly aware that a divorced woman was a social anomaly. Moreover, she was already a controversial figure. As a resolute and courageous suffragette, well educated and articulate, she had overcome her natural reserve, braved her husband's disapproval and courted notoriety in the interests of her cause. She had organized the first meeting of Emmeline Pankhurst's Women's Social and Political Union at Newport; she had leaped on to the running board of Prime Minister Herbert Asquith's car and harangued him; she had even been arrested for attempting to blow up a letterbox with a chemical bomb. In Usk prison she had refused to be bailed out by her husband and was released only after she had been on hunger strike for five days. For these and other political activities she would come to be known as the Welsh Boadicea.

Shortly after departure Staff Captain Anderson found himself dealing with an unexpected emergency: three German stowaways were discovered hiding in a steward's pantry on the port side by the master-at-arms. They had slipped past the cordon of Secret Service men at embarkation. Some versions of the story claimed the three men had photographic equipment with them, giving rise to the speculation that they had hoped to record the presence of concealed munitions. With the assistance of Alphred Pederson, a passenger who spoke fluent German, Inspector William Pierpoint, a detective with the Liverpool City Police secretly tasked with apprehending any German spies who might have boarded the vessel, interrogated the men. He asked if they had planted explosives, among other things, but the Germans proved uncooperative, merely boasting that they would teach the First Lord of the Admiralty, Winston Churchill, 'how to trim his Navy'. The *Lusitania*'s deck plans do not indicate the presence of a gaol, so the trio were probably locked in an empty cabin below decks to await trial when the ship reached England.

The presence of these three men may have been connected with the espionage activities of Captain Boy-Ed. It has also been surmised that they may have been linked to John Neil Leach, a known German sympathizer who had obtained a position as a waiter on the liner through connections with Captain Anderson. Twenty-five-year-old Leach was the son of a judge in Jamaica. A British citizen, he spoke fluent German and frequented German sympathizer circles, staying with one of them, Gustav Stahl, at a boarding-house located at 20 Leroy Street in New York, which German spy Kurt Thummel was also known to frequent. Leach's uncle, a provisions importer in New York, was acquainted with Captain Anderson and recommended his nephew for a job. Stahl later testified under oath that he and Leach had sneaked on board the night before the *Lusitania* sailed and that the ship was armed. Stahl was later convicted of perjury.

The *New York Times* of 4 June 1915 reported on the rigorous inspection to which the *Lusitania* had been subjected: the ship was inspected every day she was berthed in New York by members of the so-called 'neutrality squad', eighty men from the government specially selected for their ability and familiarity with conditions in New York Harbor. On the day she sailed the vessel was once more inspected by none other than Dudley Field Malone, US Collector of Customs.

On the face of things an unimpeachable expert, Malone's dubious personal reputation served merely to reinforce certain aspects of subsequent conspiracy theories. He had obtained his post in 1913 on the personal recommendation of President Wilson, supported by Malone's father-in-law, New York senator James A. O'Gorman, who was a friend of the President's. Malone appears to have been an inveterate social climber whose closet contained several skeletons. In short, he seemed to be a man who might entertain few qualms about issuing a clearance certificate for a ship, usually the day before its departure, based solely on a 'Loading Manifest'. A more accurate manifest, the 'Supplemental Manifest', would then be filed three days later, after the ship had sailed and it was too late to intervene. During the outcry over the *Lusitania*, Malone was asked by a reporter from the *New York Times* whether projectiles such as those used by the Artillery could be classed as explosives. His response was quoted in the paper to the effect that if no fuse was fitted to them such projectiles theoretically had no means of detonation, and could therefore be classified as non-explosive and legitimately loaded aboard a passenger liner under US law, so long as they featured on the ship's manifest. (Malone, many times married, bankrupt and pursued by irate clients, would die in 1950 after being beaten up in 1949 at a roadside by two hired thugs.)

Little Barbara Anderson was almost three, and she thought the ship was just beautiful. She had stood with her mother, peeping through the railings, scanning the crowded pier below, trying to see her father, but there were too many people and too much confusion. After a while, Barbara and her mother Emily left the rail and went into the second-cabin deckhouse to their cabin with its bunk beds.

The 460 second-class passengers were allotted accommodation located in the far end of the stern, behind the aft mast, on the Shelter, Upper and Main Decks. Those who shared two- and four-berth cabins found they were more spacious and comfortable than first-class cabins on other vessels. Many professionals, such as teachers and lawyers, travelled second class. The last-minute gutting and rebuilding of the ship's second-class section in the stern had skilfully integrated the bracing support columns into the decor. The second-class public rooms were situated on partitioned sections of boat and promenade decks housed in a separate section of the superstructure, aft of the first-class passenger quarters.

Design work was deputized to Robert Whyte, the architect employed by John Brown. Although smaller and plainer, the design of the dining-room reflected that of first class, with just one floor of diners under a ceiling with a central well, featuring a smaller dome and balcony that gave an impression of space. Walls were panelled and carved with decorated pillars, all in white, disguising the support braces. As in first class, the dining-room was situated lower down in the ship on the saloon deck. The breakfast menu, although less lavish than the first-class menu, offered fried whiting, smoked herrings and broiled Wiltshire bacon; the dinner menu featured, for example, curried mutton with rice, corned pork with vegetables and boiled chicken with parsley sauce. The smoking- and ladies' rooms occupied the accommodation space of the second-class promenade deck. The smoking-room had mahogany panelling and a white plasterwork ceiling and dome. One wall was decorated with a mosaic depicting a river scene in Brittany; the sliding windows were tinted blue. For the first time ever, Cunard had provided a separate lounge for second class, a pleasant room with mahogany tables, chairs and settees set on a rose carpet. The lounge featured finely finished wooden columns and panoramic view of the ocean.

Outside, on the second-class promenade, passengers could enjoy the bracing sea breeze – although there was always the danger of flying smuts from the funnels. Second cabin was overbooked on this voyage, and meals had to be served in two sittings. Tables also had to be placed in hallways to accommodate the overflow. Professor Ian Holbourn had more important things on his mind than this minor inconvenience. In his early forties, Holbourn was a man of many parts – explorer, athlete, mathematician, popular lecturer on a broad spectrum of subjects ranging from archaeology to ethics and co-founder of the Ruskin College for Working Men. He had fallen in love with the remote and beautiful island of Foula, off Shetland, which he purchased in around 1900, becoming its laird. In September 1914 the White Star transatlantic liner RMS *Oceanic*, commissioned as an armed cruiser by the Royal Navy on the outbreak of war, had been wrecked off Foula. Before he set sail on the *Lusitania* Holbourn had had a recurring dream that the liner would be torpedoed. His wife Marion would later claim to have had what she would describe as a 'waking vision' on 6 May.

Holbourn had been invited in 1913 by the Lecturers' Association of New York to give a lecture tour of the USA. He had given more than a thousand lectures before returning home and had returned to the USA in the autumn of 1914 with the manuscript of his magnum opus, *The Fundamental Theory of Beauty*. He had worked on this for twenty years and hoped to publish it in 1916.

Aboard the *Lusitania*, missing his three sons, the professor, a kindly man who liked children, struck up an unlikely friendship with twelve-year-old Avis Dolphin who was travelling in second class on her way to England to attend school. He spent time with her, taking her mind off her seasickness with stories. Avis's mother, the proprietor of a nursing home in St Thomas, Ontario, had emigrated to Canada from England ten years earlier but insisted that her daughter receive a British education. Avis was looking forward to seeing her homeland; she had only heard stories about it and seen pictures. Accompanying her on the voyage were two nurses who worked for her mother. Avis's nurses had left her very much to her own devices.

Forty-one-year-old Commander J. Foster Stackhouse, formerly of the US Navy, was sailing on the *Lusitania* to be reunited with his wife and twelve-year-old daughter in London. He was travelling with Robert Dearbergh, a Quaker who worked with the Belgian Relief Fund Commission. In New York Stackhouse had stayed at the Lotos Club, one of the oldest literary clubs for gentlemen. He was planning to lead the British Antarctic and Oceanographical Expedition to survey the Antarctic coastline, continuing the exploratory work of Captain Robert Falcon Scott. He had hoped to purchase Scott's ship, the *Discovery*, from the Hudson Bay Company. He had put down a £1,000 deposit on the ship, hoping to be ready by 1916. An article in the *New York Times* of Sunday,

9 May 1915 stated that he had been in the USA with the aim of raising funds for this expedition and had obtained promises of financial support amounting to almost $900,000. While in the USA he had handed over a letter from Sir Edward Grey to US Secretary of State William Jennings Bryan. The Commander had also met with President Woodrow Wilson and had dined with former President Theodore Roosevelt and ex-President Howard Taft.

On the morning of their departure Stackhouse and Dearbergh had stopped by the studio of portrait artist Henry R. Rittenberg to pick up a portrait for which the Commander paid Rittenberg a huge sum of money. Rittenberg asked him why he was choosing to sail on the *Lusitania* in view of the warning from the German Embassy that the ship would be destroyed. Stackhouse scoffed at the notion. The ship, he said, was too fast to be torpedoed; moreover, the presence of so many US passengers would act as a deterrent. It was widely rumoured among Stackhouse's fellow passengers, including Harold Boulton, that he was a British agent on a secret mission.

Second-cabin passengers Theodore and Belle Naish, enjoying a belated honeymoon, had heard of the warning telegrams received by some of their fellow passengers, but Theodore told Belle that, if the Germans were truly serious about destroying the *Lusitania*, such telegrams would have been delivered to every single American passenger aboard.

Leslie and Stewart Mason were also honeymooners; they were travelling to set up home in Woodbridge, Suffolk. They were accompanied by Oliver Bernard, an artist from Covent Garden who had been working in Boston for Leslie's millionaire father William Lindsey, an arms manufacturer and would-be playwright. Bernard had been designing a stage set for a play set in medieval Picardy written by Lindsey, which Bernard thought deplorable.

Julia Sullivan pretended that this trip was a second honeymoon for her and her husband Florence, too, but her heart was heavy. She found the prospect of leaving her comfortable existence in the USA for life on her husband's family farm in Ireland depressing in the extreme. Florence Sullivan originated from Clounlea, Kilgarvan, in County Kerry. After emigrating to the USA he had met Julia, who was living in Long Island, New York, with a wealthy old couple, the Branders. The Branders helped Flor find work at the fashionable Stuyvesant Club in New York City, and Julia often visited the club when Flor was on duty.

After Flor and Julia married and moved into the city Flor's father often wrote asking them to come back to Ireland to manage the family farm. But they were enjoying their life in the USA and kept putting off the trip. Now Flor's father had died. The Sullivans knew they had to go back to Ireland or lose the farm. They decided to make the best of it. Flor was friendly with the ship's purser, James McCubbin, who promised the couple the best cabin and table in second class if they arrived early enough. He allocated them an end cabin next to the saloon promenade and a table next to his own in the second-cabin dining saloon. McCubbin also showed the Sullivans the saloon-class dining-room and a corner where they could hide unnoticed to watch the dancing and entertainment. Julia Sullivan thought their sailing day was like a day at the races. Flor had seen several of the millionaires on board at the Stuyvesant Club and knew many of them by name.

Emigrants travelling in third class were the financial mainstay of the transatlantic shipping lines. *Lusitania* had harvested accolades for the superior travelling conditions it provided to emigrant passengers and had become popular with this group. Previously, third-class accommodations had consisted of large spaces where hundreds of people had to share open berths. The few public areas often comprised little more than a small deck space and a few tables thrown up in the sleeping quarters. The *Lusitania*'s third-class accommodations were located on the Shelter, Upper, Main and Lower Decks at the forward end of the ship, and, although simpler than first or second class, were surprisingly comfortable and spacious by comparison with steerage accommodations on other ships of the time. Indeed, they offered more agreeable living conditions than those to which many of their occupants were accustomed in their lives ashore. Cabins contained two, four, six or eight berths, a significant improvement on the previous 'mass dormitory' system. There was sheltered deck access, although, unlike saloon passengers, steerage passengers had no access to the open decks.

In steerage functionality replaced opulence. Walnut and mahogany panelling was replaced by pine; exposed bulkheads and rivets and simple white-painted gangways made no attempt to create the illusion of a five-star hotel. The compact cabins nestled deep within the bowels of the ship.

Outside cabins had a single porthole, and each cabin had metal beds, a steel wash-basin and a small closet. Plain but hearty meals were served at long tables in the communal dining-room. Breakfast might typically feature porridge; lunch might be steak and onions, corned beef, curried veal or an omelette; dinner menus offered roast beef or pork, fish or steak with a side dish or vegetables, rice and bread. The large third-class dining-room on the saloon deck, forward, was – like the smoking-room and ladies' room on the Shelter Deck – finished in polished pine.

When the *Lusitania*'s third-class accommodation was fully booked, the smoking- and ladies' rooms could easily be converted into overflow dining-rooms, where meals were eaten at long tables and there were two sittings. A piano was provided so passengers could create their own entertainment if they wished.

Although third-class passengers travelled in comparative comfort aboard the *Lusitania*, Alice Middleton, who had almost missed the ship, counted herself lucky that not only had she managed to scramble aboard at the last minute but she had also secured an upgrade from third to second class. She felt especially fortunate after she noticed handsome Richard Preston Prichard. Alice smiled at him often but never got the chance to speak to him. Much to her chagrin he seemed more interested in Grace French, an attractive Scottish milliner and dressmaker. French claimed she was the last passenger to be transferred to the *Lusitania* from the requisitioned *Cameronia* and had almost missed the ship – in an interview in 1975 she would say she wished she had missed it.

Richard Preston Prichard, who was twenty-nine and studying medicine at McGill University in Montreal, was a realist. He had put his papers in order before embarking and had instructed a fellow student where to find his will if anything should happen to him. He spent many afternoons on board with Grace French, when her seasickness permitted. Other time she spent in the company of Archibald Donald and his friends.

Donald, a Canadian engineer of Scottish descent, was travelling to attend an officer-training course at the University of Edinburgh. His cabin-mates aboard the ship were John Wilson, a chemist, who had been his roommate at Cambridge, and George Bilborough. Despite the luxurious appointments of the vessel there was a fault with the ventilation system in their quarters, so Donald stayed out of the cabin most of the time, playing bridge from ten in the morning with Bilborough, Thornton Jackson and the Reverend Herbert L. Gwyer. He took a break in the afternoon to be with Grace and 'the ladies'.

The very tall Reverend Gwyer and his new wife Margaret were Donald's table companions, together with Lorna Pavey, who had been working as a governess in Canada but who was returning to volunteer for the Red Cross. Margaret saw little of her new husband those first few days aboard ship, such was his passion for cards.

Travelling in third class were Annie Williams and her six children: Edith, Edward, George, Florence, Ethel and four-month old David. Annie was in desperate straits. The Williams family had emigrated to America years earlier, but soon after their arrival in the New World John Williams had deserted them. Annie suspected that he had gone back to England without telling her. So she had saved as much money as she could, sold all their possessions and booked passage on the *Lusitania* to take the family back to England where she hoped to track down her errant husband.

Twenty-three-year-old Harold Boulton had been in the USA on medical discharge from the British Army. He was travelling with his Oxford friend Frederic Lassetter and Lassetter's mother Elisabeth. At twenty-two Lassetter was already a veteran. A lieutenant in the Scottish regiment the King's Own Light Infantry, he had been wounded fighting in Flanders in September 1914 and had been convalescing and visiting relatives in Los Angeles.

The war was on everyone's minds. Surgeon Dr James Houghton of Troy, New York, a graduate of Harvard Medical School, was the son of Supreme Court Justice James Houghton. He was twenty-nine years old. On board the *Lusitania* he encountered the charismatic and courageous Belgian Red Cross fundraiser Marie Depage. Depage, born into an aristocratic family, had joined the humanitarian efforts of her doctor husband Antoine, head of the Belgian Red Cross and surgeon to King Albert. Finding herself appalled by the lack of resources available in Belgium to care for the wounded, she had been in the USA on a fund-raising mission to obtain support for Belgian military medical aid. She was returning home on the *Lusitania* to see her son Lucien, who had been called up and was about to join his older brother in the trenches. Depage solicited Houghton's help in the Western Front field hospitals, inviting him to work with her, her husband and the heroic and ill-fated nurse Edith Cavell. Houghton told Depage that he had signed a new will the night before leaving New York. She in response described herself a 'happy fatalist'.[3]

While some passengers planned war work or reflected on their resolution to join the forces, others whiled away the voyage with card games; these included Sir Hugh Lane, born in 1875, aged thirty-nine, an art collector and philanthropist. Lane had established the first known public gallery of modern art in the world, Dublin's Municipal Gallery of Modern Art. He had also made significant contributions to the visual arts in Ireland

and South Africa. Aboard *Lusitania* he was travelling with fellow connoisseurs Charles and Frances Fowles. There was a rumour circulating that Lane was bringing with him, sealed in circular lead containers, paintings by Monet, Rembrandt, Rubens and Titian insured for £4 million. If these existed they were never recovered.

On board the *Lusitania* Lane could be seen playing cards in the smoking-room with fellow passengers Marguerite, Lady Allan, and Dr Fred Pearson. A prominent Montreal socialite, Marguerite was travelling with her daughters Anna, sixteen, and Gwen, fifteen, to be reunited with her family. At meals Lady Allan and her daughters shared a table in the dining-room with Frederick Orr-Lewis, a Canadian businessman who was the president of Canadian Vickers, Ltd, the Canadian division of the British shipbuilding and armaments corporation. He owned an estate in Enfield, Middlesex, named Whitewebbs, to which he was returning after a business trip to Canada and was accompanied by his valet George Slingsby.

Many of the first-class passengers travelled with an entourage – maids, valets, secretaries, nursemaids. Often, for their employers' convenience, these servants were accommodated in cabins close at hand. Lady Allan's maids Emily Davis and Annie Walker were accommodated in B-4930. Lady Allan herself occupied regal suite B-47.

Frances Stephens shared Lady Allan's table. A Canadian philanthropist of Scottish descent, and a leading member of Montreal high society, she was the widow of landowner and lawyer George Washington Stephens, a Cabinet minister of Quebec. She was travelling on the *Lusitania* with her infant grandson John Harrison Chattan Stephens, her maid Elise Oberlin and baby John's nurse Caroline Milne. John, aged eighteen months, was the son of Frances's only son, Lieutenant Chattan Stephens, who had abandoned his career as a stockbroker in order to fight on the Western Front. His wife Hazel had departed for England ahead of him, accompanied by the couple's daughter Frances. John and his grandmother would follow later aboard the *Lusitania* upon hearing the news that Chattan had fallen ill with trench fever and developed endocarditis.

Beautiful, frail 25-year-old Dorothy Braithwaite was Frances Stephens's dining companion. Her journey, like that of so many, was linked to the personal tragedies of wartime. Both her sisters had lost their husbands on the same day. When Braithwaite learned that her brothers-in-law had been killed in action she at once took ship to join her young widowed sisters.

Personal tragedy and war also meant that for wealthy Canadian mother and daughter Mary Amelia Ryerson, aged fifty-six, and Laura, aged twenty-three, this voyage was hardly a pleasure trip. Two of Mary's sons had been fighting for Britain. One had been killed; the other was recuperating from being shelled. Mary's husband George, founder of the Canadian Red Cross, had already crossed on the *Lusitania* in April to deal with the heartbreaking family situation, and now Mary and Laura were following. George's cousin, Arthur L. Ryerson of Haverford, Pennsylvania, had lost his life on the *Titanic.*

The Ryersons shared their table with fifteen-year-old William Robert Grattan Holt who was being sent back to school at Marlborough. When the First World War broke out, his parents had kept him home in Montreal for fear of a German invasion of England, and thus he had missed both the Michaelmas 1914 and Lent 1915 terms. Several months later, the Holts believed that the risks had diminished and their son could return to school.

Sarah Mounsey Lund was travelling with her husband Charles Lund and her father William Mounsey on a desperate errand of a different kind. Sarah's mother Fanny Mounsey had been missing since she sailed on the ill-fated Canadian Pacific liner *Empress of Ireland*, which sank in the St Lawrence River in 1914 after a collision with the Norwegian collier *Storstad.* The *Empress* went down in fourteen minutes. Fanny's body had never been recovered. Almost a year later the Mounsey family had received extraordinary news: a woman known as Kate Fitzgerald, residing in a Liverpool institution, was repeatedly uttering the name 'Mounsey' and appeared to have a pathological terror of water. This woman was believed to be a survivor of the *Empress of Ireland* disaster. William, Sarah and Charles dropped everything and hurried to New York to board the *Lusitania*, hoping that the mysterious woman would turn out to be Sarah's mother. On the train to New York the trio struck up a friendship with Eunice Kinch, a widow, and her son William Mostoe-Kinch, who were also booked on the ship.

Frederick Orr-Lewis's valet George Slingsby travelled in first class with his employer. He had his own cabin, B-62, and he ate his meals in the magnificent saloon-class dining-room with William Stainton, valet to Charles Frohman, and Emily Davis and Annie Walker, maids to Lady Allan. Their table was on C Deck of the first-class dining-room, on the starboard side facing the open deck through the window. Slingsby kept Lady Allan's teenage daughters entertained.

Dr Fred Pearson and his wife Mabel were citizens from the USA travelling aboard the *Lusitania* on business and to visit their daughter

Natalie Nicholson. Pearson was a consulting electrical engineer and a successful international entrepreneur, heading up the Pearson-Farquhar Syndicate which did extensive engineering around the world. Pearson's secretary, David Walker, accompanied them.

Flor's and Julia Sullivan's new shipboard friend Patrick Callan, also Irish-born and, like the Sullivans, returning to Ireland for family reasons – his wealthy father had fallen ill – enjoyed a game of poker. He and the Sullivans noted with disapproval the activities of card-sharps in the saloon-class smoking-room. Outraged, Flor pointed them out to Julia, noting that the professional cheats were smartly dressed and spoke in the superior accents of senators while fleecing their fellow players.

News of the ongoing war was inevitably of great interest to many passengers, including a Canadian named Ernest Cowper, a reporter with the Toronto tabloid *Jack Canuck*, who was on his way to Europe as a war correspondent. Cowper was travelling in second cabin but would cross into first class every day to interview the notorious literary icon Elbert Hubbard and his second wife Alice. Hubbard had scandalously abandoned his first wife Bertha, the mother of his first four children, proclaiming that Bertha was boring and that great men often married commonplace women. After Elbert and Alice married, they campaigned for liberal divorce laws, feminism and women's rights.

Hubbard, despite his notoriety, was held in high esteem as a sage. He had strong convictions of moral rectitude, faith in a Supreme Being (despite being an agnostic) and no fear of death. Cowper and Hubbard bonded, Hubbard calling Cowper 'Jack' after the name of the publication that employed him. Hubbard was on board through a colossal piece of effrontery that had paid off. In 1913 he had pleaded guilty to misusing the postal service to send 'filthy' material. He was fined $100 and deprived of his citizenship. Among the evidence of the 'filth' he had disseminated was a joke. A young woman who has been married for only one year enters a drugstore and asks whether they exchange unsatisfactory merchandise. Assured that it is store policy to ensure customer satisfaction or to exchange goods, she produces a whirling-spray contraceptive device, sets it on the counter and demands that it be exchanged for a bottle of Mellins Baby Food.

Having once attempted to secure an American passport, Hubbard applied to the President in person for a pardon. His request was turned down. But when war broke out Hubbard appealed to Wilson's secretary Joe Tumulty, saying he intended to go to Europe to cover the war. This time Wilson granted the pardon at once.

In October 1914 *The Philistine*, a 'periodical of protest', published Hubbard's pro-Allies article 'Who Lifted the Lid Off Hell?' in which the author said of Kaiser Wilhelm II, 'He has a shrunken soul, and a mind that reeks with egomania . . . He is swollen, like a drowned pup, with a pride that stinks . . . Caligula, the royal pagan pervert, was kind compared to the Kaiser.'[4] Hubbard had brought copies of his article with him with the intention of distributing them to his fellow passengers.

Cowper knew that on the day the liner left New York Hubbard had dismissed the German warning not as a threat but as a personal challenge. While munching on an apple in his stateroom, B-70, he had told reporters he used to be on friendly terms with the Kaiser but had no idea how he stood with him now because he had written some things that might have displeased him. However, Hubbard said, if he managed to reach his destination unscathed and the Kaiser refused to see him in Berlin he would bide his time and catch up with him on St Helena.

Hubbard went on to say that from his own personal point of view he would not mind if the ship were to be attacked and sunk. It might turn out for the best as far as he was concerned, because if he went down with the *Lusitania* and was proclaimed a hero it might well be his only chance of fulfilling his ambition to get into the Hall of Fame. Otherwise, barring accidents, Hubbard declared that he intended to live to be a hundred, there being but two respectable ways to die – either from old age or by accident. All disease, he said, was indecent. Three years previously Hubbard had said of Isador Straus, co-owner of Macy's Department Store, and his wife Ida that dying together on the decks of the sinking *Titanic*, having refused to be parted, was 'a glorious privilege'.[5]

British-born Marguerita Kay was in an advanced stage of pregnancy when she and her seven-year-old son, Robert, took passage on the *Lusitania*. She was determined that this next baby would be born in England; she was willing to brave the threat of torpedoes, the inconveniences of pregnancy, her inability to swim and a tendency to suffer from seasickness.

Twenty-five-year-old Dorothy Conner, the Red Cross volunteer, was travelling with her brother-in-law Dr Howard Fisher. They intended to establish a war hospital in France. Conner and Fisher had met Marie Depage and had been discussing the possibility of joining forces with her husband Dr Antoine Depage to provide aid to the soldiers in La Panne, France. Conner enjoyed these new shipboard friendships and found her table companions, suffragette Margaret Mackworth and her father the Liberal MP D.A. Thomas, congenial. She had also met up with Charles

Plamondon, a friend of Howard's brother Walter, but despite the pleasant company she was finding the voyage dreary and tedious and found herself hoping there might be some thrills when the ship entered the channel.

Conversely, the relaxing atmosphere of a sea voyage was just what wealthy hoteliers Gladys Bilicke and her husband Albert had been hoping for. He was recovering from abdominal surgery, and the couple had been taking a short trip to recuperate on the advice of Albert's doctor. While in New York they decided to round off their trip with a luxurious voyage on the *Lusitania*. In a postcard to his friend Leonard Brown, Albert said he had been aboard the *Lusitania* twice before and the ship's speed and officers were familiar to him. He also sent a telegram to his real estate agent, C.H. Barber, announcing his intention of taking a sea voyage because life ashore was too strenuous for him. Barber tried to stop the Bilickes from embarking, but he was too late: they had already bought their tickets. They intended to travel in magnificent comfort, occupying B-48, one of the ships' two regal suites.

As *Lusitania* cleared Ambrose Light and headed into the Atlantic sea lanes the veteran Captain Turner decided not to steer a zigzag course. He did not want the resultant rolling motion to frighten the passengers. Frequent lifeboat drills also risked alarming these delicate hothouse flowers, and ordering them to keep their port-holes closed would exasperate them. Although Turner resented having to pander to the wealthy passengers, it had been drummed into him that their physical comfort and psychological well-being were a priority. This caution may well have fatally affected the number of those who survived.

On Sunday, 2 May Oliver Bernard had observed a half-hearted attempt at a lifeboat drill. He had spent some time at sea and noted that the *Lusitania*'s somewhat desultory lifeboat drills always involved the same two boats, one on the starboard side and one on the port side. A few members of the crew would clamber into the lifeboats, secure their lifejackets and then get out again, making no attempt to lower the boats, which Oliver knew to be the riskiest and most demanding part of the procedure.

Another passenger concerned about safety procedures was wine importer George Kessler, the 'Champagne King'. In his cabin, A-23, which had cost him $380, Kessler was carrying with him $2 million in stocks and bonds. He was a firm believer in keeping his possessions within reach; he told Purser James McCubbin that it was 'safer this way'. On Sunday, 2 May Kessler had witnessed the crew's lifeboat drill. He had said to Purser James McCubbin that it was all very well to drill the crew, but the passengers needed to be familiar with safety procedures, too. McCubbin referred Kessler to the Captain. Consequently the next day Kessler called on Turner in his day cabin and asked what measures were being put in place in view of the 'torpedo scare'.

Kessler suggested a system whereby every passenger was given a ticket listing the number of the lifeboat he or she should make for in the event of anything untoward occurring. The Captain did not appear to welcome the advice, replying that a similar suggestion had been made to the company after the *Titanic* disaster but that they considered it impracticable. Kessler was not impressed by this response and made his feelings clear.

Those participating in the ship's pool that first day were annoyed to find that the *Lusitania*, known to be capable of steaming ahead at over 25 knots and making over 600 nautical miles in a single day, was travelling only about 450 miles a day. Export broker Isaac Lehmann, never the easiest of men, was disappointed to find the ship was making such slow progress and asked First Officer Arthur Rowland Jones the reason for the ship's lacklustre performance. He was informed that they were not operating all the boilers partly because the liner's current crew had been picked up here and there, it being difficult to assemble experienced crews in Liverpool at that time. Turner would later defend his crew, contending that although they were a scratch crew they were the very best available in the circumstances.

Throughout the voyage the geologist Lothrop Withington and his fellow Bostonian and seasoned traveller Charles Lauriat, of the Boston booksellers, would also check on the ship's daily run. Lauriat, too, often found the unexpected sluggishness of the 'Greyhound' frustrating. On the first day of the voyage he noted that the ship logged 501 miles; to his disappointment the second day's count was lower. He complained to Withington that the ship would not reach Liverpool on schedule at the present rate of performance.

Both men accepted the possibility that, as a ship from a belligerent nation, the *Lusitania* might be subjected to attack, but they had embarked undeterred. Moreover, Lauriat had been heartened by reassurances that the liner would be escorted through the war zone.

As the *Lusitania* headed east, her massive bow making light weather of the Atlantic waves, those aboard – even those who had suffered pre-boarding nerves – grew increasingly relaxed. Three square meals a day, the sea air, the regular and reassuring motion of the ship, the pleasant conversation and the novelty of shipboard life and new acquaintances, and the enforced suspension of cares and preoccupations that would assail them once more as soon as they set foot on dry land, all conspired to lull minds and senses and soothe spirits.

The day before the *Lusitania* sailed out of New York Harbor German submarine *U-20* had slipped out from her base at Emden on the north coast of Germany. She was under the command of her dynamic and determined young captain, Walther Schwieger, on a mission to patrol the British waters which had recently declared a war zone by the Imperial Powers. Her primary targets were to be troopships and supply vessels. Cutting off the lifeline of the Allied war effort, the supply of troops and material to the British forces currently engaged in the Dardanelles, was crucial to the German war effort. The Allied offensive relied heavily on the constant replenishment of resources, in particular from the USA. British ports, chiefly Liverpool, serviced a steady stream of vessels involved in this vital traffic. Now *U-20* was making her slow and stealthy way towards the hunting grounds off the Irish coast, through which the *Lusitania*'s course lay.

FIVE

U-20

On 6 May 1915 the *Lusitania* steamed into the designated war zone. In this particular area off the Irish coast some fifteen German submarines were prowling. U-boat crews and commanders were celebrated in accordance with their 'bag', the number of 'kills'. One of the keenest underwater hunters, the German U-boat *U-20* had rounded the southern tip of Ireland on 5 May and was now positioned some way from the coast, off the Old Head of Kinsale. The *U-20*'s career as a hunter and killer would last just over three years, from the date of her commissioning in August 1913 to November 1916 when she would run aground at Vrist in Denmark and be blown to smithereens by her own crew. In that short time the *U-20* would sink thirty-seven ships, crippling many more, gaining a respectable kill score of 145,830 tons.

From December 1914 the *U-20* had been commanded by dynamic, tough-minded thirty-year-old Kapitänleutnant Walther Schwieger. He was one of the new breed of German naval officers, technically competent, ambitious, cool-headed and popular with his 32-man crew. Born on 7 April 1885 to a noble family in Berlin, Walther von Schwieger – he disliked the aristocratic 'von' and never used it – had entered the Kaiserliche Marine as a sea cadet in 1903 at the age of eighteen. After initial training at the shore-based training establishment Stosch, he was promoted to the rank of Fähnrich zur See, comparable to that of a midshipman in the Royal Navy, on 15 April 1904. In 1905, on successfully completing specialist training at the Marineschule, he was posted to a naval reserve vessel, the liner *Braunschweig*. He was subsequently posted to the Kaiserliche Marine's Torpedo Division in 1906, and in September of that year he was commissioned as a Leutnant zur See, after which he served two years as a watch officer on torpedo boats, first the *S-105* and then the *G-110*. On 10 November 1908 he was promoted to the rank of Oberleutnant zur See and posted to the light cruiser SMS *Stettin*. In 1911, he transferred from SMS *Stettin* to the U-boat service. After serving as a Flaggleutnant on the *U-14* Schwieger was promoted to the rank of Kapitänleutnant on 19 September 1914. He took command of the *U-20* at the end of December in the same year and soon proved an inspirational and ruthless commander.

His command, the *U-20*, had been built in Danzig dockyard in 1913. She was 210 feet long, with a beam of just 20 feet and a surface displacement of 650 tons. Submerged, her displacement was 837 tons. She was propelled on the surface by two 850-horsepower diesel engines. While submerged, two 600-horsepower electric motors took over the job of driving her twin screws. Her armament comprised four 19.7-inch torpedo tubes, two forward and two in the stern, plus one 4.1-inch deck gun. She carried six torpedoes on each patrol.

On 30 April 1915 Kapitänleutnant Walter Schwieger's orders were to take his command the *U-20* to the northern tip of Great Britain, then to return southwards on the Atlantic side, turning east towards the Irish Channel with the purpose of attacking and destroying vessels entering and leaving the busy port of Liverpool. This mission completed, he was then to proceed round Ireland and head home to Germany. Since leaving her base at Emden on 31 April 1915, the *U-20* had enjoyed a moderately successful run, although three days into her patrol she had spent some time dodging enemy patrols and performing emergency dives, she had enjoyed a moderately successful run. On her journey to the Atlantic she had attacked several ships, including a Danish merchantman, released after the German look-out spotted the Danish flag.

On 5 May, when Schwieger rounded the south-west tip of Ireland, despite the lack of 'kills', his crew were in good spirits. Even a failed attempt at sinking a freighter, during which their torpedo had misfired, had not dampened their mood. They felt their luck was about to change, and they were right. Early on Wednesday, 5 May, the *U-20* bagged her first modest trophy, a small British three-masted wooden schooner of 132 gross registered tons, with square sails. The Liverpool-registered schooner, the *Earl of Lathom*, was carrying a cargo of bacon and potatoes from Limerick to Liverpool. Schwieger, like other U-boat commanders at this stage of the war, scrupulously observed the maritime code, surfacing and ordering the five-man crew of the schooner to abandon ship and bring him her flag and papers. The crew complied. As they pulled for the shore in their lifeboat the *U-20* launched twelve grenades at the schooner. The *Earl of Lathom* heeled over and sank. The *U-20* then fired a torpedo at the British steamer *Cayo Romano*, which was flying a neutral flag, but missed.

At 10.30 that night, the British Admiralty sent out a general warning simply stating 'Submarines active off the south coast of Ireland.' At midnight, they transmitted a more specific addendum: 'Submarine off Fastnet.'

The next day, Wednesday, 6 May, brought better hunting for the *U-20* as she pursued an eastward course in the Irish Channel. On that foggy morning off the coast of County Wexford, near the Coningbeg Lightship, the *U-20* encountered the *Candidate*, a British single-funneled 5858-ton steamer sailing from Liverpool on the Britain–West Indies run. Although submarine commanders were wary of attacking large merchantmen on the surface, since many were armed with deck guns often concealed behind bales or crates, the undaunted Schwieger surfaced and fired his deck gun from a distance of about 300 yards. The shells struck the *Candidate*'s funnel and superstructure. Her firemen panicked and rushed to launch lifeboats despite the orders of their commander, Captain Sandiford, to stay at their posts. The captain tried to swing his ship's broadside away from the submarine so as to expose only her stern, but when the *U-20* fired directly at the bridge Sandiford reluctantly ordered his crew to abandon ship. The *Candidate*'s second cook Fred Smyth warned the chief cook that they were being shelled; the chief officer ordered Smyth into a lifeboat. The *U-20* stopped shelling to allow the crew of the *Candidate* to abandon ship. As they did so, Smyth noticed that the steamer's deck was riddled with shell holes. One lifeboat swamped as it hit the water, but the other three lifeboats got away safely. As they retreated into the fog Schwieger ordered his crew to sink the *Candidate*. The *U-20* fired a torpedo into the *Candidate*'s engine room. The resultant loud impact rocked the submarine, but the *Candidate* stubbornly remained afloat. Schwieger ordered the *U-20* to move closer to the ship and used the submarine's guns to fire on the *Candidate*'s waterline. Now he could clearly see the ship's name on her stern, although there had been an unsuccessful attempt to paint over it. At last, slowly, the *Candidate* sank, stern first.

The survivors of the *Candidate* noted a small armed naval trawler, the *Lawrenny Castle SA-52*, hovering near the scene. The trawler's gun would not have been sufficiently powerful to sink the submarine, but it could have done enough damage to prevent it from submerging again. To the survivors' astonishment the trawler fled without resistance.

At 3 p.m. the *Candidate*'s survivors were picked up by the naval trawler *Lord Allendale*, commanded by Captain Foster. Hearing their complaint that the *Lawrenny Castle* had fled the scene of the sinking, Lieutenant

Stevens, whose patrol included *Lawrenny Castle*, ordered the captain of the fleeing vessel to proceed to the nearest Irish harbour and turn himself in for arrest.

The *Candidate* survivors specifically requested the Admiralty to relay news of their vessel's torpedoing to the *Lusitania* for the larger ship's safety. However, for some reason the message was not passed on to the *Lusitania.* Indeed another twenty-four hours passed before the Admiralty even informed the naval base at Queenstown.

The *U-20* 's look-out then sighted the White Star liner *Arabic,* but, although the liner was not zigzagging, her speed made it impossible for the submarine to attack her. About two hours later, at 12.25 Greenwich Mean Time, the *U-20* had more success with a new prey, the *Centurion*, a British ship of 5,495 gross registered tons, off the coast of County Wexford. The *Centurion's* name was covered, and she flew no flags. The *U-20* 's torpedo struck her below the foremast. As the *Centurion* began to sink, her 44-man crew abandoned ship. An hour later the small steamer was still afloat. Again *U-20* surfaced to finish the job. Schwieger had no desire to allow the ship to escape into the fog. Too impatient to wait for his pilot, Lanz, to identify the target's nationality, he ordered a second torpedo to be fired into the *Centurion*'s bow to ensure that the ship sank. Without lingering to observe the result of this latest strike Schwieger ordered the *U-20* to leave the scene.

Neither sinking involved any casualties. In both instances Schwieger had provided ample time for the crews to evacuate beforehand. Furthermore, the small ships took a long time to go down. Even though the survivors were rescued, no news of either of these successful attacks so close to *Lusitania*'s course reached Vice-Admiral Coke at Queenstown, who could have relayed this information to the *Lusitania*. The Admiralty was aware of the fate of the *Centurion* by the early hours of 7 May, but the *Lusitania* entered the war zone without having received any specific warnings.

On the morning of 7 May Schwieger gave the command to dive at 11 a.m. after sighting a fishing boat that he suspected might be a British patrol boat. Shortly after this the elderly cruiser HMS *Juno* chugged past the submerged submarine at high speed, zigzagging, leaving Schwieger no opportunity for a successful attack.The *Juno* had received warning of submarine activity off Queenstown at 7.45 a.m. and was hurrying back to port. The Admiralty was well aware of how vulnerable these older ships were to submarine attack.

Meanwhile, the *Lusitania*, still fog-bound, was steering a course south

87 east at 18 knots 25 miles off the south coast of Ireland. Captain Turner was fully expecting at any moment to meet up with the naval escort he had been promised – the same elderly light cruiser HMS *Juno* that had just passed over the *U-20* as she scuttled away. Turner was unaware that the Admiralty in London had withdrawn his escort because of the known presence of a U-boat; nor was he informed of this enemy presence.

After her flurry of activity, the *U-20* 's complement of weapons was now reduced to three torpedoes. Her fuel reserves were also depleted. Schwieger intended to save at least two torpedoes for his homeward journey, in case of such contingencies as surprise encounters with the enemy. He decided, therefore, not to take his craft into the Irish Sea through St George's Channel. He was ready to head back, to steer for the open waters of the Atlantic and home. He could not know that his greatest prize was at that moment steaming straight towards him.

It was the *U-20* 's chief engine room artificer Friedrich Sellmer who sighted the massive silhouette at 1.20 p.m. GMT. Schwieger's diary states that he caught sight of the ship in the distance while the *U-20* was surfaced. He quickly gave the order to dive to a depth of eleven metres and manoeuvred the submarine into an attack position.

Myths have proliferated and persisted around the dramatic events of 7 May 1915. One such legend concerns the alleged insubordination aboard the *U-20* of one Charles Vögele, an Alsace-born crew member who is said to have refused to obey Schwieger's order to relay the order to fire, on the praiseworthy humanitarian grounds that the target was a passenger liner with women and children aboard. Supposedly, this high-minded individual was shouldered aside by Raimund Weisbach, the *U-20* 's torpedo officer.

It is time to explode this myth, which appears to have originated in a letter published on 9 November 1972. It was sent to the editor of the French newspaper *Le Monde* by M.A. Ricklin, a professor of literature at Strasbourg University, and its contents have which been perpetuated in film and in naval historic literature. The fable of Vögele's alleged insubordination, subsequent court-martial and three-year imprisonment in the naval prison at Kiel continues to flourish and is treated as fact.

In research published in Volume 8 of *Marinenachrichten-blatt* by members of 'Arbeitskreis Krieg zur See 1914-1918 e.V.' (which translates as the Working Committee of 'The War at Sea 1914–1918') in March 2012, it appears that the story of Charles Vögele is a complete fabrication.[1] No man going under the name of Charles Vögele was on board the *U-20;* nor has any refusal to obey an order during the attack on the *Lusitania* been recorded; nor is there any documentary record of a court-martial against a Charles Vögele or of his alleged three-year imprisonment in Kiel.

Disciplinary cases, such as an open insubordination in time of war, would never have been dealt with by a court-martial at Kiel, where all units and agencies reported to the Baltic Naval Command. No court-martial of the Imperial German Navy ever passed a three-year custodial sentence in such a case. Moreover, German naval personnel sentenced to lengthy terms of imprisonment were generally incarcerated in the military prison of Cologne-Wahn – never at Kiel.

However, there are records of a Carl-Alfons Vögele, who was born in Strasbourg, a city that until 1918 was part of the German Reich. Having undertook an apprenticeship as an electrician from 1907 to 1910, this individual completed a three-year period of National Service in the Imperial German Navy and was redrafted in 1914 at general mobilization. Records state that C.-A. Vögele served during the First World War with the Second Naval Aviation Group at Wilhelmshaven and from February 1917 was a stoker on board the torpedo boat *S-142* in the North Sea. At the end of the war he returned to Strasbourg, styling himself 'Charles' (the French form of his name) rather than 'Carl-Alfons' after 1919. Even had he served aboard the *U-20* his sphere of operations would have been technical; he would have had no role in the chain of command in the operations room, nor would he have had the opportunity to view a target through the periscope.

Even if had Vögele joined the U-boat force at the outbreak of the First World War in 1914 his basic naval training – followed by his specialist U-boat training – would have lasted at least until spring 1915, making it unlikely in the extreme that he would have been detailed to a submarine on a combat mission as early as April of that year.

From the available technical formation such an untoward intervention also appears unlikely. At the time of the attack the *Lusitania*'s speed was about 18 knots (33 km/h), and the distance between the *U-20* and the *Lusitania* was around 700 metres. The *U-20* 's torpedo travelled at a speed of some 27 knots (50 km/h). To cover a distance of 700 metres it would take a torpedo about fifty seconds from the moment of firing; in that time the *Lusitania* would have covered about 400 metres. These data are fundamental for the determination of course, speed and cruising depth relevant to the operation of the torpedo aiming device.

In addition to estimating the target's course and speed as accurately as possible, the establishment of the correct angle is crucial, because the target continues to move while the torpedo travels through the water towards it.

Schwieger's war diary states that the torpedo struck the *Lusitania* amidships, just aft of the bridge. Had there been any incidence of insubordination on board the *U-20* this would have entailed a delay in firing of at least thirty seconds. In that time the liner would have travelled another 200 metres. In this case the impact of the strike might well have failed to cause fatal damage. The *U-20* war diary makes no mention of any insubordination. On 13 May 1915 the *U-20* returned to Wilhelmshaven from her war patrol, which had started on 30 April 1915 at Emden. However, the next portion of the war diary notes that on 14 May 1915 an unusual personal mustering of the crew of the *U-20* was called by the Commander-in-Chief himself. The reason for this may have been that the leaders of the Imperial Navy wished to ensure future procedure by submarine crews, the sinking of the *Lusitania* having inevitably assumed a major political dimension in view of the resultant international outcry.

Ralf Bartzke, a distinguished student of U-boat tactics, spent much time researching the *U-20*'s attack on the *Lusitania* in order to input all the relevant data into a specially designed computer simulator. Bartzke ran two alternative versions of the attack, using essential data taken from Schwieger's war diary, supplemented with other known torpedo data and contemporary U-boat operational procedures.

The first scenario he passed through the computer simulator was the attack according to the information known to us today; the second incorporated an estimated delay of five seconds in the firing of the torpedo, putatively caused by Vögele's alleged insubordination and Weisbach's intervention. The simulator results revealed that if the Vögele legend were true the resultant delay would have meant that the torpedo would have struck the *Lusitania* aft of her four funnels. It is known that this is not what happened: the liner sank by the bow.[2]

In early December 2011 Bartzke's findings were published on the Lusitania.net website. In April 2012 Bernd Langensiepen of the *Marine Nachrichten Blatt* obtained the relevant official crew list of the *U-20*. No crew member by the name of Vögele was recorded.[3]

Schwieger's opportunistic attack on the *Lusitania* was, of necessity, a case of rapid response planning. Once the *U-20*'s pilot Lanz had positively identified the target as one of the two mighty Cunard sisters, either the

Mauretania or the *Lusitania*, Schwieger had little time in which to study his target's movements as thoroughly as he might have wished. The first stage of the plan of attack was for the submarine commander systematically to assess all available information about the target, using a system known as UZO (U-Boot Ziel Optik, targeting optics). As Schwieger peered into the precision optics of his periscope he needed to estimate the target's speed, then calculate her course, distance and bearing to the U-boat's bow. Schwieger knew that this particular target was capable of at least 26 knots, but his experienced eye told him that she was not sailing at her top speed. Supported by data based on a positive identification of the target he estimated her speed as 22 knots. This was an educated guess. To ensure an effective torpedo strike on such a fast-moving target Schwieger planned to hit the vessel amidships, between her first and fourth funnels, preferably close to the second funnel. In order to achieve this aim he used the 'Stadimeter', the range-finding device contained within the periscope itself. This instrument was basically a split-prism range-finder. Using a double-image of the target vessel, it provided a reasonably accurate calculation up to a maximum range of 6,000 metres. If it was possible to factor in other information, such as known masthead or funnel height, even greater accuracy could be achieved. Because marine publications such as *The Shipbuilder* had published a great deal of information about the *Lusitania* – including, for instance, the fact that her masthead towered 165 feet above her waterline – Schwieger was familiar with many of the liner's particulars.

Contrary to popular belief, the periscope of a U-boat contained no cross-wire type of target sight. A target-bearing ring was located on the outside of the periscope's control column. The target-bearing ring gave the compass bearing, measured in degrees, of the intended target in relation to the U-boat's bow. This information was usually read out by an officer standing at the elbow of the officer at the periscope, as they clustered closely around the base of the conning tower. All the UZO data was then processed manually, using a slide rule and pre-determined tables, in order to calculate the firing angle with as little loss of time as possible. Torpedoes travelled at different speeds, depths and bearing to bow, and all these factors were manually programmed into the torpedo itself. When the torpedo was ready for firing, the loaded tube that contained the now fully primed torpedo displayed a light. These were Schwieger's final firing calculations:

> Target's speed estimated at 22 knots. Shot distance: 700 metres. G6 Torpedo, optimal speed: 35 knots = 18.01 m/s (metres per second.) Torpedo running depth: 3 metres. Time to Target after firing = 700 metres @ 18.01 m/s = 38,9 seconds. Angle of intersection: near 90 degrees.[4]

Having run submerged at full speed, following Schwieger's firing plan, the *U-20* arrived at the designated firing point. Schwieger had not been optimistic about the success of his strike. Therefore he was amazed when saw the liner change course, noting in his war diary that the ship veered to starboard, heading for Queenstown.

By following his coded wireless instructions from Vice-Admiral Coke to divert the *Lusitania* into Queenstown, Captain Turner had now unwittingly shortened the range between his ship and the lurking *U-20*. The submarine reduced speed, swung to port into the firing position and fired. Schwieger consulted his stopwatch and made further periscope observations to check the accuracy of his attack calculations.

Ninety-seven years later, with the same data fed into the simulator, Ralf Bartzke's computer simulation projected that the impact point would have been between the *Lusitania*'s second and third funnels, amidships, almost exactly where Schwieger had aimed his strike. However, as Schwieger observed through his periscope that his torpedo had hit the *Lusitania*, his first thought was that the strike was forward of the point at which he had aimed. He realized immediately that he had slightly miscalculated, over-estimating the *Lusitania*'s speed (she was in fact making just 18 knots at the time, rather than 22). Then he saw and noted the almost immediate second, larger explosion. He was at a loss to explain this. In his war diary he ascribed it to possibly 'Boilers, coal or powder?'

> Clear bow shot at 700 [metres] . . . Shot struck starboard side close behind the bridge. An extraordinarily heavy detonation followed, with a very large cloud of smoke (far above the front funnel). A second explosion must have followed that of the torpedo (boiler or coal or powder?) . . . The ship stopped immediately and quickly listed sharply to starboard, sinking deeper by the head at the same time. It appeared as if it would capsize in a short time.[5]

Schwieger was not to know that by a combination of chance and miscalculation his shot had in fact hit the ship at the one point that would do her deadly damage. The computer simulator confirms that Schwieger's torpedo did indeed hit the ship in the aft end of her forward cargo hold, in the vicinity of her foremast and certainly three metres below her waterline. This was also where 5,000 live artillery shells were stacked in unprotected wooden crates. Schwieger's war diary records the events of the early afternoon of 7 May 1915:

> 2 p.m. Straight ahead the 4 funnels and 3 masts of a steamer with a course at right angles to ours . . . Ship is made out to be a large passenger liner.
>
> 3.05 p.m. Went to 11 metres and ran at high speed on a course converging with that of the steamer in the hope that it would change course to starboard along the Irish Coast. The steamer turned to starboard, headed for Queenstown, and thus made it possible to approach for a shot. Ran at high speed till 3 p.m. in order to secure an advantageous position.
>
> 3.10 p.m. Clear bow shot at 700 metres . . . angle of intersection 90 degrees, estimated speed 22 nautical miles. Shot struck starboard side close behind the bridge. An extraordinary heavy detonation followed, with a very large cloud of smoke (far above the front funnel). A second explosion must have followed that of the torpedo (boiler or coal or powder?). The superstructure above the point of impact and the bridge were torn apart. Fire broke out; light smoke veiled the high bridge. The ship stopped immediately and quickly listed sharply to starboard, sinking deeper by the head at the same time. Great confusion arose on the ship. Some of the boats were swung clear and lowered into the water. Many people must have lost their heads; several boats loaded with people rushed downward, struck the water bow or stern first and filled at once. On the port side, because of the sloping position, fewer boats were swung clear than on the starboard side. The ship blew off steam; at the bow the name 'Lusitania' in golden letters was visible. It was running 20 nautical miles.
>
> 3.25 p.m. Since it seemed as if the steamer could only remain above water for a short time, went to 24 metres and ran toward the sea. Nor could I have fired a second torpedo into this swarm of people

who were trying to save themselves. [It has been widely suggested that this last sentence may have been added later.]

4.15 p.m. Went to 11 metres and took a look around. In the distance straight ahead a number of lifeboats were moving. Nothing more was to be seen of the *Lusitania*. The wreck must lie 14 nautical miles from the Old Head of Kinsale lighthouse at an angle of 358 degrees to the right of it, in 90 metres of water (27 nautical miles from Queenstown), 51 degrees 22' 6" N and 8 degrees 31' W. The land and the lighthouse could be seen very plainly.

4.20 p.m. When taking a look around, a large steamer was in sight ahead on the port side, with course laid for Fastnet Rock. Tried to get ahead at high speed, so as to get a stern shot . . .

5.08 p.m. Conditions for shot very favourable: no possibility of missing if torpedo kept its course. Torpedo did not strike. Since the telescope was cut off for some time after this shot the cause of failure could not be determined . . . The steamer or freighter was of the Cunard Line.

6.15 p.m. . . . It is remarkable that there is so much traffic on this particular day, although two large steamers were sunk the day before south of George's Channel. It is also inexplicable that the *Lusitania* was not sent through the North Channel.[6]

In fewer than twenty minutes the great liner had slipped beneath the waves, with huge loss of life. The *U-20* log chronicles the chaos and panic an apparently horrified Schwieger observed while the ship's crew and passengers struggled to launch the lifeboats as the liner listed sharply to starboard. Only six of the forty-eight lifeboats had made it safely into the water.

Schwieger returned home to a hero's welcome amid German press reports that the *Lusitania* was an armed auxiliary warship packed with munitions and Canadian troops. 'An Extraordinary Victory', trumpeted the *Frankfurter-Zeitung* of 8 May. But the Kaiser and the German authorities and diplomatic corps, desperate to keep the USA neutral, were appalled by the outcry and revulsion expressed by the Americans. Schwieger was summoned to Berlin where, according to Admiral Tirpitz, the foremost advocate of unrestricted submarine warfare, the U-boat commander was 'treated very ungraciously'. Shwieger's war diary may have been doctored to suggest humanitarian scruples and imply a level of British incompetence; this 'official' version does not appear to have borne his signature.

Many of the dead were Americans. In the USA there was an upsurge of anger, placing President Wilson in a quandary. 'I wish with all my heart that I saw a way to carry out the double wish of our people,' Wilson wrote privately to Bryan on 7 June 1915, 'to maintain a firm front in respect of what we demand of Germany and yet do nothing that might by any possibility involve us in the war.'[7] Wilson's notes demanding reparations for the loss of life and an end to unrestricted submarine warfare were an attempt to maintain an essential balance of restraint and perceived action. US public opinion had turned against Germany. The war of words between Washington and Berlin continued, with more American casualties, until May 1916 when a declaration of war was narrowly averted. Germany pledged to abide by the Cruiser Rules and to abandon her policy of unrestricted submarine warfare that allowed attacks on merchant ships without warning. She was convinced into compliance by President Wilson's threat to break off diplomatic relations.

Alarmed by international opprobrium, the tendency in the Kaiser's administration was to play down the sinking of the passenger liner.

The second explosion aboard the *Lusitania*, recorded by Schwieger and others, including survivors and the crew of the first rescue boat, the Manx fishing smack *Wanderer*, would prove the cornerstone in the conspiracy theories that sprang up and have persisted since the day the *Lusitania* was lost. A contemporary illustration of the attack shows the liner struck by two torpedoes. This was the official explanation offered at the time for the two explosions and the rapid sinking of the ship.

Fury erupted on both sides of the Atlantic. In Liverpool and in the East End of London there were riots. The *Daily Mail* of Monday, 10 May 1915 proclaimed, 'British and American Babies Murdered by the Kaiser.' A correspondent asked the question on everyone's minds: 'Like a prairie fire indignation and the bitterest resentment is sweeping today over the American continent. The only question is: Will this universal feeling of horror and mingled grief for the innocent victims of the greatest crime in history overwhelm the Government and force it into a declaration of war?' The *New York Times* wrote with greater restraint, 'President Sees Need of Firm and Deliberate Action.'

There was wild speculation about how Woodrow Wilson would

respond. But Wilson remained firm in his conviction that the USA should stay neutral. 'The example of America must be a special example,' he said in Philadelphia three days later. 'The example of America must be the example not merely of peace because it will not fight, but of peace because peace is the healing and elevating influence of the world and strife is not. There is such a thing as a man being too proud to fight. There is such a thing as a nation being so right that it does not need to convince others by force that it is right.'[8]

It is tempting to adopt the popular but essentially facile conclusion that the sinking of the *Lusitania* was the trigger that brought the USA into the war. The atrocity certainly brought home to many Americans the reality of the war that was raging in Europe and forced them to re-examine their own convictions and moral position. It also helped demonize the Germans.

But in reality the loss of the *Lusitania* was a catalyst rather than a causal factor, and despite the outpouring of revulsion and anger its after-shock did not take concrete effect until 1917 after many more attacks. When in April 1917, in a desperate bid to sever Britain's transatlantic lifeline, the Germans reneged on their promise to abandon unrestricted submarine warfare, the President had little choice but to ask Congress for a declaration of war. It was almost two years after the sinking of the *Lusitania*.

Yet there was an air of inevitability determined by the position President Wilson had adopted in 1915. There is a useful distinction to be made between neutrality, or non-involvement in conflict, and the forceful upholding of rights of neutral countries and their citizens to engage in trade and travel in times of war without let or hindrance. During previous European conflicts the New World had been able, as Thomas Jefferson remarked, to observe events from the sidelines and to profit from the belligerence of others, to 'fatten on the follies of the Old'. This position of availing oneself of the miseries of others had included becoming the carriers for all parties at sea. But this was not Wilson's world-view, nor was it a position that could be maintained indefinitely, either ethically or practically.

Pragmatically, Wilson's aim was to assume world leadership for his country after the Old World had exhausted, depleted and bankrupted itself. Wilson clung to the hope of US neutrality, reiterating that the American people relied on him to keep their country out of the war. Despite his Anglophile predisposition, he was sufficiently acute to perceive the flaws in the moral arguments advanced in defence of the stance and actions of belligerents on both sides. Yet events overtook him, and in April 1917 he reluctantly concluded that US engagement in the conflict had become inevitable. In his speech before the special session of Congress, as was his custom he assumed the moral high ground. He declared that the decision to enter the conflict must be motivated not only by the fact that the USA's rights as a neutral been violated but also the more high-minded notion that the world must be made safe for democracy. Americans must fight 'for the rights and liberties of small nations' and to 'bring peace and safety to make the world itself at last free.'[9]

Myths about the *Lusitania* took wing. Speculation was rife, in particular among the international diving community, that the ship was carrying a fabulous cargo of gold bullion. But this would appear unlikely in view of the fact that she was on her return voyage from the USA. Britain was buying munitions; America was selling. The bullion, if any, would have been travelling in the opposite direction.

As for more dubious cargo, the Germans were certainly well aware that war materials were being carried on passenger ships. On 23 June 1915 the front page of the *New York Times* carried a story reporting a visit to President Wilson by the German Ambassador Count Bernstorff. On page 2 the subhead 'Shells on the *Lusitania*' appeared. In their meeting Bernstorff laid a copy of the ship's manifest before Wilson and then proceeded to quote from a copy of Bethlehem Steel's shipping note: 'The consignment of 1,250 cases of shrapnel was in fact 5,000 shrapnel shells, filled; and the total weight of this consignment was 103,828 lb.'

Bernstorff left a memorandum with Wilson listing these and other figures as irrefutable proof of this practice and called the President's attention to the 'deliberately incorrect marking' of this consignment as 'Non-Explosive Shrapnel', claiming that the shrapnel shells were known to have been filled.

This was hardly news: the transporting of munitions aboard passenger ships was an open secret. It made sense. Liners were faster than cargo ships and arguably less likely to be targeted by U-boats. Moreover, US newspapers habitually published details of the cargoes three to five days after the ships had sailed and therefore after their manifests had been cleared by the US port customs authorities. It would not have been difficult for Bernstorff to obtain such accurate information.

In the light of the *Lusitania*'s known cargo of war materials, the justification for Schwieger's attack and the cause of the mysterious and fatal second explosion on board the *Lusitania* have been the subject of study and debate for a century. It has been regularly suggested that if the sinking of the *Lusitania* was a war crime the British authorities were as guilty as the Germans.

SIX

Friday, 7 May 1915

As Thursday, 6 May dawned, the *Lusitania* was travelling at reduced speed in the fog 750 miles west-south-west of the southern tip of Ireland. In these waters, in the course of a single week, between Saturday, 1 May and Friday, 7 May, German submarines would sink twenty-three merchant ships.

At five-thirty in the morning the piercing strains of the ship's bugler roused Theodate Pope from her slumbers in her new, supposedly quieter cabin. Glancing out of her window, she observed a flurry of activity on deck and noted with curiosity that members of the crew – cooks and stewards, as well as sailors – were releasing the lifeboats and swinging them clear of the railing.

Pope would perhaps have welcomed some extra beauty sleep that morning, for that evening she and the erudite Edwin Friend, her young travelling companion, were invited to attend a party given by wealthy wine importer George Kessler. It promised to be a sparkling occasion. George 'Champagne King' Kessler's glittering events ashore were legendary for their extravagance and glamour; on a whim he might order the Savoy Hotel to be transformed into Venice or the North Pole. That night's shipboard festivities would be attended by other members of the travelling élite: millionairess Goldiana Morell, who was a septuagenarian Canadian widow; the arms dealers Fred Gauntlett, Samuel Knox and Albert Hopkins; Charles Lauriat of the famous Boston bookselling company; Isaac Lehmann, the international export broker; and Mabel and Fred Pearson. Fred, businessman and scientific polymath, had earned his first fortune before the age of thirty; his properties included a game park stocked with exotic creatures.

Among these pampered socialite saloon passengers the expectation was that shipboard life would mirror the luxury and unremitting round of engagements and diversions to which they were accustomed on shore.

In the afternoon of 6 May yet another social gathering took place. Charles Frohman was entertaining the theatrical and literary set in his stateroom. The star-studded guest list included luminaries from the world of the arts, such as the fêted stars Rita Jolivet and Josephine Brandell and the writers Charles Klein and Justus Miles Forman. Staff Captain Anderson, the social face of Cunard, dropped in. Anderson called in again at Kessler's party that evening. Kessler, his concerns about safety still preying on his mind, seized the opportunity to quiz Anderson about why Captain Turner had still not held a lifeboat drill for the passengers. Anderson replied diplomatically that the decision rested with the Captain.

But Kessler was not alone in his unease. As the voyage progressed, Professor Ian Holbourn would reiterate his concern that passengers were unfamiliar with proper evacuation procedures and did not know how to put on lifebelts properly. He had voiced these fears openly on several occasions, and on the evening of Tuesday, 4 May he had been approached by a deputation who exhorted him to cease from spreading alarmist talk. Exasperated with their obtuseness, Holbourn nicknamed people who refused to face the brutal facts of their situation the 'Ostrich Club'. Despite others' disapproval, on Wednesday, 5 May Holbourn had approached Captain Turner and broached the subject of the lack of lifeboat drills; however, he sensed immediately that his interference was unwelcome.

The refusal to face facts and address safety procedures was too much for Nottingham-born lace merchant Arthur Jackson Mitchell. He decided to take matters into his own hands. He and a group of like-minded people got together to form a committee whose aim was to instruct passengers in the correct use of lifebelts. At last, perceiving that there was a genuine will among his passengers to face up to potential risks at sea, Turner relented and gave his approval to the plan on the provision that it be stressed that it was merely a precaution and that there was no real danger. Panic must be avoided at all costs.

That evening, at 7.50, Turner received the first of four signals from the British naval centre at Queenstown, now Cobh. The first two warned about submarine activity in the stretch of water known as 'Torpedo Alley'. Turner felt these messages were vague and unsatisfactory, but none the less he instigated what he felt to be adequate safety measures, ordering watertight doors to be closed, posting double look-outs and directing a black-out. The skylights in the public rooms were to be covered up, and all lights were to be extinguished after nightfall. During the early hours of the next morning he commanded the lifeboats to be swung out on their davits in readiness for speedy launching in case of emergency. It was the noise of this operation that roused some of the passengers, including Theodate Pope, from their slumbers.

That evening saloon passengers Charles Plamondon, the industrialist, and his wife Mary were celebrating their thirty-sixth wedding anniversary. Charles recorded in his diary that it had been a day of pleasant and sunny weather and that the ship had travelled 488 miles. He also noted seeing the Irish coast from the *Lusitania* around 11 a.m. – although in fact the ship approached the coast at about noon. This confusion may have arisen because clocks were set one hour ahead each day as the ship travelled westward.

The Seamen's Charities concert that evening, held in the saloon lounge and music room, was one of those rare occasions when saloon and second-cabin passengers mingled. Several second-cabin women – including young Charlotte Pye who was travelling with her eighteen-month-old daughter Marjorie and 65-year-old Phoebe Amory who was on the way to see her sons off to war – sold programmes in aid of the charity. When Phoebe sold a ten-cent programme to Alfred Vanderbilt in his suite the tycoon insisted on paying her five dollars, saying gallantly that he was paying for her lovely smile.

A sombre note was struck at the concert when Captain Turner made a brief public announcement that as the ship had now entered the war zone passengers were requested to refrain from smoking on deck lest their burning cigars be visible to lurking submarines. But the temporary grim reminder caused little more than a frisson, and the show went on. A pianist played Irving Berlin's 'I Love a Piano'; there was a Scottish comedian whose jokes fell somewhat flat on American ears; a Welsh choir offered a medley of songs and operatic arias; and a lady singer sang, with unwitting prescience, 'When I Leave this World Behind'.

The celebrated leading ladies Josephine Brandell and Rita Jolivet declined to perform, despite entreaties from their many admirers. The saloon passenger architect and theatrical set designer Oliver Bernard, who had noted the inadequacy of the ineffectual lifeboat drills on board, was a cynical social observer and unimpressed by the airs of the rich and famous. Noting how the passengers congregated in their own social cliques, he reflected wryly that a submarine attack might break the ice and force people from different classes into social interaction. He could not have known that within twenty-four hours his sardonic speculation would be proved correct.

Bernard was the son of a theatrical couple from Camberwell. His father was a theatre manager, Charles Bernard, and his mother, Annie Allen, an actress. As a child little Oliver had overheard his nurse, who was gossiping with another nanny, say that when baby Oliver was shown to his mother for the first time she had said, 'Very nice, but please take him away.' This remark, if true, set the tone for his unhappy childhood. His parents, unwilling to be encumbered by a child on their travels, handed him over to the care of his aunt. Oliver was an ambitious child and worked tirelessly to become a designer. He educated himself by reading the works of John Locke and John Ruskin.

Months before the outbreak of war Bernard had been in Berlin for a production of *The Ring* at Charlottenburg. Here he later claimed to have been followed by a German officer, lured into a quarrel with a group of German men and aggressively informed that Germany would soon show his Mr Churchill how to trim his Navy. (If true, this was in curious anticipation of the phrase that was reportedly used by the three German stowaways apprehended aboard the *Lusitania* by Captain Anderson. Presumably these prisoners were still languishing under lock and key somewhere in the bowels of the liner when she sank.)

When war broke out Bernard applied in succession to the British Army, the Royal Flying Corps and the Royal Naval Air Force but was repeatedly rejected because of his poor hearing. Ashamed of being a non-combatant he left his job and moved to New York. When he learned that the British armed forces would be changing their requirements in order to admit more men, he planned to return to London after fulfilling a commission for designing theatrical sets from the Boston millionaire William Lindsey. Fortunately for the healthy state of his portfolio Lindsey's wealth did not depend on his dubious skill as a playwright but, instead, resulted from his invention of the ammunition belt. Lindsey had persuaded Bernard to take his daughter Leslie, dark, lithe and a beautiful dancer, and his new son-in-law Stewart Mason under his wing on the voyage. Leslie and Stewart had been married on 21 April 1915. The *Lusitania* trip was to be the highlight of their honeymoon. Bernard, who found the billing and cooing of the infatuated profoundly tedious, was relieved that the young couple seemed absorbed in each other.

Third Officer Albert Bestic glanced into the ballroom. The festive scene, the music and the dancing reminded him of the legendary ball given in Brussels by the Duchess of Richmond on the eve of Waterloo. Later he would wonder if this thought had been a premonition of what was to come.

There was music in second class that night, too. Hilda Stones entertained second-class passengers with her beautiful voice.

And in third class that last evening romance was in the air. Blonde, blue-eyed Norwegian-born Gerda Neilson had met John Welsh, a mechanical engineer from Manchester, on deck the first day out. It was love at first sight. John invited to Gerda to sit with him at dinner, where they shared a table with widower George Hook and his son Frank and daughter Elsie, who were returning to England from Toronto. The conversation around the table often turned to the possibility of being torpedoed.

Elsie Hook, aged twelve, was tall for her age, while Frank was small and adventurous. Although Elsie was a year over the appropriate age, her father George had booked her half-fare. When the family was about to board ship George urgently whispered instructions to his daughter to duck down and try to look as small as she could, so as not to arouse suspicion. The Hook family had disliked New York, finding the city noisy and dirty after Toronto, but the children were excited to be travelling on the big ship. George had originally planned to travel second cabin, but when he discovered that their housekeeper Annie Marsh was travelling on the same ship with her husband and son, in third class, George declared that rather than be separated they would all travel together. He changed his family's tickets to third class, as third-class passengers were not allowed to mix with the other classes. On the night of 6 May John Welsh and Gerda strolled along the covered third-class deck, and John proposed. The happy couple resolved to marry as soon as the *Lusitania* reached Liverpool.

To his immense amusement burly British cotton dealer Robert Timmis noticed a Greek man strapping on a lifebelt and climbing into a lifeboat. Nobody managed to persuade the anxious passenger to get out, and he slept in the lifeboat all night. Timmis later said it was the funniest thing he had ever seen. The man may have been Michael Pappadopoulo.

By 5 a.m. on 7 May the *Lusitania* had reached a point 120 miles west-south-west of Fastnet Rock off the southern tip of Ireland where she met the patrolling boarding vessel *Partridge*. By six o' clock there was an increased level of activity: heavy fog had rolled in, and Turner once more posted extra look-outs. As the ship came closer to the Irish coast, Captain Turner ordered depth soundings to be made. At 8 a.m. he called for the ship's speed to be reduced to 18 knots, then to 15 knots, and for the foghorn to be sounded. This alarmed some of the passengers. They felt that the ship appeared to be advertising her presence to any enemy lurking beneath the waves.

The booming foghorn woke Charles Lauriat. Glancing out at the weather he decided it was not worth getting up. He waited until the fog had cleared before he rose, shaved, dressed and headed to the smoking-room to check the day's run. Finding, to his disappointment, that the *Lusitania* had travelled only 462 miles, he went for a stroll on deck before lunch, noting that the ship was still only 'lounging along' within sight of the Irish coast.[1]

The German submarine *U-20* was low on fuel. During the night Schwieger had surfaced, taken bearings from the twinkling lights of Irish lighthouses, and recharged his batteries. Nothing stirred on the face of the sea. He had allowed the crew to play their gramophones. The couple of pet dogs aboard had enjoyed a welcome airing on deck. On his first wartime mission Schwieger was filled with confidence. He knew that in the few days since the *Lusitania* had sailed from New York twenty-three merchantmen had been sunk off the British Isles. The fog was exasperating. But by 10 a.m. the next day it began to clear.

As the *Lusitania* broke through the fog into hazy sunshine, and the blurred outline of the Irish coast appeared on the distant horizon, a messenger from the Marconi Room brought Captain Turner a short message from Vice-Admiral Coke in Queenstown. Although it contained only twelve words, because Turner did not recognize the cypher he took it down to his day cabin to work on it. At 11.55 a.m. a messenger brought him another message from the Admiralty which stated, 'U-boats active in southern part of Irish Channel. Last heard of twenty miles south of Coningbeg Light Vessel. Make sure *Lusitania* gets this.'

Alfred Booth, Chairman of Cunard, like other concerned parties in Liverpool, had learned of the *U-20* 's sinking of the *Centurion* and *Candidate*. The Admiralty had known about these incidents since the early hours of the morning. Their various signals to Turner were to play a sinister role in the aftermath of the disaster, as various parties would seek desperately to wriggle out of responsibility and apportion blame.

As things stood, this latest message complicated matters for Turner. His instructions from the Admiralty were to sail through the middle of the channel; now he was told a U-boat was prowling around the entrance to the area he needed to pass through. He desperately needed to determine his precise position if he was to have any hope of successfully dodging an attack in a potentially deadly game of cat-and-mouse. He decided to finish decoding Coke's earlier message. This took him until 12.10. When he had finished deciphering the signal he sprang into action, hurried to the bridge and immediately altered the ship's course 20 degrees to port. The vessel veered to port so sharply that many passengers momentarily lost their balance. The *Lusitania* was now closing to the land at 18 knots on course north 67 east. According to the clock on the bridge, the time was 12.15.

The *U-20* blew her tanks and surfaced. The fog that had been frustrating her commander had finally cleared. The submarine headed back toward Fastnet at full speed. Schwieger checked his watch: it was 12.20. Just before 1 p.m., while the *Lusitania* was still steaming ahead on course north 67 east, another Admiralty signal was received. It read: 'Submarine five miles south of Cape Clear proceeding west when sighted at 10:00 a.m.' This message was misleading: no submarine had been at that location. Turner felt relief. If the signal was correct the immediate threat was past. Cape Clear was already many miles astern of the east-bound *Lusitania*. Turner did not realize that this signal referred to the submarine's position the previous day.

Assuming perhaps that submarines would be more likely to keep to the open sea and that his ship would have better chances closer to land, he adjusted his course north-east. The entrance to St George's Channel, and therefore the next notified U-boat threat, would still be four to five hours away if he had maintained his original heading. For now he was safely in the middle. As far as Turner knew, there were no enemy submarines in his immediate vicinity.

At 13.20 the submarine was still running on the surface, heading back toward Fastnet. Schwieger was up on the conning tower with the look-outs when the starboard look-out sang out. He had spotted smoke off the starboard bow. Schwieger focused his binoculars. He estimated the target was some twelve to fourteen miles away. It would be a long shot. He ordered the submarine to dive to a periscope depth of eleven metres. As the klaxon blared and the *U-20* plunged to the depths, Schwieger altered course to intercept the target at the *U-20*'s maximum submerged speed of 9 knots. From thirty-five feet below the surface Schwieger settled into the classic submarine procedure of stalking his prey.

At 13.40 Turner caught sight of the reassuring landmark he knew so well, the black-and-white horizontal bands of the lighthouse perched high on the looming promontory, the Old Head of Kinsale. He ordered the *Lusitania*'s course to return to south 87 east steady. He urgently needed to fix his position in order to plot a new course to Queenstown rather than Liverpool. The message from Vice Admiral Coke, sent in the high-grade naval code, had advised him to divert the *Lusitania* into Queenstown immediately, in accordance with standard Admiralty procedure in situations of grave peril. Turner calculated that his ship was now fourteen miles offshore, west of the Old Head of Kinsale. He now needed to plot a course through the mine-free channel into Queenstown Harbour. Turning back to the bridge Turner noticed the ship's newest officer, Third Officer Albert Bestic. (Turner persisted in calling him 'Bisset', perhaps as part of a subtle but elaborate wind-up, a kind of unstated initiation process. Although young Bestic was Dublin-born, his surname was originally Huguenot French.) Bestic was due to go off watch in fifteen minutes' time. The captain asked him whether he knew how to take a four-point bearing. Bestic knew that a four-point bearing was no trifle: the process took almost an hour to complete, and the ship needed to maintain a steady course and constant speed while the operation was conducted, but he told his Captain he knew how to do it. Turner ordered him to take a four-point bearing of the lighthouse. With that Turner spun on his heel and left the bridge, entering the chartroom and leaving Bestic to take the bearing. This was typical of Turner's quirky nature. On Wednesday evening he had challenged his officers to tie a Turk's Head, an elaborate decorative knot from the days of sailing ships. Turner sent Bestic to deliver the completed knot to Chief Officer Piper, who was annoyed to be disturbed at a crucial point in his game of bridge. Piper snapped that he had not heard of a Turk's Head in twenty years and told Bestic to go and tie the next one. Bestic, not to be outdone, completed the challenge.

If Bestic was worried about the four-point bearing he was reprieved ten minutes later when he was relieved from duty. Some sources state that John Idwal Lewis, the Senior Third Officer, well aware of what the 'old man' had done, came back at 2 p.m. to relieve Bestic. Others, including Bestic himself in his testimony to the British Wreck Commissioner's Inquiry, stated that he was relieved at 2 p.m. by another officer, Mr Stephens, who did not survive.[2]

Bestic left the bridge, taking the first set of bearing figures to his captain in the chartroom on his way below. He was back in his own cabin and just about to write up his log when Baggage Master Crank came and asked him to oversee the working party under orders to bring the baggage up on deck in readiness for disembarkation at Liverpool. Bestic realized that he was still wearing his new uniform and changed into the old one he habitually wore for baggage-room duty. He had just changed and by his own account had stepped into the officers' smoke-room when the torpedo struck.

As the ship's horn blared out at intervals during that foggy morning of Friday, 7 May Dorothy Conner had been getting ready to leave the ship. She and her brother-in-law Dr Howard Fisher were so busy packing for imminent disembarkation that they arrived late in the dining-room for lunch. Some diners were already leaving the tables, many intending to enjoy a stroll on deck since the weather had cleared. Conner had no made no secret of the fact that she found the voyage tedious and longed for something to happen to enliven the proceedings. As her table companions Lady Mackworth and her father D.A. Thomas finished their coffee her father said jokingly to Conner that perhaps they should stay up on deck that night to see whether they got their thrill.[3]

When the *U-20* 's Chief Engine Room Artificer Friedrich Sellmer called the submarine commander to the periscope, at first the *Lusitania's* forest of masts and funnels appeared to belong to several ships, but then the image resolved itself into one enormous vessel. Schwieger studied the huge ship and called out to his Pilot, Lanz, that he had identified a ship with four funnels, over 20,000 tons, travelling at an estimated speed of 22 knots. Lanz checked in his copies of *Jane's Fighting Ships* and *Brassey's Naval Annual* and called back that the ship was either the *Lusitania* or the *Mauretania*. He added that both were listed as cruisers and troop-carriers. Schwieger was well aware that if they were sailing at full speed the two ocean-going giants were too fast to be caught by a submarine, but he gave the command to prepare for action anyway on the off-chance that he might get lucky. Accordingly, one G6 torpedo was loaded into one of the *U-20* 's forward launching tubes. The distance between the two vessels had closed to two miles, but then Schwieger's heart sank: the *Lusitania* altered course and turned away. The German commander feared he had lost his target. 'I had no hope now, even if we hurried at our best speed, of getting near enough to attack her,' he wrote.[4]

But then, as he watched, Schwieger could not believe his luck: the great ship abruptly altered course again. Suddenly, the range and angle were ideal for an attack. Schwieger later told a friend, 'She could not have steered a more perfect course if she had deliberately tried to give us a dead shot.' He noted in his logbook, 'The ship turns to starboard then takes a course to Queenstown . . .' It was a unique opportunity for a textbook shot. The time was 14.10, and the range was 700 metres. Schwieger yelled the order to fire. There was a shriek and a deafening hissing sound. The whole submarine juddered, and Wiesbach, the Torpedo Officer, shouted the standard confirmation, 'Torpedo los!' The G-Type torpedo had cleared the tube and was streaking towards the target at a speed of 38 knots and a running depth of three metres.

The Manx fishing-boat *Wanderer* had been at sea for weeks. The night's catch had been good: 800 mackerel lay in the hold. The sea air had sharpened the crew's appetites for Manx broth and corned beef and duff. They were 'stodged' and exhausted from fishing through the night, and they were lying six or seven miles off the Old Head of Kinsale that Friday morning. When the haze lifted, the day was bright and clear, the sea flat calm, which was a bit of a problem. There was too little wind to be sure of reaching Kinsale in time to put to sea again for the shoals that would rise again that Friday night.

Skipper William Ball took the decision to sprinkle salt over the catch and stay out at sea, 'dodging' without sails, putting one man on watch while the others turned into their bunks and caught up on some sleep. Tommy Woods took over the watch at 1 p.m. Before an hour had passed he sent young John MacDonald below to make tea. Raking the calm sea with his old seaman's gaze, something caught his eye. A huge four-funnelled liner was approaching in the distance, some three miles south-south-west of the *Wanderer*. Tommy watched her with interest; he reckoned she would pass close by. Ten minutes later, when the big ship was still about half a mile away, without warning the boom and crack of a massive explosion shattered the peaceful scene and before Tommy's horrified eyes the great ship seemed to blow up. The first loud explosion was quickly followed by a second, a roar and a rumbling crash. Within minutes the great liner tilted, listing sharply to starboard. The thought that flashed through Tommy's mind was: Torpedo! He yelled to the crew, and they leaped out of their bunks and stumbled up on deck, bewildered, rubbing their eyes.

Captain Turner had come out of the chartroom and was standing on the port side of the *Lusitania*'s bridge, according to some sources, watching John Idwal Lewis working out the four-point bearing. (This differs markedly from Lewis's own account, given in his testimony to the inquiry, which states that he was in the dining-room at lunch with First Officer Arthur Rowland Jones, having come off watch at 12.45.)

Eighteen-year-old Leslie Morton, look-out on the starboard bow, spotted a sharp ridge of foaming bubbles slicing through the water towards the liner. 'Torpedoes coming on the starboard side!' he shouted through his megaphone, but his warning went unheard.[5] Morton's first impression was that there were two torpedoes. Seconds later Able Seaman Thomas Quinn in the crow's nest sounded the alarm over the ship's telephone. But it was too late.

The torpedo struck the ship with a loud bang that, Turner later recalled, sounded like the slamming of a heavy door. Almost immediately the first impact was followed by a second, much more deafening explosion. The great liner rocked and swayed violently. Bestic ran back to the bridge just in time to see the track of the torpedo. He told the Mersey inquiry later that the torpedo seemed to have been 'fired in line with the bridge, and it seemed to strike the ship between the third and fourth funnels, as far as I could see'. (In reality the torpedo must have struck closer to the bridge, since the ship sank by the head and not the stern.) Bestic heard Turner shout out the orders 'Hard-a-starboard' and 'Lower the boats down level to the rail.'[6] As Bestic rushed from the bridge, heading for his boat stations, he noted that an eerie silence had fallen over the ship, broken only by the whimper of a frightened child and the cry of a seagull. Then in the unnatural stillness a confused babble arose, like the sighing of the wind in a forest.

Captain Turner, still on the bridge, understood at once that his ship had suffered a body blow from which she could not survive. The *Lusitania* was doomed. He shouted out the order to abandon ship and rushed out on to the port bridge wing. Staring back along the boat deck he could see that all the portside lifeboats had swung inboard: launching them would be impossible. He knew all the starboard boats must have swung outwards: these would be usable, but lowering them would be tricky, technically difficult and dangerous, especially if passengers panicked. Each wooden lifeboat weighed five tons unladen and was fastened to the deck by a metal snubbing chain fixed with a release pin. In order to release the boat the pin had to be hammered out. Collapsible life rafts were stowed beneath the boats.

The liner plunged on through the waves. Turner ordered Staff Captain Anderson not to lower any of the boats until the ship had lost sufficient momentum to make the launching operation safe. But on the port side passengers had begun a desperate scramble into the lifeboats, which now hung inboard over the deck. The people who had rushed into the boats would have to be persuaded to get out again so that the boats could be safely launched, but many terrified passengers resisted and refused to budge.

The list indicator had just gone through the 15-degree mark. The Irish shore was fourteen miles away. Turner knew there was no chance of reaching it and beaching the ship, because of the rapid rate at which she was sinking. If the lifeboats were to be successfully launched he needed to stop the stricken liner from ploughing on lopsided through the waves. He rang down to the engine room demanding full speed astern; but the *Lusitania's* steam pressure had now dropped: her great turbines were virtually powerless.

Bestic, for his part, was doing his utmost to calm the situation and maintain some kind of order at portside Boat Station No. 2. Standing on the after davit, he was trying to explain to the frightened passengers that the ship's list made it impossible to lower the boat when it was full of people as the vessel was still moving so fast and was listing so precipitously. Then someone grabbed a hammer and struck the link-pin to the snubbing chain. As Bestic cried out a horrified protest, the chain rattled free and the heavy lifeboat, crammed with fifty or more passengers, swung inboard, crushing people waiting on the boat deck. The sudden weight overwhelmed the crewmen manning the davits, and under the sudden strain they released the falls. Both Lifeboat No. 2 and the collapsible stowed beneath it slithered down the deck, dragging screaming injured people along, and rammed into the base of the bridge wing right beneath where Captain Turner was standing. Bestic, hoping to prevent the same catastrophe from happening at the next boat station along, sprang to No. 4 lifeboat, but he was too late: somebody was already knocking out the link-pin. Bestic had to jump aside to avoid being crushed as No. 4 boat slid down the deck, maiming and killing countless more people before crashing into the wreckage of the first two boats. Then it was chaos.

Terrified passengers stampeded, swarming into boats 6, 8, 10 and 12, and each lifeboat in turn was freed in a frenzy of hacking and hammering. One after the other they all went careering down the deck and smashed into the other ruined boats. On the deck the bridge was already awash with swirling water.

Then the *Lusitania*'s stern began to settle back and a surge of water flooded the bridge, sweeping Turner out of the door and off the ship. As the *Lusitania* sank beneath the waves, the surge caught Bestic, too, and swept him off his feet and out through the first-class entrance hall into the roiling sea.

Leslie Morton, the teenager who had first sighted the torpedo, had signed on as a deckhand with his brother John only so they could drink up the money their father had sent for their fares home to England. In New York the Morton brothers had been persuaded to sign up by one of the *Lusitania*'s officers. They were experienced seamen, and ten hands had jumped ship in New York to avoid the draft. Leslie, unaccustomed to alcohol, passed out on Broadway after a night drinking Manhattan cocktails, but none the less he turned up promptly to report for duty early the next morning. The brothers had also recruited others to join the *Lusitania*'s scratch crew. When Leslie first set eyes on the ship he had contracted to join, he had described her as 'as big as a mountain'. The brothers would save many lives in the disaster. Leslie said later that he saw what appeared to be the top of the submerging submarine's conning tower, 'like the top portion of a silk hat just going into the water'.[7] As he helped people into the boats his eyes ranged around the empty sea. On the horizon he saw only one tiny vessel, the *Wanderer*, appearing on the distant horizon as a black dot.

On the Old Head of Kinsale six-year-old George Henderson was enjoying a picnic lunch with his family in the spring sunshine. From their vantage point they had been gazing out to sea, admiring the impressive passenger liner with her four raked-back funnels steaming steadily eastward. Suddenly, before their astonished eyes, a mighty fountain of water and smoke shot up from the ship. Within minutes the family saw the great ship tilt over, her bows starting to plunge into the sea. As her stern rose skyward they could see her huge propellers churning ineffectually in the empty air. Then, unbelievably, she was gone. George never forgot the sight. As an old man he told a television crew in 1994, 'I can still sit here now and see that great liner just sliding below the waves.'[8]

SEVEN

Disaster

George Kessler was enjoying a post-prandial cigar on the starboard A Deck when something caught his eye. He would recall later that he distinctly saw the wake of the approaching torpedo. In his published account he described the experience. 'It came rushing at us. It struck us at exactly 2.03 o' clock. I know this because my watch was in my hand at the time.'[1]

Young George Slingsby spotted the torpedo, too.[2] He had been relishing the voyage, both the luxury and the company. His previous employment as a butler had been tinged with loneliness. As 'gentleman's gentleman' to the wealthy Canadian Frederick Orr-Lewis he not only occupied a first-class cabin but enjoyed first-class dining, sharing a table in the first-class dining-room on the starboard side of C Deck, with other personal servants to the wealthy: William Stainton, valet to Charles Frohman, and Emily Davis and Annie Walker, maids to Marguerite, Lady Allan, a friend of Orr-Lewis's. Slingsby would later recall that at about 1.30 p.m. the ship seemed to alter course so abruptly that glasses fell crashing off the bar. He and his companions were listening to the band's rendition of 'It's a Long Way to Tipperary' when he happened to glance out of the window. A flash caught his gaze – a long white streak – the distinctive wake of a torpedo. He leaped from his seat and dashed out of the saloon just before the violent impact smashed against the portholes with horrific force. The torpedo had struck the *Lusitania* under the bridge, sending a plume of debris, steel plating and water shooting upwards with a force that knocked Lifeboat No. 5 off its davits. One passenger thought it sounded like a million-ton hammer hitting a steam boiler a hundred feet high. A second, more powerful explosion followed almost immediately, shooting another geyser of water, coal, dust and debris high above the deck.

John Idwal Lewis had noted that the weather was clearing, although the Irish coast still remained hidden in the haze. He finished his duties around 12.45 p.m. and changed for lunch, where he joined First Officer Rowland Jones at a portside table in the first-class dining saloon. The band was playing 'Tipperary', the catchy tune that would haunt the minds of many. Pathetically, some survivors would still be attempting to sing it in the midst of the nightmare. Lewis and First Officer Arthur Rowland Jones were just finishing their lunch when Lewis heard something that sounded like a report of a huge gun some two or three miles away but which was in reality much closer, coming from the forward starboard side. This was followed by another loud report and a rumbling crash, like a clap of thunder, and the sound of breaking glass, from the starboard side again. This sound seemed to be closer to where the officers sat, further aft of the first crash. They stood up and left the table. They had to walk rather than run, because of the press of people ahead of them. The ship was listing at about 10 degrees. Idwal Lewis made his way up the staircase to C Deck on the port side and then to the boat deck by way of the exterior stairways. As the two officers left the saloon Rowland Jones ordered any portholes that were open to be closed.[3] He stated later that he had not seen any portholes open when he gave the order. John Idwal Lewis would always maintain that all the portholes had been shut as the *Lusitania* entered the war zone and that he was not aware that any portholes were open on that last day. But the testimony of many passengers contradicted this statement.

Isaac Lehmann had noted that all the portholes were open on that beautiful day, and Charles Lauriat would state that, as he sat at lunch, he had found the dining-room drafty, the portholes being open, and had in consequence asked a steward to turn off an electric fan above his head.[4] Lauriat expressed his surprise that steps had not been taken to seal up the portholes as soon as the ship entered the war zone. James Brooks, who had been sitting at his dining table facing the bow, quite close to the entrance, on the port side of the centre line, also stated that the portholes had been open. Actress Rita Jolivet concurred: her recollection was that they were open. Frederic Gauntlett went further. He left his coffee and nuts and rose from the table, shouting to the stewards to close the portholes.[5] Oscar Grab, the Austrian immigrant who would later become a fashion millionaire, also noticed that they were open.

Little Barbara Anderson and her mother were seated at a small table on the upper level. When disaster struck, Emily Anderson, who was five months pregnant, was able to lead Barbara straight out on deck. Even after being scooped up and placed in the lifeboat by Assistant Purser

William Harkness the toddler carried on gripping her pudding spoon in her fist. Helen Smith was three years older than Barbara, old enough to enjoy playing on deck with her cousins Ronald, also six, and Reginald, four years older. The boys' mother, Helen's aunt Cecelia Owens, who was minding Helen's baby brother Hubert in the cabin, had given the older children permission to play on deck for another half an hour. She never saw them again. Cecelia heard the crash and thought the ship had run aground or struck a reef. But the second blast left her in no doubt. It was an explosion. Seizing baby Hubert, she hurried up to the open second-class decks calling for the children. She encountered, instead, her brother and sister-in-law frantically searching for their daughter. Cecelia handed over the baby, and they set off separately to find the missing children.

On deck six-year-old Helen Smith couldn't find her family; lost and scared, she was clearly a child with great presence of mind. She ran up to a tall man she did not know and begged him, 'Please, mister, take me with you!' Cowper, the Toronto journalist, picked her up and carried her to a lifeboat.

Twelve-year-old Avis Dolphin had been enjoying her lunch. Her first thought was: What a shame. I'm going to miss dessert. Professor Ian Holbourn, who had befriended her, had been seated nearby in the second-class dining-room with his coffee. He shouted to Avis and her nurses, 'Stay where you are!' Holbourn had appreciated the gravity of the situation immediately but decided to wait until the first rush was over.

Archie Donald was finishing lunch in the company of Reverend Gwyer, the minister's wife Margaret and the Canadian nurse Lorna Pavey who was travelling to join the Red Cross. Amused, Donald was observing Lorna eat a grapefruit. He teased her gently about her choice of dessert, and the Gwyers joined in the banter. Donald would remember not an explosion but a shattering of glass, as if someone had fallen through a 'glass house'. Reverend Gwyer laid his hand on his shoulder. 'Let us quieten the people,' he suggested with great dignity. The two men moved calmly to the door of the dining saloon and called out loudly that everything was going to be all right and there was no need for panic. They didn't really believe this themselves, but they managed to muster sufficient conviction to reassure others, and diners began to file out of the dining-room quickly in an orderly fashion. The courageous Gwyers waited until the crowd had thinned out before making their own way up the stairs. They had contemplated going to their cabin to get lifebelts but were afraid of being trapped. Lorna stayed in the dining-room until it was almost empty. John Wilson, who had been rushing round closing the portholes, found her standing there. He grabbed her by the hand and dragged her through the debris of ruined floral arrangements and heaps of silverware, glass and dishes that had crashed to the floor.

Herbert Ehrhardt, too, was finishing his lunch when the torpedo struck. Noticing that several of the second-class dining-room's portholes were open, he and his roommate (probably John Wilson or William Gardner) and a number of other passengers and stewards swiftly slammed the them shut and fastened them to buy more time for the ship. None of them was in any doubt that the liner was sinking. Ehrhardt noticed the lack of panic as the dining-room cleared. As the smell of smoke crept in, he decided it was time to fetch his lifebelt.

John Wilson and Lorna Pavey managed to make their way up to C Deck, but they had to use the rungs of the banister as stairs because the ship was tilting so steeply. They saw a lifeboat already lowered and half full of water as well as people. Wilson told Lorna to slide down a rope.

At about 1.30 p.m. Charles Lauriat had returned to his stateroom to put on a sweater before embarking on a walk. On deck he encountered Elbert and Alice Hubbard standing by the port-side saloon-class entrance. Hubbard had lent Lauriat a copy of *The Philistine*, which contained his essay 'Who Lifted the Lid Off Hell?', an attack on the Kaiser. Hubbard had asked, still consumed with the notion of his own relationship with the Kaiser, 'Do you really think I'll be a welcome visitor in Germany?'

Just then they all felt a muffled impact that shook the ship. Turning towards the sound they saw 'smoke and cinders flying up in the air on the starboard side'. A second explosion soon followed, but to Lauriat this appeared to emanate from an exploding boiler rather than from a second torpedo strike. Lauriat suggested to the Hubbards that they go back to their portside B Deck cabin (B-70) and retrieve their lifebelts, especially in view of the fact that he knew Alice Hubbard could not swim. To Lauriat's surprise the Hubbards made no attempt to move. Alice seemed stunned. Elbert 'stayed by the rail, affectionately holding his arm around his wife's waist'.

'Stay here if you wish,' Lauriat said quickly. 'I'll fetch some lifejackets for you.' Hurrying to his own B Deck cabin forward on the starboard side, Lauriat grabbed his leather attaché case, secured his own lifebelt and seized two more. He intended to give them to the Hubbards, but when he got back they were nowhere to be seen. Lauriat searched the decks, but they seemed to have vanished into thin air. Archie Donald said later that he saw them refuse a place in a lifeboat.

Ernest Cowper, carrying little Helen Smith, who had run up to him when she got separated from her family, also bumped into the Hubbards. Helen was still wearing her white hat and clutching her doll. Hubbard said, 'Well, Jack, they have got us. They are a damn sight worse than I ever thought they were.'

Cowper remembered:

> They did not move . . . As I moved to the other side of the ship, in preparation for a jump when the right moment came, I called to him, 'What are you going to do?' and he just shook his head, while Mrs Hubbard smiled and said, 'There does not seem to be anything to do.' . . . Then [Hubbard] did one of the most dramatic things I ever saw done. He simply turned with Mrs Hubbard and entered a room on the top deck, the door of which was open, and closed it behind him. It was apparent that his idea was that they should die together, and not risk being parted on going into the water.[6]

In his philosophical writings Hubbard had stated, 'We are here now. Some day we shall go. And when we go we would like to go gracefully.' Other witnesses claimed to have seen the Hubbards after this point.

Then an Italian family from third class – grandmother, mother and three children – approached Lauriat, who was still holding the lifebelts he had collected for the Hubbards, imploring his help, so he put life-jackets on the women and found another for the oldest child. The family then squatted meekly on a collapsible boat, patiently waiting for some-one to tell them what to do. Lauriat, affected by the spectacle, found this 'one of the most pathetic things' he saw that day. He then went round trying to help other people who had not put on their lifebelts correctly, but some of them feared he was trying to steal their belts and recoiled in terror. Returning to his stateroom Lauriat found there was no electricity and struck a match. He collected his passport and personal papers. It was just ten minutes after the explosion, but the ship was flooding and keeling over rapidly.

Lifeboat No. 7 was still attached to the ship. Amid a great commotion Lauriat jumped on to the small craft and tried to loosen the after falls. He then attempted to assist a steward who was trying to saw through the forward falls with a pocket knife, but he was blocked by the mass of panicking people. The ship's stacks towered menacingly over them. Lauriat, despairing that the lifeboat would not be freed in time, shouted to others in the boat to jump into the water.

Few listened. Abandoning his futile attempt to persuade them, Lauriat jumped. As he swam away from the sinking liner, followed by the few intrepid souls who had heeded his advice and example, he glanced back and saw the lifeboat and its howling occupants dragged under by the sinking liner. Then he felt a crushing impact as a heavy Marconi aerial tumbled on to his shoulders, pushing him head first into the water. Kicking, tearing himself free, he fought his way to the surface. The plaintive cries of those struggling in the water ringing in his ears, he managed to climb into a collapsible boat with Leslie Morton, the young look-out. Hearing Fred Gauntlett call out his name, he helped him into the boat also.[7]

Former senator Samuel Knox and James Brooks also climbed in the boat.[8] Knox had been dragged down to the depths by the sinking liner's smokestack before fighting his way to the surface. 'Jay' Brooks had been planning a game of shuffleboard with his friends Montagu and Chastina Grant when he saw the torpedo streaking towards the ship. He felt 'a solid shock' go through the *Lusitania* and 'instantly up through the decks went coal, debris of all kinds . . . in a cloud, up in the air and mushroomed up 150 feet above the Marconi wires'. This was accompanied by 'a volume of water thrown with violent force' that knocked him flat on his face. Brooks got back up again and heard Chastina weakly call for her husband. Jay ran between the second and third funnels to find Montagu and Chastina lying on the deck on the starboard side. He experienced the second explosion as 'a slight second shock'; it enveloped him in suffocating steam. When the steam cleared there was no sign of the Grants.

Panicking now, Brooks saw Captain Turner hold up his hands and shout, 'Lower no more boats! Everything is going to be all right!' As he passed a lifeboat station Brooks heard one crewman mutter to another, 'To hell with him. We'll damn well get this one away!' Brooks saw the first lifeboat spill its occupants into the sea. He thought that maybe if the *Lusitania* dropped speed the lifeboats would get away safely. But the ship ploughed on relentlessly straight towards the Old Head of Kinsale. A crewman was brandishing a gun, bellowing that nobody was to get into the boats. Brooks retorted, 'Who in hell is trying to?' He saw Staff Captain Anderson, coatless, running towards the stern where at least

Right: The Cunard liner the *Lusitania* being launched from the John Brown and Company shipyard, Clydebank, Scotland, on 7 June 1906

A postcard depicting the new ocean liner – at one time the largest in the world

The Cunard Line proudly announces 'the largest, finest and fastest ships in the world'

The 32,000-ton *Lusitania* at sea

The *Lusitania*'s captain, William Turner

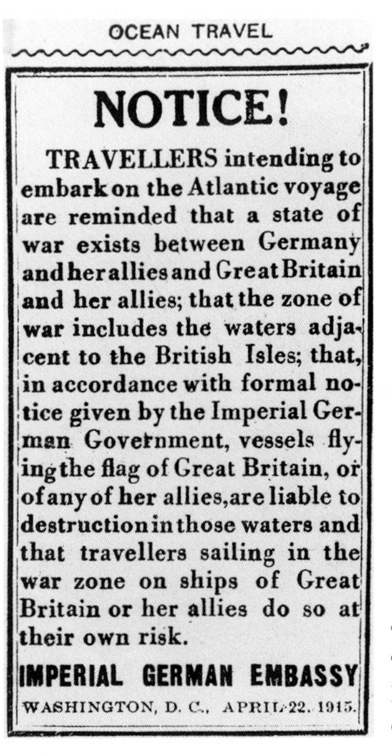

OCEAN TRAVEL

NOTICE!

TRAVELLERS intending to embark on the Atlantic voyage are reminded that a state of war exists between Germany and her allies and Great Britain and her allies; that the zone of war includes the waters adjacent to the British Isles; that, in accordance with formal notice given by the Imperial German Government, vessels flying the flag of Great Britain, or of any of her allies, are liable to destruction in those waters and that travellers sailing in the war zone on ships of Great Britain or her allies do so at their own risk.

IMPERIAL GERMAN EMBASSY

WASHINGTON, D. C., APRIL 22, 1915.

The warning notice inserted within the 'Ocean Travel' section of a number of US newspapers by the Imperial German Embassy before the *Lusitania*'s departure on what proved to be her last voyage

An illustration based on reports of the sinking of the *Lusitania* off the coast of Ireland on 7 May 1915 after it was torpedoed by the German submarine *U-20*; the artist's impression may not be entirely accurate, as the ship's livery at the time is still in dispute.

One of the lifebelts that was salvaged from the floating remains of the liner

The dandy-rigged, eighteen-ton fishing-boat the *Wanderer* at Port Erin on the Isle of Man; its crew saved 160 lives after the *Lusitania* sank.

The *Wanderer* and its crew at its moorings, Peel, Isle of Man

The crew of the *Wanderer* wearing the medals they received for their rescue of 160 passengers from the *Lusitania*'s lifeboats; in a letter its skipper, William Ball, wrote, 'It was an awful sight to see her sinking, and to see the plight of these people. I cannot describe it to you in writing.'

The Manchester Manx Society had a medal struck for each member of the *Wanderer*'s crew; these were presented on Tynwald Day, the Isle of Man's national day, in July 1915. The example shown here (obverse and reverse faces) was awarded to Thomas Woods.

Reaction to the tragedy put to propaganda uses:
Top left: A poster by Fred Spear, featuring a painting of a mother and child drowning, states simply, 'Enlist'.
Above right: A recruitment poster detailing the official verdict of the inquiry
Above: An unofficial postage stamp commemorating the sinking of the *Lusitania*

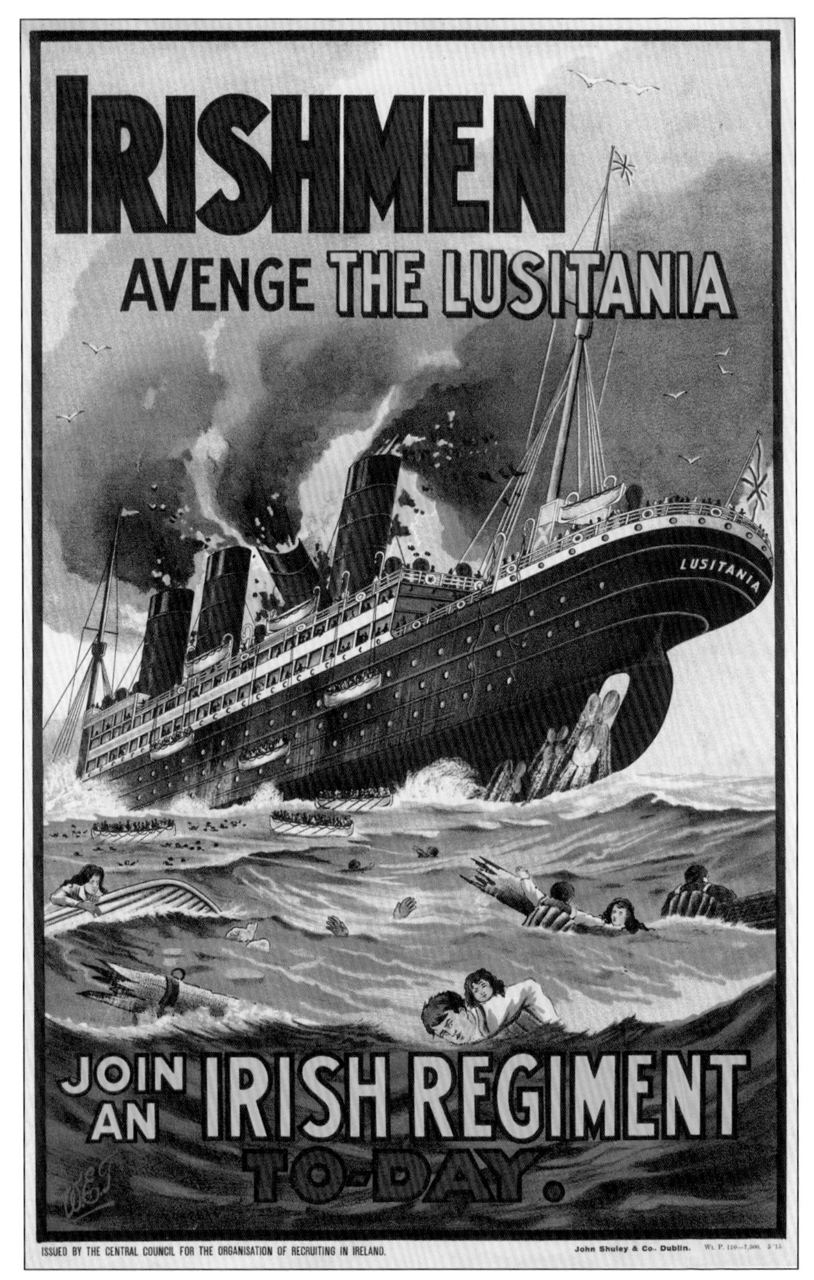

'Irishmen, avenge the *Lusitania*': the Central Council for the Organisation of Recruiting in Ireland published this colourfully dramatic poster shortly after the attack on the Cunard liner.

sixty women were clinging to an iron railing, afraid to let go and lower themselves into a lifeboat. Brooks helped, holding on to a lifeboat davit with one arm and with the other assisting women into the lifeboat one by one. The deck was almost submerged, but the chains prevented the lifeboat from being freed.

Before the clamps could be released, the boat's keel was afloat and the waters smashed the lifeboat into the davits, spilling most of the women into the sea. Without removing his shoes Brooks leaped into the ocean. The water was not freezing but was clogged with wreckage. He swam away as fast as he could. The hazardous Marconi wires came crashing down on him, threatening to trap him. As he shoved them aside they sliced into his hand. He saw the *Lusitania*, which was pointing towards the land just out of reach, go down 'with a thunderous roar as of the collapse of a great building during a fire'. He thought perhaps the innards of the ship had broken loose and crashed towards the bow.

Fred Gauntlett would recall, 'Women and children under the protection of the men had clustered in line on the port side, and as the ship made her plunge, down a little at the head and heeling at an angle of 90 degrees, this little army slid down toward the starboard side, dashing themselves against each other as they went, until they were engulfed.'[9] Gauntlett said he heard only one explosion and the whole tragedy was over in twenty minutes.

Jay Brooks, together with Leslie Morton, Fred Gauntlett, Samuel Knox and Charles Lauriat, had managed to clamber aboard the collapsible, and they set to work to raise the sides. With great difficulty they tried to persuade the desperate people in the water who were clinging on to the sides to hang onto the ropes attached instead, so the sides could be raised. But those in the water fought them off, convinced that the men were trying to push them off and abandon them. Nothing was easy: after they eventually managed to get the sides raised the seats had to be slid in place. There were no oars. They had to cast about to find ones among the 'the dead and living among the debris'. They started to pull for the shore, aiming for the tall lighthouse they could see on the massive headland, and as they rowed they continued to haul more and more people into the life-raft until it had sunk 'flush with the water'. The indomitable Lauriat refused to give in to despair. He told himself optimistically that at least they had a good crew.

When John Idwal Lewis reached the boat deck he saw Chief Officer Piper by Lifeboat No. 2 on the port side. Lewis crossed over to the starboard side and saw land. Clearly the *Lusitania* had swung towards Ireland. Lewis went to the bridge. Encountering Quartermaster Hugh Johnston, he shouted out to him, 'What is the list on the telltale, on the compass?' He was told, 'Fifteen degrees.' Second Officer Hefford tossed several lifebelts to Lewis, but Lewis passed them all on to other people, keeping none for himself. He hurried to his assigned boats, Nos 1 to 11 on the starboard side, where First Officer Rowland Jones had assumed control. Lewis noticed that Lifeboat No. 1 had already been lowered into the water and contained just two sailors. Lewis did what he could to occupy his boats, filling them up and lowering them as best he could, but the steep list swung the boats out from the rail with the result that few got away successfully. The officers brought women passengers to the edge of the collapsibles so they could get in, but they were afraid of the yawning gap and drew back frightened. While Lewis tried to persuade them to get into the boats he had to stop groups of men from rushing up and throwing themselves in by force. He caught a glimpse of a small fishing boat far away on the horizon, almost certainly the *Wanderer*, and gazed at the distant Irish coast, wishing that either were nearer so he could make a swim for it. He then went to fill the forward boats, but when he saw that others were already doing this he returned aft to assist First Officer Rowland Jones. They each took charge of one end of the lifeboat as they lowered it, and then Lewis returned to his own section, going continuously between No. 1 and No. 9, making sure the boats that could be lowered got away safely. As he lowered Lifeboat No. 9 a woman in it yelled to him, 'For God's sake, jump!'

Lewis bravely called back, 'Goodbye and good luck. I'll meet you in Queenstown!'

Up until then nurse Alice Middleton had been feeling luck was on her side. She had nearly missed the ship in New York but had just made it. Then, having originally booked third class, she had managed to obtain an upgrade to second class. She had been sitting in the second-class dining-room with three Irish girls when one of them glimpsed land through the porthole and the girls began singing 'There Is a Green Hill Not Far Away' – in a corrupt version of the hymn. Then all hell broke loose. The *Lusitania* listed so suddenly and violently that dishes crashed to the floor. The stewards shouted, 'No danger. Keep to your seats!' There were a few shrieks, but in general the atmosphere in the dining-room was calm. Then the lights went out, and people began a desperate scramble towards the exits in the semi-darkness.

Middleton was now on the lower promenade deck, and her euphoric mood had evaporated. She felt she was losing her mind with terror. Her eye fell on Richard Preston Prichard, whom she had noticed and smiled at several times during the voyage but to whom she had never spoken until that moment. He saw that she was terrified, and tried to calm her. Another man handed her a lifebelt and helped her to fit it. This second man may well have been Alfred Vanderbilt, and this was his perhaps last gallant action in the final half-hour of his life, when the notorious millionaire playboy metamorphosed into a hero. His life up till then had been distinguished by excess and indulgence. He had left a trail of scandal and extravagance behind him as he squandered his immense fortune on horses and women; indeed four of these women were said to have committed suicide because of him. In the *Lusitania* crisis the millionaire sportsman became the saviour of many people in distress; he reportedly gave away his own lifejacket, fixing it securely round Charlotte Pye as she hugged her baby daughter Marjorie. Then, with Charles Frohman, Vanderbilt devised a system to rescue the infants. They tied lifejackets to Moses baskets containing babies. These contraptions were swept off the ship and floated, but, tragically, the infants did not survive. However, the disaster of the *Lusitania*'s sinking was Vanderbilt's finest hour. He seemed to have no care for his own safety. Oliver Bernard would remember his handsome face wearing its customary quizzical grin as he attempted to rescue women and children.

The next minute Alice Middleton and Richard Preston Prichard were washed off the deck. He was never seen again. She found herself underwater with her head trapped in an open porthole. Despite the agonizing pain in her ears, somehow she struggled free and kicked her way upwards to the surface. Gasping, staring about her aghast, she found herself surrounded by corpses. The pathetic dead children looked to her like 'drowned dolls'. And there was more horror in store. Close by a woman was in the throes of childbirth in the water. It was stated that at least four pregnant passengers went into labour and gave birth in the sea. Alice looked on, appalled. Powerless and sickened, she slipped into unconsciousness.

The unfortunate woman who had gone into premature labour may have been Marguerita Kay. Two days previously, on Wednesday, 5 May, the ship's doctor had diagnosed her seven-year-old son Robert as having measles and had placed him in quarantine. When the torpedo struck she led Robert up to the top decks. He would recall that his mother was tense, yet strangely composed. She said she was afraid they would not manage to reach the upper deck, but she bundled him into whatever garments were to hand and out of the cabin. She moved with difficulty because of her advanced state of pregnancy. It was strangely quiet except for the muffled shouts and cries filtering from the upper decks. They reached the ship's rail, Marguerita still gripping her son tightly. Water swirled over the deck beneath their feet. The next moment, they were torn asunder . . .

The electrical engineer and inventor Robert Rankin had been enjoying the voyage. His table companions were agreeable, and he became friends with Clinton 'Bill' Bernard, Robert Dearbergh and Thomas Bloomfield. At 2 p.m. he was standing by the rail on the starboard side with Bloomfield and Dearbergh when one of them caught a glimpse of something. 'There's a whale,' someone said. But Rankin, looking out on the dazzling blue sea, knew at once that the black ridge was something more sinister than marine wildlife. As they stared, a white, foamy streak sliced through the water. Rankin saw the torpedo speeding straight for the ship. It was aimed ahead of her and was evidently going to hit. Then it struck under the bridge. In suspended animation, for a brief moment that yet seemed endless, the friends stood transfixed, holding their breath, waiting for the explosion. A crazy hope sparked in their minds: perhaps the thing would fail to detonate. But then the inevitable happened. According to Rankin, 'The explosion came with a terrific crash, clear through the five decks destroying the boiler room and the main steam pipe . . . A mass of glass, wood, etc. came pouring on our heads, 200 feet aft. We ducked into the smoking-room shelter, and I never saw my companions again.'[10]

He had sensed that the *Lusitania* was doomed. He crossed the smoking-room to the port side and tried to help some men who were attempting to push a lifeboat over the side. Realizing their efforts were futile, as the ship was listing too far to starboard, he abandoned the endeavour and made his way down the stairs, trying not to get entangled in the throng of passengers who were surging up the stairs. Rankin got as far as D Deck when he heard the disconcerting sound of water close by. Looking down he saw that E Deck was flooding fast. Crossing the darkened passageway on D Deck he peered through a porthole and saw to his horror that the water was within twelve inches of the port. In the stairwell he bumped into Clinton Bernard, who asked him if he had a lifebelt. They found that they were all gone. They decided that if they did find one they would share it 'fifty–fifty'. They made their way along B Deck where passengers were milling about in wild confusion, casting about desperately for anyone who could tell them what to do. The friends mounted the stairs to A Deck and watched the boats on the starboard side begin loading. To their dismay, lifeboat No. 1 drifted away with what appeared to be just one or two people aboard. Rankin spotted one of the 'doughnut life-preservers' attached to the rail and handed it to Bernard. They were just about to jump overboard holding it between them when a steward shouted that there was an old lady who needed it. Bernard selflessly handed it over. The last minutes were a blur to Rankin. He knew the ship was sinking rapidly. 'Bernard said, "Goodbye, old chap", and grabbed me by the hand, at the same time pulling out his money and throwing it away. The sixty-foot deck was, by now, within six to ten feet of the water, and I pulled off my coat and jumped, feet first, as far as I could and started to swim on my side. Looking straight up I saw the funnels coming over and thought that I would certainly be hit on the head. Then the funnels went back and the bow plunged and the ship went down.'

Ernest Cowper raced down below to snatch up a lifebelt for little Helen Smith whom he had told to wait for him by the funnel. The terrified child was overjoyed when he returned and cried out, 'You came back for me just like you said you would!' When they reached Lifeboat No. 13 Cowper saw there was a yawning gap between the lifeboat and the side of the ship. He tossed the little girl to Elizabeth Hampshire, who was already seated in the boat beside her foster-sister Florence Whitehead. He explained, 'She asked me to save her. Says she can't find her mother and father or baby sister Bessie, but her grandparents will be waiting in Liverpool.' (There was, however, a misunderstanding somewhere. Helen later confirmed that her sibling was baby Hubert. Bessie was the nickname of her mother Elizabeth.)

In the lifeboat Helen sat quietly on Elizabeth's knee. Elizabeth and Florence Whitehead had been about to leave the lunch table and start their packing when the torpedo hit. Elizabeth remembered a 'terrific explosion' that seemed to shatter the vessel. Her first thought was: My God, they've got us! A steward, his face 'as white as death', took control of the situation, telling the two women, 'Follow me.' Elizabeth and Florence seized their purses, so that they would have money with them after the ship sank. The steep list of the vessel made negotiating the stairs difficult; when they reached the debris-strewn deck Elizabeth lost her footing and began to slide down the slope towards the ship's rail and the water churning below.

Florence seized Elizabeth by the hair and hauled her to safety. When the women recovered their composure they approached Lifeboat No. 11, but Florence was disconcerted because she thought the boat already looked overcrowded. She urged Elizabeth to wait for the next one. Florence's fears were justified: as Lifeboat No. 11 was lowered its stern suddenly dropped, and the shrieking occupants were tipped into the sea.

Cowper climbed into Lifeboat No. 13 and watched as John Davies and William Harkness helped lower the craft. Elizabeth Hampshire saw the four-year-old Riley twins, Ethel and Sutcliffe, thrown into the boat, but their parents were left behind because the boat was already being lowered. When it reached the face of the sea, as soon as the falls were detached, the lifeboat rowed slowly away from the mother ship. A crew member shouted at those manning the oars, 'Row! Row! Hurry up, before the ship goes under and the suction gets us.'

The sight of the sinking ship, her decks crowded with doomed passengers and crew, was too much for Elizabeth Hampshire. She bent over little Helen, welcoming the chance to comfort the child. Meanwhile Florence went on staring in fascinated horror. In spite of the danger their lifeboat stopped to pick up more people flailing around in the water; these were survivors of Lifeboat No. 17, which had been swamped during lowering. Cowper saw how the mast aerial dangled down into the water and the ship's great funnels loomed over the little boat. Elizabeth finally turned her head to view the last of the ship. She watched as people leaped into the water from the stern, still pitched high in the air. Then the *Lusitania* plunged downward and disappeared from sight. The two women spent several hours in the lifeboat. During a quiet moment Helen, with extraordinary composure, said to Elizabeth, 'If I can't find my mama and daddy I'll go with you ladies.' Florence and Ernest took Helen on their laps in turn to give Elizabeth opportunity to stretch her legs.

George Kessler had felt no alarm; he noted the lack of panic among the saloon-class passengers. Indeed, he thought many of them were smiling. Nobody seemed to believe it was a real emergency. 'We lived in a fool's paradise of disbelief,' Kessler later said.

But businessman Isaac Lehmann had been convinced catastrophe was looming even before the torpedo. So unnerved was he during the voyage by the talk of submarines that he had sat up throughout the previous night in his stateroom, fully dressed, ready for disaster. After lunch on that fatal Friday, he was sitting in the A Deck smoking-room chatting with the antique jewellery merchant and noted bigamist Maurice

Benjamin Medbury when they were startled by a booming sound like a cannon. Lehmann said to Medbury, 'They've got us at last!' Medbury thought he was joking. Lehmann retorted, 'Let's get outside and see if I am joking.' Hurrying through the smoking-room to the deck, he saw the torpedo powering straight for them through the water. 'The time from the noise of the report until it struck us was less than a minute. I said, "Let's get away from here; it looks like it is going to strike right under us."' Lehmann never saw Medbury again. He hastened to the other side of the deck to reach the last portside Lifeboat No. 20 before the second-class passengers arrived. The deck was already crowded, and the ship was still shuddering from the violent impact. Lehmann reached the first lifeboat but found nobody had made any attempt to prepare it for lowering. Lehmann told them to get on with it, and a large number of people crowded into the boat. There were three or four men on each rope, and another stood with a hatchet in his hand ready to cut the blocks, but they failed to coordinate their movements. One side started lowering the boat, but the other did not, and on the side let go the rope severed, freeing the boat and pitching everyone in it into the sea.

Lehmann, appalled, ran down to his D Deck stateroom to collect his life-preserver only to find somebody else had taken it. The liner had already begun to settle into her dying list. Lehmann, with mounting hysteria, whipped his revolver out of his dress-suit case. He later said he 'figured this would come in handy in case there was anybody not doing the proper thing'. He rushed up to B Deck, gun in hand. He met his steward, William Barnes, whom he ordered to procure a life-preserver for him. He waited until Barnes came back with one and helped him into it, then walked out on to B Deck where he encountered the ship's doctor, James McDermott, and the ship's purser, James McCubbin, both calmly puffing on cigarettes. Meanwhile water was already surging along the starboard side and flooding on to C Deck. The two men told him there was not a chance the boat would sink, advised him to stay calm and said he was foolish to wear a lifejacket. Lehmann later said, 'I did not take very much notice of this outside of the fact I laughed at them and said it was better to be prepared if anything did happen. This was the last I saw of these men. I understand they have been drowned.'

He made his way to the boat deck on the port side. Seeing that Lifeboat No. 16 was gone he then looked aft to Lifeboat No. 18 and noted that between thirty and forty people were sitting in the craft but nobody appeared to be making any attempt to lower it. By now the

Lusitania's bows were plunging beneath the water. He asked a seaman with an axe in his hand, 'Why aren't you putting this boat into the water? Who has charge of this lifeboat?' The man replied, 'It is the Captain's orders not to launch any boats.'[11]

Furious, Lehmann produced his revolver and waved it about in plain sight of everyone. He bawled, 'To hell with the Captain! Don't you see the boat is sinking? And the first man that disobeys my orders to launch this boat I shoot to kill.' The seaman stopped arguing and swung his axe, releasing the link-pin holding the boat. As the boat descended, the ship gave an 'awful lurch . . . There were about thirty to forty men and women standing on the collapsible boat where I was, and the boat in receding smashed all these people, who were trying to get into the boat, up against the smoking-room, killing pretty much all. They could not move, I being knocked down as well, and hurting my leg severely, but I succeeded in crawling out and was able to hold on to the rails when the water from the funnels commenced pouring over us.'

He saw blood streaming from his injured foot. Somehow the crew in charge of Lifeboat No. 18 had managed to regain control and were lowering it efficiently when suddenly one of the men in the lifeboat sprang to his feet and yelled, 'Don't you drop this boat!' The startled crew lost control, and the lifeboat tipped its howling human cargo into the water. Lehmann grabbed on to a rail, but the water 'commenced coming over the smokestack' and washed him 'right off the deck and into the ocean'. (The water probably did not come over the smokestack but swirled around the ventilators.)

'A terrific explosion occurred in the front of the steamer, and then I noted the lifeboat which had killed these people had gone back into its original position. By this time the ship was sinking fast, and this boat finally got away safely. I was then thrown high into the water, free and clear of all wreckage, and I then went down twice with the suction of the steamer, and the second time I came up I was 400 or 500 feet away from the ship. I clung to an oar, and just then I saw the *Lusitania* take her final plunge. It sounded like a terrible moan.'[12] (Lauriat was reported to have used the same expression.)

Almost immediately, the crew had scrambled to launch the lifeboats that were accessible. The *Lusitania* carried lifeboats and rafts sufficient to accommodate 2,605 persons. These included twenty-two lifeboats which carried 68 persons each, twenty Chambers collapsible boats carrying 54 each, twelve McLean-Chambers collapsible boats with a capacity of 49 each, two Henderson collapsible boats carrying 43 each and fourteen life-rafts, with capacities varying from 20 to 40 each. *Lusitania* also carried nearly 3,000 life-preservers on board.

While the number of lifeboats should have been adequate, the conditions of the sinking made their usage extremely difficult, dangerous and in some cases impossible, because the ship heeled over so quickly and at such a steep angle. In all, only six lifeboats were launched successfully; several others overturned, splintering to pieces and breaking apart. Most of the boats that did get away had no plugs in them, and the collapsible boats that were floating had no oars in them. Eighteen minutes after the torpedo struck, the liner's bow hit the seabed while her stern still towered above the surface, a situation that mirrored that of the *Titanic* three years earlier. When the stern slid beneath the waves hundreds of people were left struggling in the water, calling for help from the debris-strewn sea.

Fortunately the weather and sea temperature were relatively mild, and the water was calm. Survivors able to do so scanned the horizon for possible rescue vessels. They caught sight of what they took for a sail about a mile away but later decided it must have been the periscope of the submarine that had torpedoed them. In the water Lehmann and another man tried to save a baby by lifting it on to a steamer chair floating by. They managed to keep it alive for an hour and a half, but in the end it died. Lehmann tried to retain the infant's body warmth by moving his arms and left leg, but as the sun began to sink the water grew cold and his limbs grew numb. Lehmann was picked up by First Officer Rowland Jones at about 6.15 p.m. after some four hours in the water. His watch had stopped at 2.28 p.m. Lehmann weighed in at 200 pounds. Wearing his waterlogged clothing and lifejacket it took six men to haul him into the boat.

Lehmann recalled, 'After leaving the lifeboat I was transferred [first to the *Wanderer* (Peel 12), then] to the tender known as the *Flying Fox* [in fact the *Flying Fish*], and after leaving the scene of the disaster we did not arrive in Queenstown until eleven o'clock that night. We tied up at the Cunard Dock, and the arrangement for the reception of the survivors was just as hard and difficult as it was to get saved from the *Lusitania*.'[13]

Although they could not believe that a torpedo could harm the *Lusitania*, Kessler described how, together with Robert Timmis, the middle-aged Texan cotton magnate, and his colleague Ralph Moodie, he had helped women into the lifeboats 'in a spirit of convention'. However, a sudden violent lurch threw him into a lifeboat that had not yet been lowered and which still hung about fifty feet above the water. The next moment the boat was violently launched. Before it hit the water the *Lusitania* had settled some twenty feet. 'Scarcely had we got the boat clear of the rails when the *Lusitania* disappeared before our very eyes. It was too sudden to describe. It just happened.'[14] The violent suction as the great mother ship sank overturned the lifeboat, tossing Kessler and the other fifty or sixty occupants of the lifeboat into the water and then sucking them down. After what seemed to him an eternity Kessler surfaced. All signs of the boat and its other occupants had vanished. He swam, finally reaching a collapsible boat half full of water. There were already eight men in it: six big, burly stokers. He climbed into the boat, and the men tried bailing and balancing, but the boat kept tilting and turning, clearly damaged, finally capsized again. It overturned eight times, and all the while about fifty others were fighting to get into the craft. After three hours some of them were picked up by a trawler, but the strong young stokers were dead.

George Kessler was later asked, 'How long was it between the striking of the torpedo and the sinking of the *Lusitania*?' He replied, 'Exactly twenty-five minutes. She was struck at 2.15 and sank exactly at 2.30. Look! Here is my watch – see, it is stopped just at 2.30, when I was thrown into the water when the vessel sank.' Dramatically he drew forth a gold watch from a case tarnished by salt water. About him, listening to his tale, were a dozen fellow survivors. There were cries of 'You are right – look at my watch', and a dozen watches were flashed, all but one showing the hour to be 2.30 (one showed 2.33). Asked what became of Alfred Vanderbilt, Kessler said, 'I am certain he perished.' Kessler also had the melancholy task of identifying the dead body of Charles Frohman, who had tried to help Vanderbilt save the youngest children.

Big Robert Timmis had lugged a woman on his hip up the precipitous stairs to A Deck, gripping the balustrades. On deck he met stewards who were striding about proclaiming that there was no danger and urging people to get out of the lifeboats. Timmis found himself surrounded by steerage passengers, 'some Russians and other foreigners. I tried to re-assure them. I could not talk to them, but I put up my hand and nodded my head and said, "All right, all right," and they seemed to understand that, and one of them kissed my hand, the first time I had ever had my hand kissed.'[15] Timmis saw Sarah Lund standing with her father William Mounsey who had been travelling to England to see the woman in a Liverpool institution they hoped might prove to be Sarah's mother Fanny.

(Sarah's father and her husband Charles Lund would be lost with the *Lusitania*, and the woman in Liverpool would turn out not to have been Sarah's mother.) Having been ordered to vacate a lifeboat by crewmen who kept repeating that the ship was not going down, Sarah and her father stood at a loss, wondering what to do. She told her father she was sure the ship was going to sink, despite what they had just been told. She had no lifebelt. Timmis removed his own and gave it to her. Then all was confusion: the ship seemed to fly to pieces, and Sarah and her father were swept into the sea in what seemed a downward swirling vortex. Sarah managed to cling to a board until she was rescued by Robert Timmis, a strong swimmer who clung to various pieces of wreckage for almost three hours before he was taken into a lifeboat 'which he still had the strength to assist in rowing'. Timmis bent down to shake her hand as she lay cold and exhausted in the bottom of the boat.

Timmis later described Sarah's rescue. 'There was a woman further on I thought might be alive. She was face down with a belt on but seemed shoulders high out of the water. Her golden hair which was loose over her shoulders showed up well.'[16]

After the worst of the crush in the dining-room had passed, Professor Ian Holbourn escorted his young friend Avis Dolphin back to his cabin to fetch lifebelts, as her accommodation was on a lower deck. He put on her a lifebelt that belonged to a fellow passenger. The other passenger helped him. Ian gathered a few of his most precious manuscripts. Carrying his own lifebelt, together the three made for the top. When they had almost reached the deck all the lights went out. On deck they spotted Avis's nursemaids Hilda Ellis and Sarah Smith. Sarah had no lifebelt and Ian offered her his, but she refused, saying that 'his life was of more value than hers as he had a wife and children'.[17] Holbourn would later make trenchant observations regarding the lack of lifebelts available on the boat decks. He agreed to keep his lifebelt and try to find a boat for Avis and her nursemaids. He wanted to get them away in a port-side lifeboat, but of those they saw one was smashed to pieces while it was being launched, and another was launched with nobody in it, and a group of men stripped off and swam for it. Knowing the starboard-side crafts were their only hope, Holbourn placed Avis, Sarah and Hilda in a starboard lifeboat, possibly No. 17. He kissed Avis and, fearing that he would not survive, asked her to 'find his wife and children and kiss them goodbye for him'.[18]

Almost a quarter of an hour had passed since the impact. The *Lusitania* now wallowed very low in the water. Holbourn put on his lifebelt, stuffed his manuscripts into his clothing and found a clear space to jump. As he did so, to his horror he caught a glimpse of Avis's lifeboat capsizing. Avis was sucked under and disappeared. Horrified, Holbourn knew he had no chance of getting to her through the confused mass of debris and panicking people. The sight would haunt his dreams for years afterward. In the water he became entangled in ropes. Struggling free, he witnessed the death throes of the great ship. He made for the nearest lifeboat, No. 15, kicking hard, propelling another survivor in front of him. It was only when he reached the craft that he realized that the other man was dead. The people in the overcrowded boat refused to let him on.

Fearing that his manuscripts would be lost, he threw them into the boat so that least his papers would be saved. He then grabbed on to a rope trailing from the stern of the lifeboat. The people in the lifeboat saw another empty craft (perhaps No. 1 Lifeboat or a collapsible) a few yards off and made towards it. As No. 15 was full of people fished from the water, the oars moved slowly. It took perhaps three-quarters of an hour to reach the other boat, which seemed to Holbourn 'an interminable age'. Weakening from the cold water, he asked one of the men in the boat to hold his hand. Those in the boat were all in such a state of shock that they refused. Seeing and hearing so many people drowning painted a picture 'too ghastly to describe'. He thought he was going to die alone.

A the last minute, however, he was dragged to safety with the help of Francis Luker. He even managed to retrieve his precious manuscript. Luker was a Canadian postal worker on his way to enlist in the war. He later gave an imaginative, not to say fanciful, account of events in which he described seeing the *U-20* 's periscope and the two torpedoes striking the ship, sending up clouds of smoke and steam. He recalled alarmed passengers rushing to the starboard side and being 'thrown into a heap' by the ship's lurching and then pitched into the sea. He saved himself by gripping hold of a piece of iron fixed to the woodwork on deck. Then he hurried to the second-class accommodation to find a lifebelt. On his way he said he passed the nursery forward on C Deck. Seeing a baby inside, he tried to run in to rescue it, but the ship lurched and the door jammed shut. Outside, on the starboard side, he saw a lifeboat that was over-full and another that had pitched all its occupants into the water. He jumped into Lifeboat No. 11. The boat had drifted some distance away from the mother ship, so Luker used the boathook to haul it close enough for more people to get into it. Phyllis Wickings-Smith tossed her baby Nancy to him. He also caught another child thrown to him whose identity Luker did not know. The boat rowed away but narrowly escaped being dragged under by the wireless masts. After the ship went down Luker had to change boats five times. He would remember that one of the boats had a defective plug and that he was waist-deep in water on board.

Elizabeth Duckworth, a twice-married textile worker, had left Connecticut to return to Blackburn, her birthplace. She shared a cabin with Alice Scott and her son Arthur, aged eight. Alice had a dream before embarking that the *Lusitania* would be destroyed, and her family teasingly suggested that she should cancel her reservation. She replied that she could die only once.

After lunch on 7 May she went to the cabin to lie down while Elizabeth and young Arthur went for a stroll on deck. When the torpedo struck, Elizabeth felt the ship shake from 'stem to stern'. Dodging through a rain of hot cinders, she and Arthur rushed to the forward deck. Someone shouted that there was a 'gaping hole' in the *Lusitania*'s side and that the ship was going to sink by the bow just where they were standing. As the liner pitched and rolled it seemed the sea would soon have them. Panicking, Elizabeth and Arthur started climbing the ship's rigging. An officer, perhaps Second Officer Hefford or First Officer Piper, ran up and persuaded them calmly to come down. He said there was a lifeboat ready for them on the promenade deck. Elizabeth told Arthur to slide down the rope ladder and that she would catch him. He panicked, but Elizabeth shouted encouragement, and he finally plucked up his courage and slid down. She muffed the catch and the boy landed on the deck on his back, winded. His mother Alice had now caught up with them and the three of them headed towards a lifeboat on the starboard side. An officer told them there was room for the child but not for the women.

Elizabeth told them to take the little boy, and she sped off with Alice heading for the next boat down, only to be told there was no room in that one either. A sailor pointed them to a boat that was 'the last one down the long line of swaying starboard-side boats'.[19] Elizabeth stumbled, but an officer helped her up and dragged her bodily to the 'last boat', Lifeboat No. 17. With his help the two women managed to scramble into it. Elizabeth was mortified when she accidentally trampled on someone's leg in the process.

The sailors seemed to be having trouble with the rollers; it was taking an age to lower the boat. Elizabeth didn't like this. She hitched up her skirts and got out again, but Alice remained in the boat. The launch was bungled: the boat overturned, hurling the occupants against the ship's side before they landed in the water. To Elizabeth's horror she saw Alice go under and never saw her come back up. Elizabeth started to recite the 23rd Psalm. Beside her, the three Irish girls who had been singing a version of 'There Is a Green Hill Far Away' during lunch were now singing it again in thin, frightened voices.

Arthur Mitchell, who had been concerned about safety, allegedly told the *New York Times*[20] that he was 'in the storeroom of the *Lusitania*' – other sources state that he was resting in his Deck E stateroom – when he heard a 'thud accompanied by the sound which I can best describe as of an iron safe falling from a height of thirty or forty feet'. Passing through the passageway outside his cabin, which smelled of sulphur and powder, Mitchell found himself beside Lifeboat No. 15. He managed to persuade Sarah Fish to enter the boat, although she was worried about her sister, Elizabeth Rogers, who still had the youngest of Sarah's three daughters, baby Joan, with her. Mitchell threw Sarah's middle daughter, Marion, into the boat. The eldest Fish daughter, ten-year-old Eileen, took a running jump and leaped in of her own accord. After he had assisted Ellen Hogg into the boat – she was in her stocking feet – Mitchell was told to get in. Lifeboat No. 15 had terrible trouble trying to get away from the ship. Wallace Phillips, in the same boat, later claimed that the lifeboat only got away in the end because a collapsible slid off the ship and nudged No. 15 forward. The Marconi aerial tumbled on to the lifeboat, but fortunately the wire snapped and the craft floated free. When the *Lusitania* went down, Lifeboat No. 15 was whirled around the vortex a few times but managed to escape. Several people clinging on to the sides, including Ian Holbourn, were pulled into the boat, but eventually it became so overcrowded that they could only urge people to 'hang on' while they sought another boat to offload the surplus passengers.

Norman Stones told his wife Hilda to get undressed to her stockings. Norman and Hilda were vocalists who also farmed on Texada Island in British Columbia. The previous evening Hilda had delighted the second-class passengers with her singing. Norman, a veteran of General Pershing's expedition after Pancho Villa on the Mexican border, intended to join a University Officer Training Corps when they reached England. Having helped his wife strip off, he strapped her into her lifebelt and started ripping the canvas cover off a collapsible boat.[21] This should have been done earlier, but no one seemed to have thought of it until then. Norman and Hilda went down with the ship. Norman survived; Hilda did not.

Dorothy Conner and her brother-in-law Dr Howard Fisher climbed up to A Deck port side where a scene of frantic confusion met their eyes. People were rushing the lifeboats; men were not giving up seats to women and children. Meanwhile the crew seemed at a loss. Margaret Mackworth joined Dorothy and Howard, unable to find her father. She remarked, 'I always thought a shipwreck was a well-organized affair.' 'So did I,' Dorothy said, 'but I've learnt a devil of a lot in the last five minutes.' They saw that a couple of sailors were beginning to lower the overcrowded boat but that their efforts were uncoordinated.

Margaret later said:

> One man lowered his end quickly, the other lowered his end slowly; the boat was in an almost perpendicular position when it reached the water. Half the people fell out, but the boat did not capsize, and I think most of them scrambled back afterwards. I do not know. We turned away and did not look. It was not safe to look at horrible things just then. Curious that it never for a moment struck any of us as possible to attempt to get into the boat ourselves. Even at that moment death would have seemed better than to make part of that terror-infected crowd. I remember regretfully thinking something of this sort.
>
> That was the last boat I saw lowered. It became impossible to lower any more from our side owing to the list on the ship. No one else except that white-faced stream seemed to lose control. A number of people were moving about the deck, gently and vaguely. They reminded one of a swarm of bees who do not know where the queen has gone. Presently Dr. F— decided to go down and fetch lifebelts for himself and his sister-in-law. While he was away, the vessel righted herself perceptibly, and word was passed round that the bulkheads had been closed and the danger was over. We laughed and shook hands, and I said, 'Well, you've had your thrill all right.'
>
> 'I never want another,' she answered. Soon after, the doctor returned bearing two lifebelts. He said he had had to wade through deep water down below to get them. While we were standing, I unhooked my skirt so that it should come straight off and not impede me in the water. The list on the ship soon got worse again and, indeed, became very bad. Presently Dr F— said he thought

> we had better jump into the sea. (We had thought of doing so before, but word had been passed round from the captain that it was better to stay where we were.) Dr F— and Miss C— moved towards the edge of the deck where the boat had been and there was no railing. I followed them, feeling frightened at the idea of jumping so far (it was, I believe, some sixty feet normally from A Deck to the sea) and telling myself how ridiculous I was to have physical fear of the jump when we stood in such grave danger as we did. I think others must have had the same fear, for a little crowd stood hesitating on the brink and kept me back. And then, suddenly, I saw that the water had come over on to the deck. We were not, as I had thought, sixty feet above the sea; we were already under the sea. I saw the water green just about up to my knees. I do not remember it coming up farther; that must all have happened in a second. The ship sank, and I was sucked right down with her.[22]

Margaret recalled that she had no acute feeling of fear while floating in the water, only a sense of relief that she had her head above water.

> The lifebelt held one up in a comfortable sitting position with one's head lying rather back, as if one were in a hammock. At moments I wondered whether the whole thing was perhaps a nightmare from which I would wake, and once, half laughing, I think, I wondered, looking round on the sun and pale blue sky and calm sea, whether I had reached Heaven without knowing it – and devoutly hoped I hadn't.[23]

Howard managed to find an upturned craft, although it was in danger of being swamped by a crowd of people clinging on for their lives. Luckily another collapsible boat had drifted out from underneath it, and this relieved some of the pressure. Meanwhile actress Rita Jolivet recognized Howard in the vessel. During the next four hours in the water Howard would help treat the injured as best he could. Marie Depage and Dr James Houghton, too, behaved heroically, calming children and women and assisting them into lifeboats. Houghton had been in his cabin, E-64, when the *Lusitania* was struck. He found Depage and Richard Freeman on A Deck where they had seen the submarine and observed the torpedo strike the ship. Houghton recalled that Depage and Freeman, who was on his way to a job as a mining engineer in Siberia, were soaked with spume and black with soot. Freeman, exhilarated at having witnessed the torpedoing, was energized, assisting in the lowering of lifeboats and generally making himself useful. Houghton and Depage calmed women and children and helped them into the lifeboats. Houghton saw Freeman give his lifejacket to a woman, and then the two men spent a moment or two in jocular banter. Not long after, Freeman disappeared from sight. Houghton later wrote to Freeman's parents saying they might think it strange that there should have been banter in the midst of tragedy, and he could only explain it by saying that it seemed to relieve the terrible tension. He also told the Freemans that their son had died nobly, thinking only of others.

Albert and Agnes Veals, who had been living in Orange, New Jersey, for the past three years, were travelling with Agnes's brother Frederick Bailey to see the Baileys' father in England. They had finished lunch and were sitting on starboard deck when one of them got up, looked into the water and cried, 'Look, there's a porpoise.' But it was no porpoise. After the strike, in the resulting confusion, Frederick was separated from Agnes and Albert. As the ship listed to starboard the couple almost tumbled headlong into Lifeboat No. 15, which soon cast off. There was a moment of sheer horror as the funnel hung over the boat and the Marconi wires entangled it, but then the aerial snapped and they were able to pull free.

Theodate Pope and Edwin Friend had been enjoying ice cream when a wag quipped that 'he would hate to have a torpedo get him before he ate it.' Conversation then turned to how slowly the ship was running, almost as 'though the engines had stopped.' As they left the dining-room the orchestra was playing 'The Blue Danube.' They exchanged greetings with Oliver Bernard and went out on to the B Deck promenade. They agreed that the sea was a 'marvellous blue and very dazzling in the sunlight.'[24]

As they rounded the aft corner of the promenade they heard a 'dull explosion.' Water and timbers flew past the deck, and Friend struck his fist with his hand and remarked, 'By Jove, they've got us!' The two ran inside, dodging a shower of soot, only to be hurled against the wall as the ship lurched to starboard. Recovering their balance, they headed toward the boat deck portside, where they and other friends had agreed to meet in the case of an emergency. The deck was crowded. They passed two women crying 'in a pitifully weak way' and heard an officer shout orders to stop lowering the boats and for passengers to go to B Deck for the lifeboats. Nobody was paying any attention. For a moment, before going down to B Deck, they saw a lifeboat being filled and lowered as the ship was still forging ahead.

The lifeboat (possibly Lifeboat No. 12) upended, spilling its load into the water. Sickened, the pair walked past Margaret Mackworth and Dorothy Conner and went down to B Deck starboard. There they watched another boat get away safely, but as the ship was listing so far over and sinking so quickly the *Lusitania* threatened to roll on top of the starboard lifeboats and anything or anyone on that side of the ship. Pope said to Friend, 'It's not a good place to jump from.' Side by side, with their arms around each other's waists, the two made for the companionway leading back to the boat deck. They passed Marie Depage and James Houghton along the way. Depage was helping bandage the hand of either crewman Matthew Freeman, the amateur lightweight boxing champion of England who had wounded it while helping to lower lifeboats, or the heroic Richard Freeman, a passenger who would not survive. His friend and colleague classmate James Houghton believed the man with the injured hand was Richard. Pope would recall with admiration that Depage's eyes were 'startled, but brave.'

Up top they saw a boat being filled rapidly and Friend told Pope, 'You better get in.' She refused to get in without Friend, and he in turn would not get into one as long as there were women still on the ship. They made for the stern as water came over the forecastle, and Pope's maid Emily Robinson appeared. 'Lifebelts!' Friend cried. Ducking into the nearest room they found themselves three lifejackets. Friend tied them on to the women. The ship was moving so fast that they could see the funnels moving and the bare steel of where the waterline began. They had to jump. 'You go first,' Pope urged Friend. He grabbed a rope from a davit of a departed lifeboat and jumped. Seconds later he resurfaced, smiling and encouraging the two women to join him. Pope turned to Emily and said, 'Come, Robinson.' She did not see whether her maid followed her or not.

Pope jumped and was sucked down and trapped between decks. Sure that she was about to die, she shut her eyes and hoped that during her life she had 'made good'. She opened her eyes and saw, through the green water, the keel of a lifeboat immediately above her. Floating up, she hit her head, but her hair and straw hat saved her from serious injury, although the bump temporarily affected her sight. Surfacing, she found herself with 'hundreds of frantic, screaming, shouting humans in this grey and watery inferno'. A panicked man without a lifebelt jumped on to her shoulders, grabbing at her as he struggled to keep afloat. His weight pushed her under and she shrieked, 'Oh, please don't.' The man let go. She lost consciousness and went under again.

When she came to she found herself floating on her back gazing up into a brilliant blue sky. To her left was 'an old man upright in the water', floating high above the water. Pope asked, 'Do you see any rescue ships coming?' 'No' was the response. She looked around for Friend, but he was nowhere to be seen. She managed to grasp an oar. Deciding that the whole scene was 'too horrible to be true' and could only be a dream she lost consciousness once more. Somewhere, further away, frightened voices arose from the water. People in Lifeboat No. 15 were singing 'It's a Long Way to Tipperary'. A young man who had been hauled into the boat died with his head resting against Agnes Veals's knees. Another man died while laying against the knees of Dora Wolfenden. She was already distraught, as her husband John had refused to leave the ship until all the women were off it. After the deaths, there was no more singing in the boat.

As the water rose up to the decks Depage and Houghton realized they could do no more for their fellow passengers. Together they made for the portside rail, leaping clear just as water swirled across the deck. They were caught by the suction and swept apart by the force of the water. Houghton struck his head as they went under. He described the experience in his undated letter to Freeman's family, received by them on 14 July 1915.

> As I sank I was struck by some wreckage but came to almost immediately. As I was whirled about in the whirlpool created by the sinking ship I escaped death by an inch at least a dozen times. There was the most astounding [amount] of wreckage being whirled about and I am certain that all the others were struck by some of it. I like to think that this is what happened for when I go, I would ask nothing better than such a speedy and painless death.

Depage, heroic to the last, did not get away cleanly. She had become entangled in ropes lying on the deck. Houghton saw her struggling, but then he was swept away. When he surfaced there was no sign of her. One of her last acts of selflessness had been to bandage the hand of either passenger Richard Freeman or steward Matthew Freeman.

Matthew Freeman had run to the stern, now the highest part of the ship, and peered at the waves below. Pulling himself together, he climbed over the rail and jumped. As he landed his head struck the side of a floating lifeboat. Blood spurted from the wound. Although dazed, he maintained consciousness and started swimming, only to be submerged a second time by a panic-stricken passenger who grabbed him, 'eyes bulging with fear'. Freeman struggled free and grabbed a floating deckchair. He heard someone yelling out to him above the hubbub. It was 36-year-old American surgeon Dr Daniel Moore, one of a party of US surgeons who had volunteered their services to the British War Office. Moore was clinging to a keg; the lifeboat he had boarded, No. 14, had been safely lowered but had later capsized. Moore urged Freeman to grab the other side of the keg. The two of them, along with four others, struggled to hold on to the keg to keep afloat. Freeman grew faint and said that he was going to let go, but Moore spoke to him harshly, strengthening his resolve. The men kicked hard and managed to reach an upturned lifeboat with about a dozen people clinging to it. Freeman collapsed, semi-conscious. In the hours that followed, many dropped off. Freeman recalled that 'ten of them died beside me there in the water'. By the time they were picked up by the patrol boat *Brock* only five, including Freeman and Moore, were still alive and clinging to the lifeboat.

From Queenstown Moore cabled his account of the disaster to the US media. According to him the *Lusitania* had been within sight of land for three hours. The Irish coast was distinctly visible, some twelve miles away. At about 1 p.m. he and his companions had noticed that the ship was steering in a zigzag course towards the shore.

> Looking through glasses I could see on the port side, between us and the land, what appeared to be a black oblong object with four dom-e-like projections. It seemed about two miles away. This object came along swiftly at times, slowing down, disappearing and reappearing. The Lusitania was zigzagging along at a speed of about 19 knots. She had done 23 knots during some periods of the voyage. Later, she kept a more even course and we generally agreed that it was a friendly submarine we had seen. No other vessel except one or two fishing boats were visible. At 1.40 o'clock we sat down to luncheon in the Second Saloon. Of course we talked about the curious object we had seen, but nobody seemed alarmed. About twenty minutes later there was a muffled drum-like noise in the forward part of the boat. The ship shivered, trembled, and almost immediately began to list to the starboard. She had been struck on the starboard side.[25]

Moore assumed there had been a second submarine involved in the attack, although he denied hearing a second explosion. Initial panic was soon quietened by assurances from the stewards that the ship had struck a small mine. Many passengers left the saloon in an orderly fashion. When Moore reached the deck he realized that moving about would present difficulties, owing to the steep angle at which the stricken ship was listing. He hurried to the promenade deck, which was packed with people. He peered over the side to see if he could spot any damage but was unable to do so. At first he thought he would go back to his cabin to fetch his lifebelt, but because the ship was listing so badly to starboard, he abandoned the idea and remained on deck. Moore described in his account how he had struggled to D Deck and forward to the first-class cabin where he met a Catholic priest, but they could find no lifebelts. Returning again toward E Deck he saw a stewardess struggling to dislodge a belt.

> I helped her with hers and secured one for myself. I then rushed to D Deck and noticed one woman perched on the gunwale, watching a lowering lifeboat ten feet away. I pushed her down and into the boat, then jumped in. The stern of the lifeboat continued to lower, but the bow stuck fast. A stoker cut the bow ropes with a hatchet, and we dropped in a vertical position. A girl whom we had heard sing at a concert was struggling, and I caught her by the ankle and pulled her in. A man I grasped by the shoulders, and I landed him safe. He was the barber of the first-class cabin, and a more manly man I never met. He showed his courage and will later on. We pushed away hard to avoid the suck, but our boat was fast filling and we bailed fast with one bucket and the women's hats. The man with the bucket became exhausted, and I relieved him. In a few minutes she was filled level full. Then a keg floated up and I pitched it about ten feet away and followed it. After reaching it I turned to see the fate of our boat. She had capsized and covered many.[26]

It was then that Moore caught sight of young Matthew Freeman and yelled out to him to grab the other side of the keg. After being in the water for about ninety minutes the two of them managed to scramble aboard a life-raft. Moore vomited violently and felt chilled from the exposure, but 'by beating myself I restored my energy and was soon handling an oar'. His description of the scene of the catastrophe is grimly detailed.

> There was no suction when the ship settled. She went down steadily and at the best possible angle. The lifeboats were not in order and they were not manned. Most of the people rushed to the upper decks . . . The surface of the water seemed dotted with bodies. Only a few of the lifeboats seemed to be doing any good.

> The cries of 'My God!' 'Save us!' and 'Help!' gradually grew weaker from all sides and finally a low weeping, wailing, inarticulate sound, mingled with coughing and gurgling, made me heartsick. I saw many men die. Some appeared to be sleepy and worn out just before they went down; others grew gradually blue and an air of hunger gave their features a sardonic smile.[27]

Joseph Myers, a lace manufacturer from New York whose business concerns in Europe ensured that he was a frequent transatlantic passenger, had made over a hundred round trips during the course of his career. Consequently had a better understanding of how ships operated than most passengers on board the liner on her final voyage. Myers had transferred to the *Lusitania* from the American Line's *St Paul*, believing that he would save at least a day's travelling time by taking the faster liner. But he soon realized that the *Lusitania* was sailing at reduced speed and would never make port by Friday, May 7 as he had hoped. Myers took a critical view of the crew's handing of the emergency. He had already noticed the men's incompetence the previous day, when the lifeboats were swung out as the ship entered the war zone:he thought they handled the ropes as though they were builder's labourers rather than experienced seamen. His misgivings were confirmed when disaster struck and he found the crew lacking in discipline.

He got into a port-side lifeboat thinking that he would be safe when it reached the water.

> Instead of that I was blown into the air when the boilers exploded and fell into the sea, where I floated about for nearly four hours clinging to some wreckage. When I was taken to the hospital at Queenstown the surgeon discovered that I had broken my right leg, torn my left one, burned my arms and broken several ribs.[28]

Margaret and Herbert Gwyer had waited until the crowd thinned out before making their way up the stairs. They had contemplated going to their cabin to get lifebelts but were afraid of being trapped. Herbert escorted Margaret to a boat and helped her in, along with three women and a baby. In his rush he failed to realize that Margaret had looked up and become so frightened that she thought the funnels were going to fall on the lifeboat, so she got out and climbed back on deck. Herbert, meanwhile, had leaped into the boat and begun to row away.

Honeymooners Harold and Lucy Taylor expected the ship to make a dash up the coast under cover of darkness, so they went to their cabin on Friday afternoon to start packing. Harold was back on deck when the torpedo struck. He ran back to the cabin to tell Lucy the ship had been hit. She threw a coat over her shoulders and the two hurried out. They had no lifebelts, but Lucy was later able to retrieve one from their cabin. They made for the first-class deck where Harold was able to get her into Lifeboat No. 15. She clung to him desperately, but he pulled himself free and dropped her in the lifeboat. She tried to climb back out to him, but the boat had started to be lowered, and it was impossible. Lucy despaired, seeing him with no lifebelt and unable to swim, standing quietly on deck waiting for the end. She gestured wildly to him, convinced that she would never see him again. People in the water crowded round the lifeboat, begging to be let on. Her boat-mates were fearful that the extra weight would capsize the craft. Appalled, she saw them pound the knuckles of those clinging on to the gunwales until one by one they succumbed to hypothermia and let go, sinking into the sea.

Detective-Inspector Pierpoint had realized that the crew would have great difficulty in launching the lifeboats because the ship was listing so severely to starboard. He helped load people into a starboard lifeboat and then jumped into the bow of another as it was being lowered. As the lifeboat was still tied to the ship, one of the crew called out and asked if anyone had a knife to cut the ropes attaching the boat to the ship. Before anyone could react, the ship gave a lurch and the davits pulled the boat over, tipping the occupants into the water. When the *Lusitania*'s deck slipped beneath the water, Pierpoint, Margaret Gwyer and Harold Taylor began to swim away. But as the funnels plunged under water it caused a whirlpool that devoured them all, together with Edward Bond, the saloon bed steward. Within the space of a minute the exploding boilers blew them all back out again in a cloud of soot. Margaret found herself in the water near the boat that had been commandeered by Charles Lauriat and Leslie Morton, who thought she was an African woman because she was so covered in soot; they helped her aboard.

Margaret Cox, cradling her seventeen-month-old son Desmond, had stood on the high port side trying to support with her free hand a fragile young mother with two children. It being impossible to lower the boats on the port side, she was directed to the starboard side. On her way there Desmond was knocked out of her arms several times. A young man in his early twenties helped her retrieve him. Margaret was turned away from the first boat because it was full. The second boat was No. 15, and she was about to be turned away there, too, but Margaret insisted. She told them whatever happened to her they would have to take the baby. She threw the child and someone caught him, and then it seemed as if she herself was thrown into the boat, too. Men lashed at the ropes to free the overcrowded craft. As it passed below the looming funnels, to her astonishment Margaret witnessed the surreal moment when Margaret Gwyer and the others were sucked into the funnel and blown out again.

There was much animation in the lifeboat but the only person crying was young Desmond Cox, who was wild with fear. The pleas of those in the water were heart-rending, but the boat was already dangerously overburdened. Margaret closed her eyes and covered her ears, unable to bear the desperate cries of the doomed passengers.

Violet James was a member of a family of several generations of dentists practising in Douglas on the Isle of Man. In her early thirties she had been working as a nurse in Edmonton, Canada, and was now travelling third class on the *Lusitania* on a visit to Britain. During her escape from the sinking ship she found herself helping Gladys Bilicke, wife of self-made millionaire Albert. Albert, a friend of Wyatt Earp, had testified on Earp's behalf at the infamous trial which followed the notorious Gunfight at the OK Corral. He once shot and killed a man who threatened his father with a gun. The Bilickes had been in one of the lifeboats that overturned, and Gladys feared that Albert, who was recovering from abdominal surgery, had been trapped beneath the wreckage. In her desperate quest to find him she clung to Violet in a manner that the young Manx girl found difficult. Violet, also traumatized, wrote a letter to her sister in Peel.

> She hung on to me all the time and she got on my nerves. We went to the Ritz, and she pleaded with me to stay, but I wanted sleep, my throat sore, limbs aching. I brought her up, looked after her all along, and considered I had done my duty.

Violet described her experience in some detail.

> At last I am able to write you a few lines from bed. Having felt so insufferably stiff, have done nothing beyond wiring you. I cannot tell you much now. I feel too fagged. My limbs are bruised and very much swollen, being in the water so long . . .

> I was on the main deck and saw the inevitable doom, and was prepared either way. I kept my head and tried to calm others. But, oh, the scene. The lifeboats I tried to help push off the davits. They were chained. I went down with the boat and was blown up with the explosion, and struck out for a spar, and there remained for what must have been two and a half hours . . .
>
> When the torpedo struck I was in my cabin. I could scarcely believe my ears. However the fact had to be faced, so I climbed up on the bunk and got my belt and put it on and then went along the alleyway when the second explosion came. Some glass hit me, but I kept quite calm and walked along the starboard side and, with hundreds of others, climbed up the railing to the boat deck. I grazed my legs then. The order was given, women below and keep calm, when she was listing heavily. I suppose they feared a terrible panic, and that was only bluff. I tried to get in a lifeboat, but it was too full and the sailor said, 'No more, lady.' The last I remember was facing the captain and second-in-command and they were facing me. Oh, their faces when the water closed over. They put their hands to their faces, poor men. Well, down we went and came up. It was nice warm water, too. Then I struck out. Thank God I could swim. I have got my lifebelt with me, and will bring it over and you may have it as a souvenir. This is an experience I shall never forget, and am glad of it.[29]

Gladys Bilicke would spend heartbreaking hours in Queenstown morgue walking up and down the rows of the dead, seeking Albert, who had been wearing his monogrammed shirt and watch, his emerald-and-diamond tiepin and sapphire cufflinks, but there was no sign of him. Violet promised Gladys to return with her to California within the next month – aboard an American ship this time – 'and will make sure of it, too!'[30]In the end, however, they travelled separately.

Back in California Gladys found herself embroiled in an unpleasant legal wrangle with her late husband's sister over his will. On 6 March 1916 she instructed W. Wilson Burns to reply on her behalf to people who had written to her and to other survivors desperate for news of their lost loved ones, that 'she does not know of any of the survivors, or crew or their addresses and is very sorry she cannot help you out in this.'[31]

Several times in the eighteen minutes before the *Lusitania* sank to the bottom of the sea the great stricken ship listed sharply, then rolled back to a more upright position. At times the angle was so precipitous that survivors described walking on the walls or using the banisters as stairs. It was a scene of terror and confusion. Understandably there are great discrepancies in the accounts given by survivors. Some, as we have seen, claimed that portholes were open: if this was true it would have added to the risk of sinking. Others stated that the ship was on fire. Some survivors described seeing the submarine surface, flying the German flag, and said that they saw members of her crew on the conning tower. While Ellen Burden was waiting to be rescued, clasping her fourteen-month-old son Robert close in her arms, she told Margaret Cox that she had seen the German submarine surface and hoist her colours. Meanwhile Robert was subdued, unlike Desmond Cox who would not stop screaming.

The *Lusitania*'s crew would later claim that their efforts were impeded by the antics of panicked passengers and the violent motion of the ship. Passengers would claim that the efforts of the captain and his crew had been inadequate and incompetent. Some would recall that there had been pushing and shoving and lamentation on the boat deck, while others remembered an eerie calm. But most agreed that, even when the inevitable outcome became evident, there was much dignity, no notable descent into mob behaviour and many individual acts of heroism.

For whatever reason, the evacuation was certainly catastrophically bungled. At least six boats overturned in lowering, ejecting their occupants, and scant evidence suggests that a seventh boat broke in half. One port-side boat was struck by the *Lusitania* and overturned, as the liner sank beside it, and one starboard boat was loaded but crushed against its davits and destroyed as the foundering ship pulled it down. Ultimately, seven boats were successfully lowered – six starboard, one port – and several collapsibles were washed clear and utilized by some of those who sank with the ship.

Emily and little Barbara Anderson, Emily's shipboard acquaintance Margaret Cox and her baby Desmond, the heroic Assistant Purser William Harkness, the Gwyers, Josephine Brandell, Isaac Lehman and at least eighty other passengers and crew members effected a last-minute escape from the *Lusitania* in Lifeboat No. 15. Barbara Anderson continued to clutch her pudding spoon throughout the crisis. Her mother, 27-year-old Emily, was not only pregnant but suffering from the tuberculosis that would eventually kill her. She was travelling to England in the hope of receiving treatment for her condition. The little girl had only made it into the lifeboat because William Harkness scooped up the child in his arms and leaped into the lifeboat, holding her close so that she came to no harm.

While in the boat Harkness pulled several other people from the water. These included the highly-strung young operatic star Josephine Brandell. When Harkness dragged her into the craft everyone thought she was dead. She had been clinging to a floating deckchair after the launch of her lifeboat, No. 12, had been catastrophically bungled and after she had failed to hang on to an oar to which others were clinging. She was appalled by the desperate cries and by encountering corpses in the water and by the fact that survivors desperately asked one another whether they had seen their loved ones.

Dozens of first-person accounts by passengers in Lifeboat No. 15 have been preserved, and most agree on the important details: the water came up so fast that the boats barely needed to be lowered; the dying *Lusitania* heeled violently to starboard, hurling water over those in the overcrowded craft as the huge funnels loomed above them. Several occupants stated that the funnels seemed almost close enough to touch, threatening to crush the lifeboat beneath their mass. Others described covering their eyes in anticipation of the impingeing death that seemed just seconds away.

However, the liner righted herself as she slid downwards, the funnels swung away, and Lifeboat No. 15 rowed clear. As it moved away, the radio antenna swiped across the boat which became entangled in the trailing Marconi wires that threatened to drag it down with the ship. As the *Lusitania* vanished from sight Harkness pushed the antenna away by brute strength. Some of the men managed to slash the ropes and cables and free the lifeboat, which was by now crammed to capacity with eighty-five people. Many more were pulled in from the ocean, bringing the total on board to near a hundred; almost an eighth of the total number of survivors. Those who were in the craft agreed that the lifeboat was so overloaded that less than six inches of freeboard remained. Many of those in the craft, including the Andersons, were transferred to Lifeboat No. 1, which had been lowered with just three or four men in it when it drew close enough.

By 2.28 p.m. on Friday, 7 May 1915 *Lusitania* was gone, taking 1,201 souls with her. Just as in the *Titanic* disaster, most of the fatalities were caused by drowning or hypothermia. In the hours after the sinking, acts of heroism among passengers, crew and the rescuers brought the survivor count to 764.

By the following morning news of the disaster had spread around the world. While most of those lost in the sinking were either British or Canadian, the loss of 128 Americans in the disaster, including the colourful, popular Elbert Hubbard, the famous Alfred Vanderbilt and other notables, sparked widespread outrage in the USA.

The appearance of the *Lusitania* on her final voyage made a strong impression on John Idwal Lewis. When asked he would say, 'A black hull, black funnels.' He was not the only one to describe the ship as having been repainted from the traditional Cunard colours. Rather than an attempt at camouflage, this may have been because the liner, in accord with Cunard's Admiralty contract, was now on the Navy List. It would in any case have been futile to attempt to disguise her distinctive silhouette: her huge size, her lofty superstructure and four towering stacks. Thomas Slidell described the funnels as 'giant grey tubes'. Sarah Lund, in her charges against Cunard, claimed that the superstructure was painted grey. Lewis disagreed with this while testifying on behalf of the company; he maintained the superstructure remained white.

The watchman on the little Manx fishing boat *Wanderer* said that the liner was recognizable by her Cunard livery and the gold painted name, as well as by her size and construction.

Stewardess Marion 'May' Bird and her friend and colleague Fannie Moorcroft, both in their early forties – although Moorcroft had lied about her age, feeling that younger women had more chance of staying employed – played an active part in the evacuation. Bird quietened screaming children and urged women to stay calm, grab lifebelts and get on deck. Before she herself made for the boat deck she collected all the lifebelts from her section. Moorcroft, too, ran to check her section of the cabins, urging her passengers up on deck with their lifebelts. She later stated that many passengers were 'running around like a bunch of wild mice'. Bird, a competent rower, helped steer the lifeboat away from the towering doomed ship. They had to row furiously before the liner rolled on top of them and were blasted with clouds of soot from the funnels.

Bird's thoughts, as she sat at last in comparative safety aboard the *Wanderer*, were of the many people still in the water. She, too, claimed to have seen the submarine surface while awaiting rescue.

Elizabeth Duckworth helped to row Lifeboat No. 21, the first to reach the *Wanderer*. Not long after Duckworth stepped aboard the *Wanderer* another lifeboat drifted by with just three people in it. Someone from No. 21 asked the people in the other craft what had happened and was told that the boat had capsized and they needed help to row back to rescue some of those who were drowning. 'I can't spare anyone!' the man, described in sources variously as an officer or a petty officer and sometimes incorrectly as a member of the crew of the *Wanderer* shouted back, shaking his head. 'You can spare me!' Duckworth cried, and having calculated the distance between the *Wanderer* and the lifeboat she jumped the gap between the two and grabbed an oar before anyone could stop her.

Elizabeth and her four companions fished about forty people out of the water. When the five of them got back to the *Wanderer* after their heroic exploits she was helped onboard and greeted with cheers.

The *Wanderer*'s yawl, or jolly-boat, was launched to make more room for the rescued. The vessel's deck, cabin, fo'c'sle and fishhold were jampacked with human bodies in various states of well-being and dress. Carrying 160 survivors, the boat was so overcrowded she was barely seaworthy, and the deck was awash. Jay Brooks had to sit with his leg dangling over the side because there was no room to put it inside. People still in the water clung to her gunwales, imploring to be taken on board. Heartsick, Skipper Ball realized that the weight of even one more person would sink the little fishing boat. Close at hand were two of the *Lusitania*'s lifeboats, each crowded with about seventy people and in danger of foundering. The *Wanderer*'s crew threw tow ropes to them and with Ball at the tiller they set course for Kinsale, towing the two lifeboats behind them. There was not another sail or mast anywhere for two hours on that lonely sea.

Teenagers Harry Costain and Johnny Macdonald brewed endless cups of tea, sometimes adding a drop of precious medicinal spirits. Stanley Ball recalled, 'We had four or five children on board and a lot of women. I gave a pair of trousers, a waistcoat, and an oil coat to some of them. Some of us gave a lot that way. One of the women had her arm broke, and one had her leg broke, and many of them were very exhausted.'[32] Costain wrote, 'There were four babies about four months old, and some of the people were almost naked, just as if they had come out of bed. Several had arms and legs broken, and we had one dead man, but we saw hundreds in the water. I gave one of my changes of clothes to a naked man, and Johnny Macdonald gave three shirts and all his drawers.'[33]

Finally, after two hours had passed, other vessels began to appear. About two miles off Kinsale the *Wanderer* met the *Flying Fish*, a civilian paddle-propelled tug known to locals as the 'Galloping Goose', which had set out from Queenstown. Most of the survivors on the *Wanderer* were in urgent need of medical attention, so it was decided to transfer them all to the *Flying Fish*, which also took over towing the two lifeboats and then set off at her full speed for Queenstown.

Skipper Ball later recounted the experience to his owner, Charles Morrison of Peel.

> We had rather an exciting experience on Friday afternoon, about 2.30 p.m. We were coming in with about 800 mackerel, the wind light and ahead, and we put off to sea again for another shot, rather than lose the night. When we were six or seven miles off the Old Head we saw the *Lusitania* sink, after being torpedoed by a submarine, about three miles SSW outside of us. We made straight for the scene of the disaster. We picked up the first boats a quarter of a mile inside of where she sunk, and there we got four boat loads put aboard us, We couldn't take any more, as we had 160 men, women, and children. In addition, we had two boats in tow, full of passengers, We were the only boat there for two hours Then the patrol boats came out from Queenstown. We had a busy time making tea for them – and all our milk and tea is gone and a lot of clothes as well, and the bottle of whisky we had leaving home. The people were in a sorry plight, most of them having been in the water. We took them to within two miles of the Old Head, when it fell calm, and there was a little air ahead. The tug boat *Flying Fish* from Queenstown then came up and took them from us . . . It was an awful sight to see her sinking, and to see the plight of these people. I cannot describe it to you in writing.[34]

Thomas Woods, the first of the *Wanderer*'s crew to see the liner, would call the spectacle 'the saddest sight I ever saw in all my life. I cannot tell you in words, but it was a great joy to me to help the poor mothers and babes in the best way we could.'[35]

Charles Lauriat, who had displayed such selflessness in saving others, described his hour on the *Wanderer*, his relief and the kindness of the crew:

> The old fishermen did everything in their power for us; they pulled up all the blankets from their bunks, they started the fire and made us tea while tea lasted, and after that boiled us water. The old ship

> was positively slippery with fish scales and the usual dirt of fishermen, but the deck of that boat, under our feet, felt as good as the front halls of our own homes. The sight aboard that craft was a pitiful one, for while most of the first two boat-loads of people that got aboard were dry, many of them had in their excitement removed much of their clothing before getting into the boat and consequently were, by this time, pretty thoroughly chilled. Those in my boat were in the saddest condition, for each one had been thoroughly soaked and some of them had been through terrible experiences. There is practically no cabin on one of these little fishermen, so all hands had to stay on deck, except a few that were able to help themselves down into the so-called cabin. The worst injured of course had to stay on deck. I gave my sweater to a chap who had on nothing but an under-shirt and a pair of trousers, and I loaned my coat to a woman until we got into Queenstown. There were not nearly enough blankets aboard for each to have one. There were over eighty people on that small boat. After being aboard about an hour we were picked up by the steamer *Flying Fish* which had come down from Queenstown.[36]

A motley flotilla of small coastal steamers and fishing boats had set out from Queenstown with no idea of how many survivors they would find. Many of the ship's lifeboats had been launched half-empty, others had been damaged or had capsized, spilling people into the sea, and others had been dragged down with the sinking ship before they could be launched because of the angle of the list. Most of the collapsibles had floated free, but many were damaged or only half assembled, so people clung to whatever bits of wreckage they could to keep afloat. As the sun began to set the temperature dropped and people's strength gave out; they slipped into the water and died. Debris, bodies, boats and increasingly piteous survivors spread for a mile in every direction. It was a challenge for would-be rescuers to spot people drifting in the twilight, and some were now too feeble to wave or cry out. Captain Turner was identified by the gold braid on his uniform sleeve. Diamond rings glittered on the hands of dead women. As the rescuers strained their eyes for signs of life, they were saddened to see the large number of people who had put on their lifejackets on back to front and had drowned in consequence. The sight of the dead infants, over a hundred of them, many in the arms of their dead mothers, touched their hearts.

First-class passenger Angela Pappadopoulo swam several kilometres towards the coast after her lifeboat capsized before she was picked up by a damaged collapsible lifeboat. She was given a sweater and pair of trousers by a sailor. Another woman, seated unconscious in a chair, came round to find she had been washed ashore and was safe. When Leslie Lindsey Mason's body was recovered she was wearing most of her jewellery. Her grieving parents sold it and erected a memorial chapel in Boston in remembrance of her.

Watching events through his periscope, Schwieger could hardly credit that a single torpedo could have had such a devastating effect. He noted in his log that 'an unusually heavy detonation' had taken place and that a second explosion had also occurred, which he surmised might be ascribed to 'boilers, coal or powder'. He also noticed that the torpedo had hit the *Lusitania* further forward than where he had originally aimed. Although some later reports would state that he surfaced, it is more probable that Schwieger brought the periscope down and headed back to sea.

He recorded in his war diary, 'Since it seemed as if the steamer could only remain above water for a short time, went to 24 metres and ran toward the sea. Nor could I have fired a second torpedo into this swarm of people who were trying to save themselves.' But was that last sentence, which portrayed the U-boat commander in a more sympathetic humane light, added later, after the sinking of the *Lusitania* had caused an international storm of protest? Some have suggested so.

When it was learned that 1,198 people had died a devastated member of Cunard's board said, 'To all of us in the company the moment we first learned of our loss will remain the most awful moment of our lives – the moment when God Himself seemed to forsake us.'[37]

EIGHT

Rescue

The Reverend William Forde, the Honorary Secretary of Courtmacsherry Lifeboat Station, received the alert at 2.30 p.m. that a large four-funnel steamer was in distress south-east of the Seven Heads. He rushed to summon the volunteer crew, and the response was immediate: when he arrived at the Lifeboat Station, then located at Barry's Point, Forde found Coxswain Timothy Keohane and his crew ready and waiting. At 3 p.m. the Courtmacsherry lifeboat, *Ketzia Gwilt*, was launched under the command of the coxswain, but the wind was too light to fill the lifeboat's sails. Indeed, most of the boats that hurried to the *Lusitania*'s rescue, sailing vessels from the local fishing fleet, had the same problem: lack of wind meant that it would have taken hours to reach the scene of the disaster, over 12.6 nautical miles offshore under sail. Oars were the answer. An extract from the Courtmacsherry Return to Service log states:

> We had no wind, so had to pull the whole distance. On the way to wreck we met a ship's boat cramped with people who informed us the *Lusitania* had gone down. We did everything in our power to reach the place but it took us at least three and a half hours of hard pulling to get there – then only in time to pick up dead bodies. The Courtmacsherry Lifeboat recovered the bodies of as many victims as they could accommodate and transferred them to the ships on scene tasked with transporting bodies back to Queenstown.[1]

The final entry from the Return to Service log, written by Reverend Forde, who also joined the crew that day, reads:

> Everything that was possible to do was done by the crew to reach the wreck in time to save life, but as we had no wind it took us a long time to pull the ten or twelve miles out from the boathouse.

> If we had wind or any motor power our boat would have been certainly first on the scene. It was a harrowing sight to witness. The sea was strewn with dead bodies floating about, some with lifebelts on, others holding on pieces of rafts – all dead. I deeply regret it was not in our power to have been in time to save some.[2]

Courtmacsherry lifeboat remained at the scene recovering bodies until 8.40 p.m. when they were towed back to the entrance of Courtmacsherry bay by a steam drifter fishing vessel. Using oars and what sail they could coax, they made the homeward journey, reaching the boathouse at around one o' clock in the morning of 8 May.

Meanwhile, the little Manx fishing nobby, *Wanderer*, had been at the desolate scene for two hours, her seven crew members hauling aboard large numbers of survivors until they could take no more on board. The fishing boat, wallowing deep under her burden, dragged two lifeboats behind her until at last, about two miles off the Old Head of Kinsale, her crew spied the welcome sight of the ancient side-wheel paddle steamer the *Flying Fish*. Although only 122 feet long, as well as serving as a tug the 'Galloping Goose' habitually operated as a tender, conveying passengers and mail out to the waiting liners from the White Star Line pier at Queenstown. Like the *Wanderer*, the 'Goose' covered herself with glory that day.

The *Lusitania* survivors, many of them half-conscious and badly injured, were transferred to the 'Goose', under the command of Thomas Brierley. The sea was so calm that the *Wanderer* was able to lie alongside the paddle steamer, and the sufficiently mobile could step across, while the injured were carried. The *Flying Fish* also took over the towed lifeboats and headed for Queenstown at top speed under Admiralty orders. Captain Brierley would make several trips ferrying survivors from the scene to Queenstown; many would owe their lives to the 'Goose' and the *Wanderer*.

Having safely transferred her human cargo, *Wanderer* returned to the scene of the disaster. By this time an assortment of other craft had arrived on the scene, but too much time had passed; rescuers found only dead bodies floating in the sea. Realizing that there was nothing more he and his crew could do, Skipper Ball put out to sea again and prepared to cast his nets for the evening's fishing. It was business as usual for the crew, although their hearts were heavy with the horrors they had witnessed, and the anguished cries of the doomed echoed in their minds.

Next day, with a catch of 700 mackerel, the *Wanderer* returned to Kinsale. Over the next few days news of the sinking of the *Lusitania* dominated the international media. The *Wanderer*'s contribution hardly featured, even though over 300 people owed their lives to her intervention. Because she had not herself landed the survivors at Queenstown, few members of the press were even aware of the part the Manx vessel had played. But news of the day's momentous events filtered through to the Isle of Man when the *Wanderer*'s crew wrote home to their families, and there arose a great groundswell of pride across the vessel and her crew had played. The Manchester Manx Society expressed island sentiment when it invited Skipper Ball and his six crewmen to accept medals designed for them by Mr F.S. Graves, of Peel. These were presented at Tynwald Hill on Tynwald Day, 5 July 1915, by the island's rather unpopular Lieutenant-Governor, Lord Raglan. In his address Raglan said, 'In remembrance of the fortunate act of charity and courage performed by you, I am quite sure we shall always feel gratitude to each one of you.'[3]

Fifty-six-year-old Captain Thomas Brierley, who commanded the *Flying Fish*, would also be awarded a medal for the outstanding gallantry he displayed during the endless trips he and his vessel made back and forth from Queenstown to the scene of the tragedy, bringing back the living as well as the dead. Brierley's participation in the rescue had not been without its frustrations. First, having heard of the disaster and impatient to head for the scene, he was forced to wait for over an hour, desperately aware that as the minutes passed increasing numbers of lives would be lost, while his vessel built up a sufficient head of steam. This would not be the only source of irritation for Brierley. Later that night, when he attempted to land his cargo of survivors at a pier not normally used by his vessel, he found himself facing obstructive red tape. His sole concern was to land his passengers safely so that he could quickly return to the site of the disaster, while there were still lives that could be saved, but he was kept hanging around waiting for 'official permission' to dock for what must have seemed like an eternity. The *Flying Fish* was ordered not to disembark survivors until the captain had reported to the proper authorities.

This caused a mutiny. The traumatized survivors were understandably furious. Arguing in robust terms, Charles Lauriat told the captain that many of those on board were in urgent need of food, shelter and medical help. The captain hurried ashore in search of a harbour inspector, leaving strict instructions not to lower the gangplank. He felt unable to let anyone disembark without clearance from the proper authorities.

Isaac Lehmann, casting round to apportion blame, later pinned the responsibility for the delay on what he saw as Brierley's stubbornness. In reality, this was probably only a desire on the captain's part to ensure that procedures were followed – a naval man's instinct that, when dealing with authority, the official path would in the end turn out to be the quickest. But to New World entrepreneurs, their nerves shattered by disaster, wet, tired, injured, cold and hungry, this must have seemed the last straw. Many people on the boat were in need of immediate medical attention.

Now Charles Lauriat defied the Captain's authority and led the survivors in a revolt. As soon as the Captain's back was turned he and several others put the gangplank over the side. A man standing on the quay tried to stop them, but Lauriat told him he had three seconds to get out of the way. Lauriat and others who were still in reasonable shape then helped the weak and injured ashore and went in search of assistance.

Lehmann wrote, 'After leaving the scene of the disaster we did not arrive in Queenstown until eleven o'clock that night. We tied up at the Cunard Dock, and the arrangement for the reception of the survivors was just as hard and difficult as it was to get saved from the *Lusitania*.'[4]

Another of the *Wanderer*'s rescued passengers shared Lehmann's smouldering indignation. French survivor Joseph Marichal would prove the most vociferous critic of what he saw as a catastrophe that had been mishandled from the outset. He and his family had endured a hellish experience, escaping from the sinking liner in a lifeboat that was found to lack rowlocks and that leaked so badly they were obliged to bail using Madame Marichal's shoes.[5]

Even when they were eventually safely aboard the *Wanderer* Marichal refused to be silenced. After their rescue craft landed them in Queenstown between 8.30 and 8.45 that night the ravenous and freezing family had to wait two hours in the Cunard company offices before 'having the privilege . . . of telling our names, where we came from, whether we had passports or not, and finally being directed to a hotel'.[6]

At seven o'clock the next morning Marichal hurried back to the Cunard office to discover how soon he and his pregnant wife Jessie and their three children could get on a train out of Queenstown. He found, to his disgust, that, emergency or no emergency, the Cunard office would not open until nine 'under any circumstances', so he was forced to wait, despite his mounting fury. He was eventually informed that the first train would leave Queenstown at three that afternoon. Marichal asked if his family could obtain any money or clothing, as they had lost everything, but to his disgust the company 'would not even lend me £1'. Marichal tried his luck with local stores but was told that he needed a written order from Cunard. He went back to the Cunard office yet again, where after much hassle and raised voices he managed to obtain a few supplies, but when it came to purchasing a coat for his pregnant wife, 'I was told I had exhausted the amount of credit given to me.'

The Marichal family duly lined up at the train station at about 2.30 p.m., but as the queue was so long they had to wait for over two hours to buy tickets and were then told they had missed the three o'clock train and would have to wait until 8.30 p.m. for the next one. They managed to procure space in a third-class compartment, reaching Dublin at four in the morning. At Dublin's Grosvenor Hotel they were given 'a single room with two beds from 5 to about 8 in the morning; one egg each, five cups of tea, bread and butter for the sum of 14s. 6d.; and they knew we were survivors of the *Lusitania*'.[7] Marichal's sense of grievance festered. He grew determined to see someone held responsible for the inconveniences he and his family had endured.

For other survivors saved by the *Wanderer* Queenstown was the scene of more joyful experiences and happy reunions. The honeymooning Gwyers were reunited after boarding the *Flying Fish*. Margaret Gwyer had had a miraculous escape from being sucked down the funnel and had refused to allow her natural optimism to be dimmed by the experience. When she eventually joined other survivors on the *Flying Fish* she caught sight of her husband Herbert, who was still sobbing like a broken man, convinced that his bride could not have survived. Another survivor described the couple's reunion. Margaret, her face still streaked with oil and soot, comforted Herbert by quipping that at least they had lost their unwanted wedding presents!

When the Gwyers finally reached London Margaret tried to get the black stains off her face by scrubbing it twice with Vim before she faced the daunting prospect of meeting her in-laws for the first time. For the rest of her life she would carefully preserve the camisole she had been wearing on 7 May in which she had suffered the dramatic plunge into the funnel. Tattered and filthy, it remained a souvenir of her extraordinary escape.[8]

In Queenstown there was a joyous reunion for another honeymoon couple. Even though Lucy Taylor had failed to find her husband Harold's body among the recovered dead, she was convinced he could not have survived and had already resigned herself to being a widow at the age of nineteen. She sent her family in Niagara Falls a bleak telegram, stating, 'Harold has gone.' But on the afternoon of the second day after the disaster, as Lucy was walking outside the lobby of a Queenstown hotel, to her amazement a man wearing a sailor's uniform rushed up and embraced her. It was Harold. She was overwhelmed with joy. The reunited couple sent their families a second telegram, stating simply, 'Both saved.'

In Queenstown big-hearted Boston bookseller Charles Lauriat, having successfully helped everyone ashore, managed to obtain accommodation at the Imperial Hotel. This proved as pleasant an experience as he could have hoped for in the circumstances: the landlady poured him a glass of good Irish whiskey and got his clothes dry for him, and Lauriat retired for a refreshing sleep, richly deserved after his exertions. When he awoke at six the next morning his first thought was for his fellow victims, and he set off to the bank to cash a check for £40, intending to try to help some of the survivors who had been left destitute. At first the bank clerk turned him down, but Lauriat had displayed his resolve throughout the tragedy: he was not a man to take no for an answer. He insisted that he needed the money for 'about twelve half-starved, half-naked Americans that needed to be fed and clothed', and his appeal succeeded. After helping as many as he could, Lauriat patrolled the sad ranks of the dead to see if he recognized anyone and was glad when this was not the case.

Unbeknownst to him, his neighbour and travelling companion Lothrop Withington had died in the disaster. His body was never identified. Passing the Cunard Wharf Lauriat noted the numbers of the lifeboats from the *Lusitania* that lay there, beached, battered and empty. He saw Nos 1, 11, 13, 15, 19 and 21: just six.

On 8 May Lauriat was one of the first survivors to leave Queenstown. He took a steam packet across the Irish Sea. In the boat's saloon he saw several *Lusitania* survivors sitting in the room in the middle of the night, many of them looking dazed; some were still wearing their lifebelts.[9]

Isaac Lehmann's experience of his brief stay at the Queen's Hotel, Queenstown, was not to his taste. He was upset at being asked to share a room with three other men and complained that he received 'no attention at all' and 'nothing to eat at all'. He was determined to get out of the place and make it to London as soon as he could. He took the 1.30 p.m. train on Sunday for London, via Kingstown. The boat train reached Holyhead at midnight and arrived in London at 6.30 on the Monday morning. He was highly critical of the way the disaster and evacuation had been handled.[10]

The valiant widow Elizabeth Duckworth, who had proved herself a tower of strength during the disaster, broke down for the first time when she reached land. She was treated for exposure and taken to the Westbourne Hotel where she spent the night. While in Queenstown she endured the further distress of identifying the body of her friend Alice Scott. She managed to locate Alice's son, eight-year-old Arthur, who was to be taken to relatives in Nelson, England, by a missionary. When word reached Elizabeth's son-in-law in Connecticut that the *Lusitania* had been torpedoed, he commented wryly that his mother-in-law had been advised not to sail, adding that some people had to learn the hard way.

Exhausted and suffering from exposure, Professor Ian Holbourn had huddled in the *Wanderer*'s hold with other survivors, many of them seriously injured. The image that depressed his spirits was of his little shipboard friend, Avis Dolphin, falling into the water from the lifeboat. When he finally reached dry land he was so debilitated that he could hardly walk, but he was determined to find out what had happened to Avis, and he set off on a desperate search for her. Suddenly he was overcome by weakness: his limbs seemed to seize up. Two soldiers helped him to the Cunard office, and he was then escorted to a hotel and persuaded to lie down, but he was frantic for news of the little girl and kept urgently demanding information of anyone and everyone, until finally, at two in the morning, he received word that she was safe. In fact plucky young Avis was not only safe; she was in better shape than the professor, whom she soon came to visit on his sickbed. When Lifeboat No. 17 had capsized she had swum to a raft, where two men hauled her aboard.

Isaac Lehmann continued to give free rein to his criticisms and pulled no punches when he expressed his thoughts on what went wrong during the sinking:

> I would say that on board the steamer when she was sinking there was very little panic; everybody seemed to be resigned, but there was no real direction on the part of the officers or men who had charge of the boats, no one to command them and no one to give orders. The portholes on the D Deck were never closed, which I understand is the work of the stewards – this is one of the causes that the boat went down so quickly.

> The greatest life-saving apparatus on the boat was the life-preservers. People ran around looking for them, but none could be found. Then the lifeboats were so heavy that it took ten men to handle one boat, and those who are not experienced in this work cannot very well get them out. Had a lot of life-rafts been thrown overboard before the sinking of the boat, and had not some of the officers and men in command issued orders not to lower the boats, and had some other members of the ship – who really believed that the steamer would not sink – done something to help, a great many more lives would have been saved.[11]

For Marichal, another bitter critic, the undaunted expression of whose views would have serious ramifications, the nightmare continued. He finally got his family to Birmingham at seven the next evening, 'two days and two nights without any help from the Cunard Company in the condition in which we were'. They had a hideous journey. Poor pregnant Jessie had to lie on the floor of the carriage to snatch some sleep, and they had to trudge a long way at four in the morning.

Jessie miscarried as a result of the trauma of her experience and was an invalid for sometime afterwards. As the family was destitute the children were separated from Marichal, living on the charity of Birmingham City Council. Marichal wrote to Cunard threatening legal action unless he received substantial compensation. He added that if he could file a claim against the German government he would do so as well.[12] Marichal would get his day in court, but it would avail him little.

In Kinsale the local county coroner, solicitor John J. Horgan, opened an inquest on 8 May 1915, the day after the sinking, into the deaths of two males and three females whose bodies had been brought ashore by a local boat, the armed trawler *Heron,* which had been on patrol between Kinsale and Ballycotton. Most of the other victims, both alive and dead, had been taken to Queenstown.

Among the rescued was the *Lusitania*'s traumatized captain. Turner, clinging to a floating chair, had been picked up from the sea by the trawler *Bluebell.* The disaster had knocked the stuffing out of the *Lusitania*'s tough old captain. Contemporary photographs show Turner shambling through the streets of Queenstown, eyes glazed, like a man in a daze. He was haunted by the memory of the disaster and by his harrowing three hours in the water, when he had witnessed seagulls dive-bombing helpless people around him and pecking out their eyes. The loss of his ship and so many of his passengers and crew weighed so heavily on him that he could not take it in. But for Turner the ordeal was by no means over. He would later be portrayed not as another victim of an aggressive act of war but, at best, as an incompetent bungler, at worst, a villain.

However, Turner was first summoned to give evidence at Coroner John J. Horgan's inquest, convened in the Queenstown's Old Market House. Horgan empanelled a jury of twelve local fishermen and shopkeepers. He took it upon himself to deliver the subpoena to Captain Turner in person. As a Sinn Fein supporter Horgan entertained reservations about the British authorities; he suspected that some attempt might be made to prevent Turner from testifying or to skew the outcome. When Turner turned up, cutting a somewhat pathetic figure in an ill-fitting suit, Horgan made no secret of the sympathy he felt for the captain.[13]

On 10 May, without legal representation, Turner gave evidence before Horgan. He stated that the ship had been struck by one torpedo between the third and fourth funnels. The impact had been followed immediately by a second explosion. Turner responded frankly to all but two questions. Asked about the wireless messages he had received concerning the presence of submarines off the coast of Ireland, he refused to divulge the content of official signals, replying, 'I respectfully refer you to the Admiralty, sirs, about the answering of that question.' He acknowledged receiving general warnings about submarines but said he had not been informed of the sinking of the *Earl of Lathom* by the same U-boat, the *U-20*, that would go on to torpedo the *Lusitania.*

Asked again whether he was at liberty to disclose to the inquest the special instructions he had received, Turner replied, 'No, sir.' He said the U-boat had fired without warning. It was 2.15 p.m. when the explosion occurred, and his watch had stopped at 2.36 p.m. He had spent between two and three hours in the water surrounded by corpses; he saw no one who was still alive. Horgan told Captain Turner that he believed he had remained on the bridge the whole time. Turner said, 'Yes, sir. She went down from under me.' Horgan replied, 'We all sympathize with you, Captain, and the Cunard Company in the terrible crime that was committed against your vessel, and I also desire to express our appreciation of the great courage you showed – it was worthy of the traditions of the service to which you belong. We realize the deep feeling you must have in the matter.' The Captain bowed his grizzled head and wept.

Horgan brought in a verdict that the deceased had drowned following an attack on an unarmed non-combatant vessel, contrary to international law. His suspicions that matters might not be straightforward were proved correct. Half an hour after the inquest had concluded and its results had been given to the press, the Crown Solicitor for Cork, Harry Wynne, arrived in great haste bearing instructions to halt the proceedings. He was armed with an injunction forbidding Captain Turner from giving evidence: no statements were to be made about any official instructions given to shipping about avoiding submarines.

The smokescreens were already being put in place. As it was, Wynne's attempted intervention was very much *post festum*: Turner had already given his evidence but out of a sense of loyalty, however misplaced, had resolutely refused to disclose information classified as privileged.

As soon as news of the disaster reached the Admiralty in London Admiral Oliver and Captain Richard Webb, Director Trade Division, scuttled into damage-limitation mode. They faced three major problems: the *Lusitania* had been sunk by a German U-boat the Admiralty knew to be operating in the area after the *Juno*, which had been intended to escort the *Lusitania* from Fastnet Lighthouse, had been withdrawn without Captain Turner's knowledge. Second, they had given the Captain confusing and inaccurate information about the position of U-boats off the south coast of Ireland and in the English channel. Third, *Lusitania* carried a cargo whose nature had not been disclosed to the public.

To ward off unwelcome questions and the embarrassment of important figures, a scapegoat had to be found with all possible dispatch.

NINE

'A Damned Dirty Business'

The *Lusitania* disaster placed the British Admiralty in a predicament of alarming complexity. The great ship had gone down with a speed that seemed incredible, sinking in just eighteen minutes, with appalling loss of civilian life. Many of the lives lost were American. It seemed almost inconceivable that one torpedo could have wrought such havoc. So what role did the second explosion, witnessed and recorded by so many witnesses, including the submarine commander himself, play in the disaster?

The cause of the second explosion was rapidly becoming the subject of heated debate. The Admiralty's Trade Department was painfully aware that the liner was carrying a large cargo of US-made munitions. The ship had been torpedoed by a U-boat known to be operating in the area, yet the Admiralty's signals had been vague, and it had withdrawn the *Lusitania's* naval escort, HMS *Juno*, without informing Captain Turner.

Were any of this sensitive classified information to become public knowledge in the course of the inquiry there was the possibility that extremely important heads would roll. It was quickly realized that it would not be enough to place the blame squarely on the shoulders of the enemy, Germany. In order to ensure an outcome that would be comfortable for officialdom, there was a clear need to establish back-up in the form of a scapegoat closer to hand.

Fortunately, such a scapegoat readily could be readily identified. Captain Turner became the easiest target because he was bound by Admiralty oath not to disclose crucial signal information. The Admiralty staff spent the weekend after the disaster, while the world at large was still in shock, cynically preparing their case against the *Lusitania*'s captain. Backdating, deliberate omission and falsification of evidence all featured in the plan.

The official inquiry was to be presided over by John Bigham, 1st Viscount Mersey, QC, Commissioner of Wrecks, for whom this must have seemed like a tragic case of *déjà vu*. Only three years previously, in May 1912, he had presided over the inquiry into the loss of the *Titanic*. Now, in June 1915, he would oversee the formal Board of Trade investigation into the 'foundering of the steamship *Lusitania* on 7 May 1915 after being torpedoed off the Old Head of Kinsale, Ireland, and the loss of 1,198 lives'. (This figure, incidentally, does not include the three German stowaway spies who were locked up below decks and who presumably also perished.)

Lord Mersey was a Liverpool man. There were some who muttered darkly that he was a 'company man' or government stooge. The outcome of the *Lusitania* inquiry would give the lie to that reputation. Although his background was in commercial rather than maritime law, the *Titanic* inquiry was not the only important maritime investigation over which Lord Mersey had presided. But no case in his career would be distinguished by the sinister and wide-reaching resonance of the inquiry into the loss of the *Lusitania*, nor cause him such personal misgivings.

Lord Mersey's inquiry would be conducted at the Central Buildings, Westminster, on 15, 16, 17 and 18 June, at the Westminster Palace Hotel on 1 July and at the Caxton Hall, Westminster, on 17 July. Lord Mersey was to be assisted by Admiral Sir F. S. Inglefield, KCB, Lieutenant-Commander Hearn, and two merchant navy captains, Captain D. Davies and Captain J. Spedding, who would act as Assessors. While the majority of the hearings were conducted in public, two were held *in camera*. Unsurprisingly, it was during these closed sessions that serious official attempts would be made to implicate the *Lusitania*'s commander and point the finger of blame. The only surviving transcript of these hearings is in Lord Mersey's private papers. The full report has never been made public.

Butler Aspinall, KC, who had previously represented the Board of Trade at the *Titanic* inquiry, was retained to represent Cunard. The Attorney-General, Sir Edward Carson, represented the Board of Trade, assisted by the Solicitor-General, F.E. Smith. These two heavyweight pit bulls appeared to set out deliberately to entangle Captain Turner in the witness-box through a combination of devious cross-questioning and confusing legalese, an enterprise that might have succeeded had it not been for the shrewd common sense of Lord Mersey and the ineptitude of their own staff.

The series of official signals sent to the *Lusitania* containing instructions for her captain, and the question of how far Turner had complied with or ignored them, became a crucial issue. Carson established from the outset that the intention was that not all of the proceedings were to be conducted in public. He stated that there were 'certain specific information and directions sent out by the Admiralty by wireless telegraphy to the *Lusitania*, and which so far as I know reached the captain'. However, having consulted the Admiralty, it was 'neither desirable nor possible to divulge these general regulations nor the communications that were made, in public, but to engage your Lordship's consideration is as to those instructions and those communications and how far in accordance with the circumstances the Captain acted upon them. I shall have in course of the case, subject of course to your Lordship's approval, to ask your Lordship to take that part of the inquiry in private.'[1]

Thirty-six witnesses were called; Lord Mersey asked why more of the 764 survivors would not be giving evidence. Carson replied that there was little point in calling droves of people to confirm the same thing. Written statements were collected from all the surviving crew. Their evidence was presented on standard forms, in identical handwriting, with similar phrasing. On 30 May the Germans had claimed that the *Lusitania* was probably armed and that she was carrying munitions and troops. The German Admiralty Staff presented the following official German version of the incident over the signature of Admiral Behncke:

> The submarine sighted the steamer, which showed no flag, on May 7, at 2.20 o' clock, Central European time, afternoon, on the south-east coast of Ireland, in fine weather. At 3.10 o'clock one torpedo was fired at the Lusitania, which hit her starboard side below the captain's bridge. The detonation of the torpedo was followed immediately by a further explosion of extremely strong effect. The ship quickly listed to starboard and began to sink. The second explosion must be traced back to the ignition of quantities of ammunition inside the ship.[2]

In Britain the Defence of the Realm Act was amended just before the opening of the hearing into the *Lusitania* disaster. This amendment prohibited any discussion about whether or not the ship was carrying 'war materials'. The boxes of 'small arms', .303 rifle cartridges carried by her had been declared on her manifest at the time. These were not classified as ammunition by the authorities and the ship was permitted to carry them under the regulations in force at the time. Lord Mersey also stated that 'the 5,000 cases of ammunition on board were 50 yards away from where the torpedo struck the ship.'[3]

The U-boat commander claimed to have fired a single torpedo. Carson stated that there might well have been a second or third torpedo but that the number was irrelevant. Nevertheless some witnesses who claimed that only one torpedo had been involved were refused permission to testify. There is evidence that Quartermaster Johnston later stated that pressure had been placed upon him to be loyal to the company and that it had been suggested to him it would help the official case if it could be alleged that two torpedoes had struck the ship, rather than the single impact he described. Giving evidence to the tribunal, he was not asked about torpedoes. Historian Diana Preston states that a record exists that Crewman Jack Roper – the same crewman to whom Captain Turner owed his life, Roper having spotted Turner's gold braided arm in the water after the disaster and pointed him out to the crew of the rescue vessel *Bluebell* – wrote to Cunard in 1919 demanding payment of expenses for his testimony in accordance with the 'party line' indicated by Cunard.[4]

During the closed hearings, the Admiralty began to reveal its hand as its campaign to shrug off any shadow of responsibility and its pre-arranged endeavour to scapegoat Captain Turner gathered momentum. The position adopted was that the captain was guilty of negligence. It was argued that, in the first place, he had ignored the instruction to avoid headlands and to steer a mid-channel course. Vice-Admiral Coke in Queenstown reported that the *Lusitania* had received warning that submarines were active on the south coast and had been advised to steer a mid-channel course avoiding headlands. She had been told by wireless telegraph that a submarine was off Cape Clear at 10 a.m.

Within a week of the sinking, Richard Webb, director of the Admiralty's Trade Division, issued a report stating, 'One is forced to conclude that he [Turner] is either utterly incompetent or that he had been got at by the Germans.' Webb compiled a dossier of signals sent to the *Lusitania* that Turner might be accused of having failed to observe and wrote to Lord Mersey, 'I am directed by the Board of Admiralty to inform you that it is considered politically expedient that Captain Turner, the master of the *Lusitania*, be most prominently blamed for the disaster.'[5]

Thus the legal experts set out with a clear agenda to discredit both Turner's character and his seamanship. First Sea Lord 'Jackie' Fisher noted in green ink on one document in the dossier submitted by Webb,

'As the Cunard company would not have employed an incompetent man, it's a certainty that Captain Turner is not a fool but a knave. I hope that Turner will be arrested immediately after the enquiry whatever the verdict.' The civilian First Lord of the Admiralty, Winston Churchill, added his own damning comment in red ink: 'I consider the Admiralty's case against Turner should be pressed by a skilful counsel and that Captain Webb should attend as a witness, if not employed as an assessor. We will pursue the captain without check.'

As it transpired, both Fisher and Churchill would be replaced in their positions before the inquiry was concluded. Fisher had quarrelled bitterly with Churchill over the disastrous Gallipoli campaign and finally resigned in frustration. Churchill in turn was demoted from his post as First Lord of the Admiralty in consequence of the campaign's failure. But the *Lusitania* inquiry proceeded without them, focusing on the matter of the appropriate evasive tactics to be adopted in the face of attacks by submarines.

Some aspects remained baffling. At 12.15 p.m. Turner had ordered the ship to swing to port, changing course so abruptly that the liner lurched heavily. Passengers spoke of being thrown about and of crockery smashing. Why did the *Lusitania*'s experienced skipper later fatefully decide, at 1.45 p.m., to turn again and hold the *Lusitania* on a course of 87 degrees east, thus creating the perfect shot for the lurking *U-20*?

There has been much speculation about precisely what official directives had caused Turner to alter course and head for Queenstown in the first place. Turner would maintain to his dying day that he had followed Admiralty instructions to the best of his abilities. The Admiralty signals record book for the First World War shows that one page is missing. It is possible that this page shows that Turner received instructions to divert the *Lusitania* into Queenstown. Transcripts of radio messages to the ship were removed from the Admiralty message log as late as 1950. The five *Lusitania* signals appear to be the only ones missing for the whole of the war. Did Vice-Admiral Coke, sitting helplessly in Queenstown, desperately concerned for the *Lusitania*'s safety and frustrated after having spent the morning badgering the Admiralty for advice and instructions, finally taken it upon himself to send a coded message to the *Lusitania* at 11.02 a.m. instructing her captain to head for Queenstown? Although the Admiralty officially denied this, a copy of the log from Valentia wireless station confirms that a message was sent. However, because it was in code its content remains a matter of speculation.

It might well have been a simple request for identification. This message, one of the missing ones, certainly seems to be from Valentia radio, from Vice-Admiral Coke in Queenstown, addressed to the Merchant Fleet Auxiliary (MFA), advising the recipient to proceed to Queenstown and her escort, the yacht *Scadaun*, to search and locate a German submarine operating in the area. The Admiralty has always maintained that this message was intended for the MFA tug *Hellespont*. However, the *Lusitania*'s call sign was MFA, and the operators aboard *Lusitania* certainly assumed the message was for them. Presumably this is why Turner altered course, inadvertently exposing the *Lusitania* to attack by the *U-20*. Turner later testified that he had received a message instructing him to put into Queenstown, perhaps the coded message from Coke.

The Admiralty had issued specific warnings to warships in the area, including the cruisers HMS *Gloucester* and HMS *Duke of Edinburgh*, but not to merchantmen. The cipher had been compromised since 27 March and new codebooks had not yet been issued to everyone.[6] The Admiralty was, moreover, reluctant to reveal to the enemy just how much Room 40's decoders had been able to decipher and the extent of their knowledge about U-boat deployment. However, when the *U-20* embarked on her killing spree on 5 May Vice-Admiral Coke in Queenstown broadcast the general warning about submarine activity off the southern coast of Ireland, followed by specific instructions to sail mid-channel, zigzag, avoid headlands and pass harbours at full speed. These two signals were received by *Lusitania* at 19.52 and 20.09 hours respectively.[7]

Many researchers have been fascinated by the messages the *Lusitania* received from Queenstown on the morning of Friday, 7 May. 'Submarine active in southern part of Irish Channel. Last heard of twenty miles south of Coningbeg light vessel.' This warning probably led Turner to believe, incorrectly, that steering a course further out to sea would have put the *Lusitania* directly in the path of this reported submarine. Nor could he have steered a 'mid-channel course', since his vessel had not yet reached St George's Channel but was attacked in the Celtic Sea. Instructions to ships travelling through a war zone were usually much more specific. These generalized instructions can only have added to Turner's confusion.

Author Patrick Beesley and other authorities certainly believed that the missing signals were still in existence and that, had they shown the Admiralty in a favourable light, their content would have been made public. The assumption is that the missing messages contain a request from Turner to divert and to adopt a course that would taken the *Lusitania* on a safer if longer route around the North of Ireland and through the North Channel and the Admiralty's refusal to grant him permission to do so. Walther Schwieger himself had noted in his war diary that fateful day, 'It is remarkable that there is so much traffic on this particular day, although two large steamers were sunk the day before south of George's Channel. It is also inexplicable that the *Lusitania* was not sent through the North Channel.'[8]

The North Channel, a longer route, was now considered so safe that ships using it were not even instructed to zigzag. Mines laid near Tory Island off the north-west coast of Donegal by the liner *Berlin*, converted to a mine-layer in August 1914, had been cleared by 15 April 1915, and merchant shipping could be permitted to take this route. If Captain Turner really was denied permission he had no alternative but to take the *Lusitania* south into the path of the *U-20*.

The explanation usually offered for Turner's second, fateful change of course is that he approached the Old Head of Kinsale because he had given orders for a steady four-point bearing to be taken, in order to obtain an accurate fix of his position. For this operation to be effectively conducted, a vessel had to proceed in a straight line for a period of forty minutes – clearly a risky strategy in a war zone – and the only logical reason for his giving the order to take such a bearing was that Turner intended to make landfall in Queenstown. He had sufficient experience of the rugged Irish coast to know that it held dangers besides the temporary inconvenience of enemy submarines and that the successful navigation of its skerries required accurate bearings. The four-point bearing would allow him to confirm the *Lusitania*'s exact position. At the inquiry Turner insisted that neither a sun-line bearing (requiring three minutes) nor a cross bearing (requiring five minutes) were as accurate as a four-point bearing.[9]

Young Third Officer Bestic, who had initially been instructed to take the bearing, revealed in an interview in 1962 that he believed the ship had already been heading for Queenstown, because the mail bags were already being hauled on deck. Liverpool landfall had been mentioned when he got the summons to oversee the baggage movement, but the operation had been started much too early if the intended next port of call really was Liverpool. Quartermaster Hugh Johnston recalled that 'at half past one . . . we altered the course two or three times in towards the land; I do not know what for'.[10]

In the light of these comments it appears possible that the *Lusitania* was not bypassing Queenstown but, rather, heading for that port. Sometimes mail and valuable cargo were unloaded at Queenstown and transferred to Kingstown (Dun Laoghaire) for transfer to Holyhead by mailboats such as the *Leinster* to avoid submarines known to be prowling in St George's Channel. Chart information also appears to indicate that the liner was on course for Queenstown before the change of course that proved her undoing.

In a final attempt to avert disaster for the *Lusitania*, Vice-Admiral Coke signalled to Rear Admiral Hood, the commander of HMS *Juno*, dispatching the old warship to the scene in a last-ditch rescue attempt. Coke then sent a signal to the Admiralty informing it in detail about what had taken place, as far as he knew, and of the action he had taken.

At Coroner John Horgan's inquest in Ireland on 8 May Turner had admitted that the second explosion might well have been internal. Now he conceded, under persistent questioning, that there could have been a second torpedo:

> Carson: Did you notice any other concussion that would lead you to believe there was a second torpedo?
>
> Turner: One immediately after the first.[11]

Witnesses' testimony varied as to the precise location of the first strike, between the first and second funnels or between the third and fourth, and about the number of torpedoes. Look-outs on the *Lusitania* thought they had seen two torpedoes – presumably fired by the same submarine – but this can be explained by a kind of optical illusion: the trail of bubbles takes a moment to rise from the depth of the torpedo, thus creating the impression of a separate track.

The only possible explanation for the presence of a second torpedo seems to be that two submarines were involved. Some witnesses claimed to have seen more than one submarine. At 1.40 p.m. official coast watchers on a headland overlooking the sea reported to Queenstown a sighting of a surfaced submarine close to shore. But the *Lusitania* was attacked from seaward, not from the land side. Surviving passengers also reported sighting a submarine on the port side before the *Lusitania* made the turn toward land. They interpreted the liner's change of course as evasive action taken by the captain. Significantly, the Admiralty removed questions 14 and 15 from the list of queries to be put to witnesses at Lord

Mersey's inquiry into the disaster. These referred to submarine sightings, and the two queries appear to confirm that there was some evidence for mystery sightings.

However, Turner was the designated scapegoat: the captain's alleged incompetence, allied with the ferocity of the foe, would be the official explanation for the tragedy. Establishing the former would exonerate the British authorities of negligence or – in the view of the conspiracy theorists – criminal complicity; insisting on the latter would fuel the massive anti-German propaganda machine, fill hearts with patriotic fire and inspire in powerful potential allies a sense of outrage, a thirst for vengeance and a willingness to make common cause.

It was put to Turner that he had failed to comply with Admiralty instructions to travel at high speed, maintain a zigzag course, and stay well off shore.[12] As to the first charge, the *Lusitania*, even with one of her four boilers out of action, was still capable of 21 knots; when she was attacked, she had reduced her speed to 15 knots because of the fog, but by midday she was steaming ahead at 18 knots, a greater speed than that of which any submarine yet developed was capable, whether surfaced or submerged. At the time no ship travelling at more than 15 knots had been torpedoed. Turner's orders were to time his arrival at Liverpool for high tide, because it would be dangerous to linger waiting for the tide at the mouth of the River Mersey, where submarines were known to lurk in wait for shipping. The practice of zigzagging was not unknown: in fact, the youngest of the *Lusitania*'s firemen to survive the disaster, John O'Connell, aged nineteen, said he was surprised at the time that the captain was steering a straight course. Attorney-General Edward Carson questioned Turner about receiving this Admiralty instruction, dated to 16 April 1915, which was read out to the captain during the inquest.

> War experience has shown that fast steamers can considerably reduce the chance of successful surprise submarine attacks by zigzagging – that is to say, altering the course at short and irregular intervals, say in ten minutes to half an hour. This course is almost invariably adopted by warships when cruising in an area known to be infested with submarines. The underwater speed of a submarine is very slow, and it is exceedingly difficult for her to get into position to deliver an attack unless she can observe and predict the course of the ship attacked.[13]

Turner confirmed that he had received the instructions, although he seemed puzzled. Later he said that they seemed very different from when he had read them. This admission could be readily exploited by Turner's critics as an indication of mental instability on the part of the captain, but in fact an examination of the time-scale of events indicates that the captain was correct: In the first months of 1915 Captain Richard Webb had been assiduously preparing new instructions for merchant shipping on the best avoidance strategies in respect of U-boats, instructions which included – for the first time in print as a *general* instruction – the adoption of the Royal Navy practice of zigzagging in war zones. These instructions were drafted around 17 April 1915 when *Lusitania* sailed from Liverpool for the last time, but they could not be finalized and disseminated before they had been submitted to Churchill for his approval. Churchill gave his approval only on 25 April. The instructions were not distributed outside the Admiralty until 13 May, almost a week after Lusitania had been destroyed.

Thus, whatever orders Turner received on 16 April, they could not have been these instructions. Small wonder then that Turner's recollection of the wording was different from what was read out by Carson during the inquiry. The order that Carson read out was not the one Turner had received on 16 April but the order issued on 13 May. It had been conveniently backdated to 16 April, the day before the *Lusitania* departed Liverpool for the last time. The order of 13 May was a general instruction for all ships, whereas the message Turner received on 16 April must have been specific to the *Lusitania*. This earlier order mentioned zigzagging but in more obscure terms, leaving it open to interpretation. Turner was under the impression that zigzagging was only to be conducted once a submarine had been sighted.[14]

The immediate effect of this stratagem of presenting backdated orders was to damage the captain's credibility, while portraying the Admiralty in a more favourable light.

According to the testimony of at least one survivor, the US physician Dr Daniel V. Moore, who had been travelling in a second-class cabin, the *Lusitania* had, in reality, been zigzagging for about an hour around noon, at a speed of about 19 knots.

In their zeal to lay blame at the captain's door, the Admiralty's legal team would also argue that the liner had been only eight miles off the Old Head of Kinsale and was therefore too close to land when she was torpedoed. 'Too close to land' in Admiralty parlance normally meant ships travelling closer than five miles from shore. Yet Turner stated that at the time of the attack the *Lusitania* was between thirteen and fifteen miles from the shore. Turner's statement was supported by the location of the wreck. Moreover, the *Wanderer* was close to the scene because she was well outside Irish fishing limits.

The legal experts hired to discredit Turner gave him little opportunity to insist that he was faithfully obeying orders. At the later New York liability trial, conducted under Judge Julius Mayer, and, indeed, to the end of his life, Turner maintained that he had been following Admiralty instructions to the best of his abilities. Even the orders Carson read out, which Turner had never received, stated that ships should change course every 'ten minutes to half an hour'. Turner had held the *Lusitania* on a straight course for only twenty-five minutes – from 1.45 p.m. to 2.10 p.m. – when she was attacked and was thus within the thirty-minute window proposed by the Admiralty. (It is worth noting, however, that in order to complete the four-point bearing it would have been necessary to maintain that course for a further fifteen minutes, thus exceeding the time limit unless the first set of orders, those Turner received on 16 April, specified something different.) Turner stated that he had discussed the matter of the ship's course with his two most senior officers, Captain Anderson and Chief Officer Piper, both of whom lost their lives in the disaster. All three had agreed that the Admiralty warning of 'submarine activity 20 miles [32 kilometres] south of Coningbeg' took priority over the instruction to maintain a course mid-channel; consequently, Turner had ordered the change of course at 12.40 p.m., intending to bring the ship closer to land and then to take a course north of the reported submarine.

The cunning scheme to entrap and convict Turner almost succeeded. He appeared incapable of grasping exactly what was going on. Some of his responses were vague, while others appeared contradictory. It seemed that the Captain had been successfully befuddled and bewildered by both the traumatic experience and the skilful interrogation. However, as the inquiry was reaching its conclusion, during the summing-up, the plot hit the buffers when the prosecuting barrister began reading out, from Admiral Sir Frederick Inglefield's master court file, Admiralty memos that Lord Mersey quickly realized had never been submitted to the court. Failing to find the relevant material in his copy of the file, and concluding that the two files differed in important particulars, Mersey called a halt to the proceedings and summoned all counsel to approach the bench. He demanded of the Crown Solicitor-General an immediate explanation for the discrepancy, and it came to light that the message he had questioned existed solely in the version of evidence handed to F.E. Smith, the Solicitor-General, by the Board of Trade Solicitor, Sir Ellis Cunliffe. An embarrassed Cunliffe attempted to explain away the discrepancy by claiming that different versions of the papers had been prepared, depending on whether the inquiry was to be conducted *in camera* or in public. However, it appeared that in reality the message in question had never existed.

It became clear that a signal sent by Vice-Admiral Coke via the Naval Wireless Station at Valentia, advising Captain Turner to divert the *Lusitania*'s course to Queenstown, had been either omitted or expunged from Mersey's file. Disgracefully, the Admiralty had relied on Turner's loyalty and his strict observance of his oath of secrecy, hoping these would prevent him from acknowledging receipt of this vital signal or revealing its contents. Oddly enough, the page recording this signal is the only page missing from the First World War Admiralty Signals Log. Such amateurish official skulduggery inevitably fanned the flames of imaginative conspiracy theories about the loss of the *Lusitania* and gave fuel to what has become known as the 'livebait' hypothesis.

At this point Lord Mersey became aware, if he had not been so before, that the inquiry had the character of an official whitewash and that the Admiralty had tampered with evidence and falsified documents. He had no intention of being bamboozled by official versions of events, nor of allowing himself to be manipulated further. Observing that it was his job to establish the truth, he adjourned the inquiry and asked all the assessors to give him their separate opinions in sealed envelopes. Of them all, the only one to return a verdict of 'guilty' against Turner was Admiral Inglefield. This was not unexpected, since Inglefield's brief from the Board of the Admiralty was to ensure that Turner was found guilty of treasonable behaviour.

Lord Mersey would have none of it. (The version of the report held in the Cunard archives at Sydney Jones Library, Liverpool University, is available to the public. It covers only the public hearings.)

Mersey had no doubt that Turner was an experienced and highly skilled captain. Indeed Cunard would hardly have entrusted its precious *Lusitania*, the jewel in its crown, to an incompetent master. The Captain was ultimately responsible for the safety of his ship, his crew and his passengers, and Turner had followed the majority of instructions conscientiously. He had posted extra look-outs, maintained lifeboats at the ready, observed radio silence within a hundred miles of land and blacked out lights at night. Notwithstanding, it could not be denied that, had all the portholes been closed and had the crew been better trained in handling emergencies, many more lives might have been saved. During the Mersey inquiry many witnesses claimed that portholes across the ship had been open at the time of the sinking, and an expert witness confirmed that such a porthole three feet under water would let in four tons of water per minute. Other witnesses denied that portholes were open. Lord Mersey gave a balanced summing-up:

> Captain Turner was fully advised as to the means which in the view of the Admiralty were best calculated to avert the perils he was likely to encounter . . . It is certain that in some respects Captain Turner did not follow the advice given to him. It may be (though I seriously doubt it) that had he done so his ship would have reached Liverpool in safety. But the question remains, was his conduct the conduct of a negligent or incompetent man. On this question . . . the conclusion at which I have arrived is that blame ought not to be imputed to the Captain. The advice given to him . . . was not intended to deprive him of the right to exercise his skilled judgment in the difficult questions that might arise from time to time in the navigation of his ship. His omission to follow the advice in all respects cannot fairly be attributed either to negligence or incompetence.
>
> He exercised his judgment for the best. It was the judgment of a skilled and experienced man, and although others might have acted differently and perhaps more successfully, he ought not, in my opinion, to be blamed. The whole blame for the cruel destruction of life in this catastrophe must rest solely with those who plotted and with those who committed the crime.[15]

Whether or not the plot to implicate the Captain succeeded from the official British point of view, political expediency dictated that the ultimate blame for the disaster had to be placed on the shoulders of Germany, in an act of aggression for which there could be no justification. The question of the transportation of armaments was a delicate one and strenuous efforts were made to ensure that it was, if possible, not raised at all and, if it were raised, glossed over. Two days after he closed the inquiry Lord Mersey waived his fee and formally resigned, with a request that he henceforth be 'excused from administering His Majesty's Justice'. Later, his last words on the subject would be 'The *Lusitania* case was a damned, dirty business!'

He also confiscated the entire contents of Admiral Inglefield's master court file and placed it with his own secure private papers. The full report has never been made available to the public. It was thought to still exist among Lord Mersey's private papers but never came to light after his death. Attempts to trace it have proved fruitless.

TEN

Causes and Conspiracy

The initial inquiry had been completed, the ruling given. Sole responsibility for the disaster had been placed squarely and unequivocally on *U-20*, operating in the service of Imperial Germany. Yet a climate of dissatisfaction continued to fester. There were certainly some who felt justice had not been done, and who were still determined to raise their voices and cry havoc, proclaiming iniquity, if not conspiracy.

One of these was family man and ex-army officer Professor Joseph Marichal. The French survivor was still resolved to sue Cunard for what he saw as its inadequate handling of the disaster and to draw attention to the presence of munitions in the liner's cargo. In what may have been a somewhat belated attempt to lend an illusion of transparency and accountability to the proceedings, ensuring that justice was not only done but seen to be done– and dissenting voices given a hearing – at Marichal's insistence an extra investigation was conducted before Lord Mersey on 1 July at the Westminster Palace Hotel.

Marichal had been one of the first people to voice publicly the theory that the second explosion was triggered by the detonation of munitions allegedly being transported in the *Lusitania*'s hold. Marichal testified that, while the prime cause of the second explosion might well have been the impact of a torpedo, its suddenness and magnitude were such that it could not have been caused by a torpedo strike alone. Comparing the sound of the blast to the brief noisy clatter of a machine-gun, Marichal stated that, having served as an officer in the French army for five years, he recognized the sound. He stated, 'I suggest that the explosion of the torpedo caused the subsequent explosion of some ammunition, and I have special experience of explosives.'[1] He described how the entire floor of the second-class dining-room aft was shaken by the impact and dismissed the notion that the sound he heard could have been caused by the explosion of a steam pipe. (The Marichals had insisted that their three children eat with them in the dining-room rather than in the nursery. It was their insistence on this that enabled them to collect their children quickly when disaster struck, with the result that all five Marichals survived.)

Marichal did little to advance his own case by launching into an impassioned full-scale attack on the Cunard Line for what he saw as its callous and unsympathetic treatment of the survivors. 'We were sixty-three in our boat, and after rowing for about five or ten minutes we sighted another lifeboat some distance away. We thought it was a fisherman's boat, because it was pretty far from us, but we could not catch it, so we came to the conclusion that it was another lifeboat going away from the *Lusitania*.'[2]

After Marichal and his family were rescued 'by a fishing smack' (the *Wanderer*) he claimed, 'Our suppositions were certain, because we caught up the boat and found in it about eighteen or twenty members of the crew, mostly stewards or firemen, and no women. We were so indignant that I, with others, shouted, "Where are the women in your boat?" They had taken every opportunity to sail away as quickly as they could without troubling to gather more people, and there were plenty to gather. The number in that boat was nineteen.'[3]

Marichal described the fleeing boat as the 'boat of cowards'. At the inquiry Marichal acted for himself without benefit of counsel, and his intemperate tone had the effect of alienating those who heard him, discrediting his testimony. His forthright and unwelcome accusations of bungling and cowardice, together with his aggrieved stance, aroused the hostility of the court. The official representatives also had at the back of their minds the alarming possibility that, in his frustration and annoyance, Marichal might go tattling to the media and give credence to the theory that the ship sank with such speed because she was carrying a secret cargo of armaments.

Lord Mersey refused to entertain Marichal's accusations and dismissed him out of hand, with the words, 'I do not believe him. His demeanour was very unsatisfactory. There was no confirmation of his story.'[4]

Geoff Whitfield, a researcher with the British Titanic Society, states that in the minutes of the pre-inquiry meetings it was alleged that Marichal was 'a fool', 'a trouble maker' and 'a damned Frenchman'. It was also suggested that Marichal should be persuaded that as an alien (although his wife, Jessie Emerson Marichal, was British) it might be against his own interests to continue with his hot-headed outbursts.[5]

When the Marichals had eventually reached Birmingham, Marichal had filed a claim in the amount of £1,050 for loss of personal effects and 'shock to [his] system' against the party found guilty by the inquiry. Marichal was now informed that if he intended to sue for compensation he would need to address his complaint to the German government and not to Cunard. Butler Aspinall, Cunard's barrister, suggested that Marichal's interest was mercenary and that he would not be above resorting to blackmail: he insinuated that Marichal hoped to obtain money from Cunard in exchange for not disclosing facts discreditable to the company. The newspapers the next morning were disparaging of Marichal's allegations. Marichal, feeling he had been the victim of character assassination, wrote to Lord Mersey requesting that he be rehabilitated; otherwise, he said, he intended to pursue his campaign against Cunard. This threat finally sparked an official reaction, and wheels were set in motion to discover unfavourable stories from Marichal's past in order to undermine his credibility and quash his grievances once and for all.

Enquiries were conducted into Marichal's background. On 8 July the British Embassy in Paris received a reply that was forwarded to the *Exchange Telegraph* and thence relayed to leading English newspapers. Referring to Joseph Marichal of Birmingham as 'Jules Marechal of Soho', the press reported that the subject, while serving as a second lieutenant in the French Army, had been found guilty by court-martial of brawling and of concealing his identity. Two weeks later, it was alleged, he had been cashiered from the army and convicted of fraud. This was a deliberate perversion of the facts. As a young army officer Marichal had forged a weekend pass and had married his sweetheart, British-born Jessie, without his colonel's permission. He had been invited to resign his commission, which he did, emigrating with his wife to Canada. Apart from misrepresenting his relatively trivial youthful misdemeanours, the report had deliberately updated them by over ten years in a gross distortion of the truth.

Accounts of the sound, cause and timing of the second explosion on board the ship varied. For a long time no adequate explanation was forthcoming. What is known is that armaments were on board; a list was supplied to New York authorities in a supplementary manifest some days after the sailing of the *Lusitania*. It seems unlikely, however, that the armaments as described on the manifest could have caused an explosion of such magnitude as to sink the entire ship in just eighteen minutes. Alternative theories about the cause of the second explosion include a coal dust or aluminium powder explosion, a boiler explosion or a failure in the steam pipes.

The British government hoped to keep the nature of the ship's cargo shrouded in secrecy, but the embarrassing spectre of the concealed munitions had arisen immediately after the sinking. On 8 May Dr Bernhard Dernburg, the former German Colonial Secretary, was regarded as the Kaiser's official mouthpiece in the USA, had made a speech to the City Club at the Hollenden Hotel in Cleveland, Ohio, in which he stated that the attack on the *Lusitania* was justified because the liner 'carried contraband of war' and was classed as an auxiliary cruiser. Thus Germany, he argued, had had a right to destroy her, irrespective of the presence of any passengers aboard. Dernburg further asserted that the warnings given by the German Embassy before the ship left New York, together with the note of 18 February declaring designated 'war zones', relieved Germany of any responsibility for the deaths of the many US citizens aboard the liner. Germany's submarine campaign, Dernburg said, was an understandable and entirely defensible reaction to Britain's attempt to starve her into submission, which itself contravened international law. US citizens were, he said, being used as a cloak for Britain's war shipments.[6]

At 2.45 a.m. on 8 May an official message was sent from Berlin by wireless to London:

> The Cunard liner *Lusitania* was yesterday torpedoed by a German submarine and sank. The *Lusitania* was naturally armed with guns, as were recently most of the English merchant ships. Moreover, as is well known here, she had large quantities of war material in her cargo. Her owners, therefore, knew to what danger the passengers were exposed. They alone bear the responsibility for what has happened. Germany, on her part, left nothing undone to repeatedly and strongly warn them [the passengers].[7]

Dudley Field Malone, Collector of the Port of New York, who had signed off the *Lusitania*'s manifest, issued an official denial to the German charges. He stated that the *Lusitania* had been inspected before her departure and that no guns had been found, either mounted or unmounted. Malone also stated that no merchant ship would have been allowed to arm itself in the port and leave the harbour. Assistant

Manager of the Cunard Line, Herman Winter, denied the charge that the ship carried munitions:

> She had aboard 4,200 cases of cartridges, but they were cartridges for small arms, packed in separate cases . . . they certainly do not come under the classification of ammunition. The United States authorities would not permit us to carry ammunition, classified as such by the military authorities, on a passenger liner. For years we have been sending small-arms cartridges abroad on the *Lusitania*.[8]

The nature of the official cargo was considered in the American investigation of 1917, but experts considered that under no circumstances could the cargo have exploded. Judge Julius Mayer's verdict was that 'the cause of the sinking was the illegal act of the Imperial German government', that two torpedoes had been involved, that the *Lusitania*'s captain had acted properly and that emergency procedures had met expected standards. He ruled that further claims for compensation should be addressed to the German government (which eventually paid $2.5 million in 1925).

In Britain the Defence of the Realm Act had been hastily amended just before the opening of the hearing into the ship's loss. This amendment forbade any discussion about whether or not the ship was carrying 'war materials'. The boxes of 'small arms' (.303 rifle cartridges declared at the time) were not classified as 'ammunition' and were permissible cargo under the regulations then in force. Lord Mersey also stated that 'the 5,000 cases of ammunition on board were 50 yards away from where the torpedo struck the ship'.[9] Notwithstanding, many of those who suspect a major official cover-up direct their attention to the presence of a mysterious and potentially lethal cargo of undeclared war munitions: the *Lusitania*'s official cargo included rifle and machine-gun ammunition, artillery fuses and shrapnel artillery shells without powder charges.

Diver and historian Patrick O'Sullivan, in his book *Lusitania: Unravelling the Mysteries*, notes that the *Lusitania*'s cargo manifest included a batch of 46 tons of aluminium powder that was being shipped to the Woolwich Arsenal. This highly volatile material is utilized in the manufacture of explosives and as an accelerant for other explosives. O'Sullivan expresses his conviction that the aluminium itself exploded, having been ignited by the first torpedo explosion. He states, 'If the

Lusitania's cargo had not included a highly explosive 46-ton shipment of aluminium powder, the second explosion would not have occurred, and the liner might well have made it to port in a crippled condition. Loss of life would have been minimal and the incident would have been recorded as a minor event in the annals of war.'[10]

Furthermore, the ship was carrying a large consignment of 'furs', somewhat incongruously dispatched by the explosives manufacturers DuPont de Nemours and some 90 tons of butter and lard destined for the Royal Navy Weapons Testing Establishment in Essex. Although it was May the butter and lard was not refrigerated; it was insured by the special government rate, but, strangely, the insurance was never claimed.

The wreck of the *Lusitania* now lies in 90 metres of water, almost 12 miles south-west of the Old Head of Kinsale. It has been dived on a number of occasions and is reported to be in a state of advanced decay. In 1967 the wreck was sold by the Liverpool and London War Risks Insurance Association to former US Navy diver John Light for £1,000. American venture capitalist Gregg Bemis acquired co-ownership of the wreck in 1968 and by 1982 had bought out his partners to become sole owner. Bemis subsequently went to court in England in 1986, in the USA in 1995 and in Ireland in 1996 in order to ensure that his ownership was recognized and legally in force. Although Bemis had thus proved his ownership in three separate courts, the Irish Office of Public Works placed an Underwater Heritage Order upon the site, which was occupied by Bemis's now acknowledged property. Any projected diving operations to the *Lusitania* wreck, therefore, needed to go through a complicated application procedure before permission to dive the site could be obtained. Bemis acquired the right to dive the ship without requiring a licence from the Irish state, while further expeditions to the wreck are planned in the coming years.

Bemis and his dive team have recovered live ammunition from the *Lusitania*. In September 2008 bullets known to be used by the British military were uncovered from the wreck by diver Eoin McGarry, dive adviser to Bemis. These were discovered in an area of the ship not previously known to have been carrying cargo.[11] Professor William Kingston of Trinity College, Dublin, has said, 'There's no doubt at all about it that the Royal Navy and the British government have taken very considerable steps over the years to try to prevent whatever can be found out about the *Lusitania*'.[12] It was suggested that the wreck had been bombarded in an effort to destroy evidence. Dublin-based technical diver Des Quigley, who dived the wreck in the 1990s, reported that the wreck is 'like Swiss cheese' and that the seabed around her 'is littered with unexploded hedgehog mines'.[13]

In February 2009, the Discovery Channel television series *Treasure Quest* aired an episode entitled 'Lusitania Revealed' in which Gregg Bemis, along with a team of shipwreck experts, explored the wreck via a remote-control unmanned submersible. In the documentary an unexploded depth charge was clearly visible in the wreckage, viewed via the remote-control submersible's video camera. Gregg Bemis and other members of his team have expressed the theory that the wreck site of the doomed liner was subjected to a deliberate barrage of depth charges by the British Royal Navy in order to discourage further salvage attempts and to prevent divers from discovering contraband cargo. No government has ever admitted ownership of the depth charge. In the 2009 documentary the narrator states that it is probable that the depth charges crushed the upper decks of the ship, causing further dispersal of the debris field.

Dives undertaken in 2011 revealed that time is running out. The wreck is deteriorating at an alarming rate, and the hull is on the verge of total collapse. After nearly a century at the bottom of the sea, and after having apparently been used for naval target practice, whatever the intention of this operation may have been, many unexploded 'hedgehog' depth charges continue to litter the ship's debris field.

During the 2011 dives, despite unfavourable weather conditions and technical problems, it was possible to introduce a VideoRay, a small underwater remotely operated vehicle, or ROV, into the forward hold. The means of access was a breach in the port side of the hull that had arisen through the wreck's natural deterioration. The device penetrated some twenty feet into the ruined cargo hold where it revealed and filmed stacks of copper ingot bars and the expected substantial quantity of .303 rifle ammunition. It also found evidence of severe damage for which the continuing disintegration of the hull did not appear to provide a satisfactory explanation.

However, the area that most crucially demands investigation is located below the cargo hold, right on the ocean floor. This portion of the wreck currently lies buried under another twenty to thirty feet of heavy wreckage likely to prove highly unstable. In order to access this area it would be necessary to remove all debris, an operation which in view of the overall condition of the wreck might well cause the port-side hull plating to collapse.

American scuba diver John Light discovered in the 1960s that the plates surrounding a huge hole in the port hull bent outward, suggesting that the deformation had been caused by an explosion within the vessel: a torpedo strike would cause them to bend inwards. Marine archaeologist Robert Ballard, who examined the wreck in 1993, also found that plates were bent outward from an internal explosion. Ballard's conclusion was that coal dust in the coal bunker, ignited by the first explosion, caused the second, fatal explosion. This theory has been described as problematic, because crewmen working near the coal bunker survived, whereas crew busy unloading the mail bags near the forward hold were all killed. This would appear to suggest that the explosion occurred in cargo held in the forward area.

The shell cases aboard the ship were not filled with explosive; however, there were the mysterious boxes originating from the DuPont chemical company. These, ostensibly containing 'margarine', were consigned to Woolwich Arsenal. Historian Steven Danver believes that they almost certainly constituted a large consignment of nitrocellulose or gun cotton, although this was not listed as such on the cargo manifest.[14] There had been previous shipments of gun cotton from DuPont: 870 tons had been transported on the *Arabic*, 400 tons on the *Georgic* and 3,200 boxes on the *Ordiana*. The product is surprisingly stable unless allowed to deteriorate, but it has been argued that in the case of the attack on the *Lusitania* it might well have exploded sympathetically with the torpedo.

A study of the consignment numbers indicates that even the supplementary manifest of the *Lusitania*'s cargo is not complete. Some items are clearly war material, while the description of others appears questionable. Certain items originated from the USA's second-largest steel works, the Pennsylvania-based Bethlehem Steel Company, a well-known arms manufacturer.

While the *Lusitania* controversy continues, in 2012 it was concluded that the latest research indicated that the munitions the ship was transporting were unlikely to have been responsible for the second, larger explosion after the initial impact of the torpedo.

Although now in his eighties, Greg Bemis continues his earnest quest for the final answer. His endeavours have encountered their share of red tape. He has often stated that although he was involved in the 2011 expedition and subsequent laboratory research he disagreed with the scientists' findings, stating his continued view that the reason the ship sank so quickly was that she was carrying explosives.

However, the theory that it was the *Lusitania*'s secret cargo of explosives that caused this 790-foot-long vessel to sink so rapidly before help could arrive appears to have been debunked by new scientific research, which has included investigations of the wreck as well as laboratory tests and a computer reconstruction of the sinking. The latest investigation found no evidence to support the claims that munitions caused the second explosion, and the experts involved came to the conclusion that the second explosion reported by survivors was caused by one of the ship's boilers exploding.

The team behind the new research conducted a series of dives of the wreck using a miniature submarine and a 'newt suit' – an atmospheric diving suit that allows a diver to operate at extreme depths. A camera was sent twenty feet into the wreck, which lies at a depth of 300 feet, to inspect the cargo hold and the blast damage. Tests were then conducted at the Lawrence Livermore National Laboratory in California, a US-government-funded research facility that specializes in explosives.

In early February 2014 a federal watchdog agency reprimanded the California laboratory for spending more than $80,000 of taxpayer's money to help National Geographic with a new documentary film, *Dark Secrets of the Lusitania*, about the sinking of the ship. The Energy Department's inspector general reported that Lawrence Livermore National Laboratory had improperly used its licensing and royalty fees to perform tests for the documentary. Rickey Hass, a deputy inspector general at the Energy Department, stated, 'The work itself was not really the issue, but it was inappropriate in that it may have competed with private-sector organizations and was funded with money that should have not been used for that purpose. It also wasn't necessarily reported with complete transparency.'[15] National Geographic's production team wanted to recreate the explosives that might have gone off aboard the *Lusitania*, and laboratory spokeswoman Lynda Seaver said that no other facility could do that modelling work. 'National Geographic approached this lab because of its expertise,' she said in an email. 'There's no other facility that can do the modelling and simulation we do.'[16]

In a series of controlled explosions and tests the scientists examined the various different theories. One school of thought suggested that the second explosion was the result of aluminium, which was used to make landmines, and gun cotton, an artillery propellent. The experts found that the manifestation of an aluminium explosion appeared markedly different from the type of explosion reported by survivors of the

Lusitania, while gun cotton would have exploded instantaneously, rather than after a delay of fifteen to twenty seconds.

The researchers also rejected the theory that the second explosion had been caused by the ignition of coal dust. This would not have caused sufficient structural damage to sink the ship. Their conclusion was that the second blast was the explosion of a boiler, but that this did not of itself cause significant damage. They found that the ship sank so quickly simply because of the massive damage caused by the initial torpedo strike.

Following the California tests, Dr Jon Maienschien, a scientist at the Lawrence Livermore National Laboratory, stated, 'I am confident that the torpedo caused catastrophic damage that was fatal to the ship.'[17]

Whatever the practical explanation for the disaster, over the years the conspiracy theories about official premeditation continued to flourish, the most potent of these being the 'livebait' or 'wilful murder' theory. In the aftermath of the sinking, speculation burgeoned that Winston Churchill engineered a malign plot which involved deliberately placing the *Lusitania* in harm's way, with the likelihood of major loss of American lives, in the hopes of forcing President Wilson's hand and embroiling the USA in the war on the side of Allies.

Key to the conspiracy theory is the widely known memo sent by Churchill to Walter Runciman, the President of the British Board of Trade.

> It is most important to attract neutral shipping to our shores in the hope especially of embroiling the United States with Germany . . . The German formal announcement of indiscriminate submarining has been made to the United States to produce a deterrent effect upon traffic. For our part, we want the traffic – the more the better and if some of it gets into trouble better still. Therefore please furbish up at once your insurance offer to neutrals trading with us after February 18th. (The more that come the greater our safety and the German embarrassment.) Please act promptly so that the announcement may synchronize with our impending policy.[18]

Yet at the time of the disaster, while the USA was neutral, the *Lusitania* was clearly a British ship rather than 'neutral shipping'. Those who advance the 'official conspiracy' theory also point out that the Admiralty's signal failure to protect the *Lusitania* on her last voyage looks like more than mere carelessness, in the light of its previous record of safeguarding the ship. The *Lusitania* represented, after all, a significant symbol of national prestige, and consequently she had enjoyed more privileges than any other vessel afloat. When she was scheduled to arrive in Liverpool on 6 March 1915 the Trade Division had signalled the *Lusitania* at Cunard's request: 'Owners advise keep well out. Time arrival to cross bar without waiting.' On this occasion Admiral Henry Oliver, the Director of Naval Intelligence, also sent two destroyers, HMS *Laverock* and HMS *Louis,* to receive and escort the *Lusitania* and dispatched the Q ship HMS *Lyons* to patrol Liverpool Bay, despite the shortage of available destroyers at the time. Captain Dow, Captain Turner's predecessor, commanding the liner, was unwilling to disclose his location to listening Germans and sailed the *Lusitania* into Liverpool unaccompanied.

This level of caution stands in stark contrast to the *Lusitania*'s last crossing, where the Admiralty took no special safety measures to protect her. No specific orders were issued, no escorts or Q ships detailed to protect her. Yet at this time the destroyers *Lucifer, Legion, Linnet,* and *Laverock* were sitting idly at Milford Haven in Wales and would have been readily available as escorting warships.

Early in the war the Royal Navy had severed Germany's transatlantic submarine cables. Churchill, as First Lord of the Admiralty, ordered the establishment of a section specifically tasked with handling the decoded intercepts, and 'Room 40' became a crucial unit in Britain's wartime operation. From Room 40 Admiral Henry Oliver, Director of Naval Intelligence, could have alerted Vice-Admiral Coke at Queenstown of the danger, even if he were unable to signal the *Lusitania.*

The *U-20* 's activities were already causing concern in the Admiralty War Room. She was known to be heading for Fastnet, as ever since she had left her home port the *U-20* had been notifying her position to the German Admiralty by wireless telegraph every four hours. Unbeknownst to Schwieger, every one of his messages and reports of his 'kills' was being intercepted and deciphered immediately by Room 40, where a whole file was devoted to *U-20* 's operations. This file is now kept in the National Archives at Kew, London, where it forms part of the ADM137 series. (The files ADM137/4152 are the U-boat history sheets compiled by Lieutenant Commander Tiarks.) Page 5 in the file follows *U-20* 's voyage home afterwards, and it clearly proves that those in charge at the Admiralty were fully informed about *U-20* 's activities throughout.

Even when the Admiralty was well aware of the dangers of the 'war zone' into which the *Lusitania* was heading they failed to relay the news of the *U-20*'s sinkings of *Earl of Lathom*, *Candidate*, *Centurion* and the attack on the *Cayo Romano*. But they knew the details of these attacks, and there had been specific requests to report them to *Lusitania*. In total, since the *Lusitania* had left New York twenty-three merchantmen had been torpedoed on or near the course the liner was following, and yet her captain was not informed. The need to preserve radio silence can hardly be advanced as a valid explanation.

All in all, on the *Lusitania*'s final voyage official measures to protect her were conspicuously inadequate by comparison with the elaborate precautions the Admiralty had previously taken to look after her and other vessels. On this occasion the Admiralty had ten days in which to organize protection for her and failed to do so. In the eyes of conspiracy theorists, this invites two alternative conclusions: either the Admiralty cynically planned to expose the *Lusitania* to danger on the off-chance that she would be targeted by a German submarine, with consequent loss of American lives calculated to engender public outrage in the USA, or else the Admiralty simply bungled the operation, and the enormous loss of life could be attributed in part to its negligence. If either of these theories proved correct, the result was bound to have led to a massive official whitewash and cover-up.

Radio exchanges between the *Lusitania* and the Admiralty from 5 to 7 May remain classified to this day. The fact that no correspondence between Churchill and First Sea Lord Jacky Fisher from the time of the *Lusitania*'s last crossing has survived has also fuelled speculation that something underhand was afoot. Conspiracy, cover-up, whitewash? Or wilful murder?

If there is a grain of truth in the 'livebait' theory, which alleges that there was a conspiracy to deliberately place the *Lusitania* in harm's way, then the plot must have entailed supplying the ship's captain with inadequate, confused or confusing information, with the result that his ship was placed in a vulnerable position where an attack was possible. At that point it would have been a gamble that one of the submarines known to be patrolling the area would be so positioned as to undertake such an attack and that this attack would be successful.

This would not only have been wilful murder; it would have been an outrageously desperate gamble because of the highly unpredictable nature of the outcome. Even the British Naval Intelligence code-breakers of Room 40 did not always have sufficient information to enable them to pinpoint an enemy submarine's precise location. More importantly, the aim of First World War submarines was notoriously unreliable. The chances that any torpedo would strike the well-designed liner in the precise spot that would deal a monster ship like the *Lusitania* her death-blow were remote. Had a whole series of circumstances not combined, had *Lusitania* not – apparently randomly – altered course, bringing her within range and on a bearing suitable for attack, and had Schwieger not overestimated his victim's speed by four knots, the impact of his torpedo, if it struck the ship, is unlikely to have done so with an impact sufficient to sink her.

Those who subscribe to the theory of an official plot would argue that the plotters probably never envisaged the annihilation of the liner. They imagined only an injured but stable *Lusitania* limping into Queenstown, the hope being that the attempt alone would be sufficient to provoke the USA into joining the conflict on the side of the Allies. If such a plot ever existed, the loss of the vessel in the space of twenty minutes, with horrific casualties, would had been unanticipated, and the putative plotters would have been wrong-footed. But if the intention was simply the maiming of the ship for propaganda purposes, this scheme would have been hazardous. If she were to be attacked, there could be no guarantee that the ship would escape relatively unscathed. If plot there was, the appalling disaster would certainly have unnerved the plotters and driven them into cover-up mode. And a panic-stricken effort at a cover-up certainly appears to have place.

However, the evidence of a government conspiracy before the event is merely circumstantial at best. Such a 'livebait' stratagem would not only have been monstrous and inhumane – although brutal tactics are not unknown in warfare – it would also have been so high-risk and unlikely of success that it would have bordered on insanity.

Churchill was a complex character, but he was not insane. One counter-argument advanced against the notion that he plotted to sacrifice the *Lusitania* in a cynical ploy to involve the USA in the conflict is that in 1915 the USA had not yet mobilized for war. Britain relied on US armaments to supply the British Army in France. If the USA had declared war on Germany in May 1915, war materials that had previously been going to Britain would have stayed in the USA, leaving the British without ammunition. However, as any military commander is aware, nothing equals the impact of boots on the ground. The US armaments would simply have come with the welcome addition of troops. Still, at that point the USA was not ready to enter the war. Her expeditionary force had neither been recruited nor trained.

Had Churchill masterminded such a high-risk plot, such was his character that he would surely have remained in Britain to oversee its execution. When the *Lusitania* was sunk, Churchill was not in France 'on holiday', as has been suggested. On Wednesday, 5 May, after a briefing in the Admiralty's War Room, he had set off for France intending to participate in a naval convention that would bring Italy into the war on the side of the Allies. Thereafter he was to visit the headquarters of Sir John French, who was to mount what would ultimately prove to be a disastrous offensive on the Aubers Ridge the following Friday, an unnecessary diversion for him.

More plausible than a conspiracy is the possibility that there was simply a major foul-up regarding the *Lusitania*. Several factors may have played a contributory role. The Admiralty's resources had been preoccupied with Churchill's pet project, the disastrous Dardanelles campaign. Then there was the matter of the characters of Churchill and Fisher, which the Dardanelles campaign had merely served to highlight.

Churchill and Fisher were both notoriously independent thinkers, poor at sharing information and reluctant to delegate, often leaving their subordinates in the dark. Both were known to micromanage the affairs of Room 40. To complicate matters, the ageing Fisher was at this stage already displaying signs of mental dilapidation.

As it was, no one in the upper ranks of the Admiralty was ever held accountable for the inadequacies that indubitably contributed to the catastrophe. Churchill and Fisher both hastened to allocate the blame to Captain Turner, aware not only that official ineptitude required a major cover-up operation as much as a conspiracy would have done but that a scapegoat or sacrificial victim would go a long way towards diverting attention and appeasing calls for accountability. If the British public got wind of official incompetence, the effects on national morale would have been disastrous. Moreover, the international repercussions, especially in the USA, would have been devastating.

Diana Preston advances a theory that, without the involvement of Fisher and Churchill, Captain William Reginald Hall could have independently masterminded such a plot.[19] Captain (later Admiral) 'Blinker' Hall, the legendary Director of Naval Intelligence, was described by US Ambassador Walter Hines Page as the 'one genius that the war has developed . . . all other secret-service men are amateurs by comparison.'[20] Hall was known to use cloak-and-dagger tactics. He had access to all the relevant decodes of Room 40 and was capable of acting independently of Fisher and Churchill. However, it is doubtful that even the powerful and intelligent Hall could have managed to devise and implement a scheme of this extreme character without Churchill's knowledge and approval.

So was the sinking of the *Lusitania* the result of inept bungling or a murderous conspiracy? Perhaps the truth lies somewhere in between.

And how much truth was there in the official allegations against the *Lusitania*'s captain? The authorities would have few scruples about discrediting those they regarded as potentially vexatious, as is indicated by the spurious 'background checks' advanced as evidence against the difficult and vociferous Marichal. They would certainly have entertained few moral qualms about denigrating the ship's captain if it served their interests.

Captain Turner was accused of disobeying a specific order to steer a mid-channel course. But Turner was not navigating through a channel. The Celtic Sea off the Old Head of Kinsale is not a channel. The nearest land lying due south of the Old Head of Kinsale is more than seventy miles away.

Nor was Turner sailing too close to shore. When the torpedo struck the captain was obeying instructions to stay at least ten miles off the Irish coastline. The *Lusitania* was fourteen miles offshore when she was hit. The wreck lies on the seabed eleven and a quarter miles offshore. The ship's bow points roughly north-east, toward land. (Turner put the helm landward at the last moment, in his desperate attempt to beach her after the torpedo struck.) Even as she was sinking, she never crossed the Admiralty's ten-mile limit. Yet the Admiralty has always maintained that Turner was deliberately sailing perilously close. Captain Webb claimed in a memorandum that Turner had been sailing about eight miles off the Irish coast, following what appeared to have been his customary peacetime route. (In reality the *Lusitania*'s 'usual peacetime route' was only three miles off the Southern Irish coast, and only ships coming closer than five miles to shore were reported for the offence of breaching their war risks insurance.)

Turner was blamed for apparently disobeying standing Admiralty orders to zigzag. Yet no such Admiralty orders were in force until after the *Lusitania* disaster. The specific order to zigzag was draft dated 16 April 1915, and it was not officially circulated outside Admiralty House until 2 May, by which time Turner and the *Lusitania* were already on the open ocean heading for home. The order was not generally circulated until a week later, and it did not become an official standing order until every ship's master had received a printed copy. Certainly nobody at the Admiralty ever relayed such an order by wireless to the *Lusitania*. The very first time Captain Turner saw that order was when it was used against him at the Mersey inquiry in June. There was an advice note dated 10 February 1915 that Turner had received, but this note only 'recommended' steering 'a serpentine course' if a submarine was actually sighted.

With hindsight, it is easy to state that Turner might have held more boat drills. Possibly, he refrained from doing so because he was reluctant to behave in an apparently alarmist manner that might upset his pampered passengers. Again, he could perhaps have ensured that the extra collapsible lifeboats were better maintained (some were rusty and had been painted fast to the deck, making their release impossible). He might have been quicker off the mark about ensuring that all portholes were closed. But excessive inspection of private accommodations might be resented as unduly intrusive; nothing was to be done to alarm the passengers or compromise their comfort.

Many elements contributed to a disaster beyond the Captain's control. These included the speed with which the ship sank; the severe list that complicated the lowering of the boats on both port and starboard sides; the immediate damage and power failure that made it impossible to steer the liner or bring her to a halt; the quality of the rather inexperienced, in some cases, scratch crew which it had been necessary to employ in these times of desertion and wartime conscription; and the terrible damage that meant many members of the crew below decks were trapped by the failure of the electric elevators.

Both the British and the US hearings cleared Cunard of negligence, and the US plaintiffs were advised to seek restitution from Imperial Germany.

In the spring of 1914, the release of government documents revealed the extent of Whitehall's secret anxiety about the official account of the loss of the liner. The episode had become one of the most keenly debated issues of the First World War. Almost seventy years after the ship was sunk a new generation of officials continued to entertain grave concerns regarding what potential spectres might one day come to light.

The disaster remained a hot topic of international discussion and speculation for many years. Germany had always maintained that the ship had been carrying munitions and that the submarine attack was therefore justified, while propagandists on the British side vilified the Germans for their unprovoked attack on civilians.

Even after the British disclosed publicly that the liner's cargo had included 5,000 cases of small arms ammunition, rumours persisted that she was also carrying dangerous high explosives and that it was these which had triggered the huge secondary explosion which allegedly caused the vessel to sink so rapidly, resulting in the massive loss of life.

Foreign Office files first released by the National Archives at Kew in May 2014 show that news of the projected salvage operation in 1982 sparked alarm throughout Whitehall at the time. These newly released secret Whitehall files disclose a warning issued by the Ministry of Defence that 'something startling' might come to light during the August 1982 salvage operation. Despite all the strenuous previous denials that the ship had been carrying explosives, divers planning to explore the wreck were warned by the Ministry of Defence in the strongest terms of the possible 'danger to life and limb' they might face when diving the *Lusitania*. There were serious official concerns that previously undeclared war materials might be discovered.

Government lawyers in the Treasury Chambers turned to the Foreign and Commonwealth Office. The Foreign Office's legal department sought to reassure ministers that there was not the 'remotest chance' of Britain being held liable for the loss of American lives so long after the event. But the Foreign Office's warning that the operation 'could literally blow up on us' reopened debate over the German rationale for sinking the liner.

Despite their reassurances, Foreign Office officials also voiced serious concerns that a final British admission that there were high explosives on the *Lusitania* could still trigger serious political repercussions with the USA even though it was nearly seventy years after the event.[21] Noel Marshall, the head of the Foreign Office's North America department, was appalled at what he was being told on 30 July 1982:

> Successive British governments have always maintained that there was no munitions on board the *Lusitania* (and that the Germans were therefore in the wrong to claim to the contrary as an excuse for sinking the ship). The facts are that there is a large amount of ammunition in the wreck, some of which is highly dangerous. The Treasury have decided that they must inform the salvage company of this fact in the interests of the safety of all concerned. Although there have been rumours in the press that the previous denial of the presence of munitions was untrue, this would be the first acknowledgement of the facts by HMG.[22]

Marshall appeared to be unaware of the government's previous acknowledgement of the 5,000 cases of ammunition cases. He stated that the disclosure of the nature of the *Lusitania*'s cargo was likely to spark a public and journalistic debate. Marshall also mentioned that the Treasury's solicitors had gone so far as to consider whether the relatives of American victims of the sinking might still sue the British government if it could be proved that the German claims had some justification.

Jim Coombes, a senior government lawyer with the Treasury, told Marshall that the Admiralty had always denied that the *Lusitania* was armed or carrying war munitions but that there had always been persistent rumours about the latter. He warned the Foreign Office that, even after the passage of time, it was still possible that there would be political fall-out detrimental to international relations if it were to be revealed that the ship was carrying explosives.

> If it were now to come to light that there was after all some justification, however slight, for torpedoing, HMG's relations with America could well suffer. (Your Republic of Ireland desk is of the opinion is of the opinion that the Irish would seek to create as much uproar as possible.)[23]

Coombes added that in 1918, in New York, Judge Julius Mayer had ruled that although there were 4,200 cases of safety cartridges, 18 fuse cases and 125 shrapnel cases (without any powder charge) on board the liner when it went down, these did not constitute 'war munitions'. Mayer stated that the cases of cartridges had been stowed well forward in the ship, fifty yards from where the German torpedo had struck, and that the *Lusitania* had not been armed, nor had she been transporting high explosives. The 1915 British inquiry, chaired by Lord Mersey, had barely touched on the issue: the secret report of the inquiry concluded that the *Lusitania* was not carrying explosives or any 'special ammunition'. The British public were not told at the time about the 5,000 cases of small-arms cartridges which had been aboard but had been deemed non-military.

The Ministry of Defence now embarked upon a thorough search of its own records but could find no reference to any munitions in the cargo other than those that had previously been acknowledged. There was no evidence to substantiate the rumours of a secret munitions store.

Nevertheless it was still felt to be prudent for the divers to be forewarned of the 'obvious but real danger inherent if explosives did happen to be present'. Harry Nicholson of the Ministry of Defence wrote, 'In view of the rumours, well known, I believe, in salvage circles, and the purpose of the project, we consider that the organizers and participants should be warned of the risks they may be taking.'[24] For good measure the Salvage Association was also told to deliver a similar warning to dive teams, both orally and in writing.

Back in 1982 in Whitehall it had been agreed to maintain the official line that there had been no munitions aboard the liner, although it had 'always been public knowledge that the *Lusitania*'s cargo included some 5,000 cases of small-arms ammunition'. Marshall, the senior Foreign Office mandarin remained sceptical. 'I am left with the uneasy feeling that this subject may yet – literally – blow up on us,' he said, adding his suspicion that others in Whitehall had decided not to tell all that they knew. As for the salvage operation, it recovered 821 brass fuses for six-inch shells but failed to settle the bigger question.

All told, the notion that the *Lusitania* disaster was planned in a cynical warmongering ploy, possibly masterminded by Churchill, appears fanciful, chiefly because it would have been a hare-brained scheme and a massive gamble. The devastating outcome would have been quite impossible to predict with any degree of certainty. But there was indubitably a subsequent whitewash, an urgent attempt to cover up official bungling; this entailed not only the inevitable wartime lies but a blatant example of buck-passing and efforts to smear the ship's captain.

A statue commemorating the *Lusitania* dominates the main square in Queenstown, now Cobh. Behind the town a secluded graveyard contains the mass graves of 160 victims of the attack that took place on that sunny afternoon in May 1915.

As we have seen, the loss of the *Lusitania* did not invoke the immediate military retaliation that other atrocities did. Yet it changed the outcome of the war in two ways. First, it was the catalyst that created a climate of distrust and hatred of Germany among the American people. It has been remarked that the sinking of the *Lusitania* had a more jolting effect upon the American opinion than any other single event of the war. When Wilson declared war on 6 April 1917 the loss of the *Lusitania* was still at the forefront of people's minds.

Second, as von Langsdorff and others surmised, had Germany

persisted in pursuing her programme of unrestricted U-boat warfare in 1915 this might well have tipped the balance and ensured a German victory or at least brought peace negotiators to the table at a much earlier stage. But the international outcry over the *Lusitania* alarmed the Kaiser. He chose to ignore the advice of Admiral Tirpitz, who advocated keeping up the pressure through unrestricted submarine warfare. Tirpitz and other German naval commanders soon began to feel constrained and hamstrung.

Another old warrior with a profound understanding of naval warfare sympathized with their feelings of frustration. In an extraordinary communication, the erratic Admiral Jackie Fisher, now relieved of First Sea Lord duties, wrote to his old colleague and adversary Admiral Tirpitz, who had been forced to resign in 1916, a chummy letter. This began 'Dear Old Tirps' and ended 'Cheer up, old chap! Say "Resurgam"! You're the one German sailor who understands War! Kill your enemy without being killed yourself. I don't blame you for the submarine business. I'd have done the same myself. Well, so long. Yours till hell freezes over, Fisher.'[25]

Epilogue

Joseph Marichal never received any compensation. Determined to restore his tattered reputation after the public drubbing he had received, both during the hearing and in the media, he enlisted as a private soldier. He was killed in action just over a year later, on 12 August 1916, at the Battle of the Somme, while serving with the 44th Infantry Regiment. France awarded him the Croix de Guerre.

George Kessler had made a vow, as he struggled for his life in the water, that if he survived he would devote his energy and some of his substantial fortune to philanthropic causes. While in hospital in England he encountered the blind newspaper magnate Sir Arthur Pearson who told Kessler about the organization he had recently founded, the Blinded Soldiers and Sailors Care Committee (later renamed St Dunstan's), for members of the armed forces who had been blinded by gas attack or trauma. The committee's objective was innovative for the times, the aim being to provide vocational training rather than charity for invalided servicemen. Kessler decided that this was the cause he would choose to embrace. In November 1915 he and his wife Cora organized the British, French, Belgian Permanent Blind Relief War Fund in Paris. When the Kesslers returned to the USA they met Helen Keller, the celebrated deaf–blind author and activist, and the three of them worked together, raising funds and establishing training programmes for Allied soldiers and sailors blinded in combat.

The Reverend Herbert Gwyer, who had sought to reassure frightened passengers and who had despaired when he feared his wife Margaret had drowned, went on to become the second Bishop of George, South Africa.

At the time of the disaster Fannie Morecroft, the stewardess who helped save many passengers, had been working for Cunard for over ten years, since her husband had died in 1901. As a teenager she had run away to marry her much older widower husband, a lawyer who had abandoned the law to become a travelling actor. As a widow her work as a stewardess supported her two children. Hence she was appalled by Cunard's decision, after the sinking of the *Lusitania*, not to employ female staff aboard any of their vessels until the war was over. However, as the huge numbers of men drafted to fight in France created a shortage in the labour force she successfully obtained various other types of employment, even doing a stint as a tram conductor. In early 1919 she was able to resume her career with Cunard and was eventually appointed Chief Stewardess on its new liner, RMS *Lancastria*, where she enjoyed her own spacious private cabin. She continued in this transatlantic role until her retirement in the 1930s.

May Bird, Fannie's friend, also went back to work for Cunard after the war. When May's husband died, she and Fannie shared a home in Sussex. Fannie died in 1958; May continued to grant interviews about her *Lusitania* experience until she was over ninety. When she died, in Birkenhead in 1975, May was almost one hundred years old.

Professor Ian Holbourn wrote a book for his young protégée, Avis Dolphin, because she complained that she found children's literature boring. Ian and his wife Marion remained friendly with Avis, who eventually met Thomas Foley, the man she would marry, while visiting the Holbourn family.[1]

Another long-term association was forged between two other survivors saved by the *Wanderer*. William Inch and Emmie Hill remained friends for life.

First Officer Arthur Rowland-Jones, who had been in charge of Lifeboat No. 15, was killed in action in February 1918, aged thirty-eight.

Francis Luker, who saved two small children from drowning, later returned to Saskatoon and his job in the Post Office. In July 1917, by the irony of fate, he drowned while swimming with friends in the Saskatchewan River.

Wallace Banta Phillips, who had so admired Rita Jolivet and enjoyed socializing with the theatrical set on board the *Lusitania*, went on to have a varied and successful career in business and, briefly, naval intelligence.[2]

The querulous Isaac Lehmann had been travelling to Paris for a business meeting in which he hoped to win a lucrative contract, supplying a bulk order of cloth to the French government for military uniforms. By the time he reached Paris, after a period of recuperation in London, it was too late to secure the contract. Lehmann brought his case before the Mixed Claims Commission. The court deemed his claim that he had lost the contract because of the sinking of the *Lusitania* to be speculative but none the less awarded him $6,000.

Harold and Lucy Taylor, the newlyweds joyfully reunited in Queenstown, put in their own claims, which included Lucy's grey Quaker wedding dress, her silver gravy ladle, her fancy cushion covers and her chinchilla coat. Harold was conscripted and fought in France but survived. After the war, in 1922, the Taylors returned to Niagara Falls, where several children were born to them. Their daughter Marjorie was given the middle name of Lusitania.

Also reunited in Queenstown were the Veals, Albert and Agnes, who had been rescued by *Wanderer*, and Agnes's brother Frederick Bailey. The three would later take an active part in the Lord Mayor's fundraising efforts for the Lusitania Relief Fund.

The valiant Elizabeth Duckworth, having recovered from her ordeal, undertook war work at the Royal Arsenal Ammunition Factory in her native Blackburn and later returned to the USA. She died in 1955 in Taftville, Connecticut, aged ninety-two. 1955. Authors A.A. Hoehling and Mary Hoehling, who communicated with several survivors of the *Lusitania*, credit Elizabeth Duckworth's life as being the catalyst for them to write their book *The Last Voyage of the Lusitania.*

In 1916 Rita Jolivet married a Venetian count and declared her intention of retiring from the world of stage and screen. However, this retirement was to be of only a brief duration. She returned to the screen and in 1918 revisited the experience of the *Lusitania*, starring in a film entitled *Lest We Forget*, the proceeds of which were donated for the alleviation of suffering caused by the war. Jolivet died in 1971 in Nice, reputedly after having broken a hip while attempting to demonstrate that she was still capable of dancing a jig. Like Fannie Morecroft, Jolivet had always lied about her age, maintaining to the last that she was only seventy-seven, whereas she was in her early eighties.

Josephine Brandell really did abandon her burgeoning career as an actress and singer after the disaster. She died childless at eighty-five, despite having been married four times.

Through the good offices of historian Michael Poirier, survivor Barbara Anderson, who died in Wallingford, Connecticut, aged ninety-five, was put in touch with the family of William Harkness, the man who had saved her as a small girl from the wreck of the *Lusitania*, and was able to express her thanks to him.

Oliver Bernard joined the Royal Engineers, was wounded and was awarded the Military Cross. Demobilized with the rank of captain, he became technical director for the Grand Opera Syndicate and Sir Thomas Beecham seasons at Covent Garden. His autobiography, *Cock-sparrow*, published in 1936, included some memories of his voyage aboard the *Lusitania.*[3]

Robert Rankin, the electrical engineer, went on to fulfil the predictions of his classmates at Cornell, enjoying a distinguished international career.

Colliery owner and MP D.A. Thomas and his secretary Arnold Rhys-Evans were rescued from Lifeboat No. 11 by the *Wanderer.* Thomas declined to recount his experience of the disaster to the press on the grounds that he had had too easy a time for it to be interesting. As a boat was being lowered on the starboard side, an officer had simply told him to take a vacant seat, and he had complied. The boat got away without problems and was one of the first to be picked up. One Welsh newspaper published the banner headline 'Great National Disaster. D.A. Thomas Saved'. This may have been penned in innocence but may also have been recalled with glee by Welsh miners as their dissatisfaction with the colliery owners gathered momentum. In 1916 Thomas was created Baron Rhondda. He was appointed Minister of Food in June 1917, and he introduced food rationing in Britain. When he died in July 1918 his title and peerage were inherited by his suffragette daughter Margaret, Lady Mackworth, rescued by the *Bluebell.*

The presence of the tiny shipwrecked children had been especially affecting for the crew of the *Wanderer.* They had seen what they thought was a bundle of rags floating past, which proved to be a child about two months old. Baby Nancy Wickings-Smith, one of the children saved by Francis Luker, to whom she had been thrown by her mother when she herself was held back from boarding the boat, was later reunited with her parents. Nancy lived until 1993. She was one of four infants to survive the disaster. Another who was saved by the *Wanderer* was Thomas Docherty. His mother, Mabel Docherty, wrote to the family for whom she had worked as a maid in New York telling them how glad she was that although she had lost all her possessions her baby son, Thomas William, had been saved. She said the child was so adorable that the women in Ireland wanted to eat him up.

Shortly after the sinking a renowned German medallist, Karl Goetz, whose forte was the creation of political cartoons in the form of medallions, cast a medal castigating Cunard for allowing passengers to board a ship bound for the war zone in British waters. Goetz incorrectly dated the medal May 5, thus predating the actual sinking by two days. This error would be exploited by British propagandists as proof positive that the attack had been cynically premeditated rather than opportunistic. As soon as Goetz realized his error he cast a small number of new medals with the corrected date, but the first medal had already been pounced upon by the British propaganda machine which made good use of the incorrect one.

The image on the medal depicts the sinking *Lusitania* (inaccurately, stern first). Guns and aircraft are visible on the liner's deck. The legend above the image reads, *Keine Bannware*! (No Contraband!) Below, in the exergue, are the words 'Der Grossdampfer *Lusitania* durch ein deutsches Tauchboot versenkt 5 Mai 1915' ('The liner *Lusitania* sunk by a German submarine, 5 May 1915'). The reverse shows a line of people queuing at the Cunard ticket office ('Fahrkarten Ausgabe') to buy tickets from a skeleton, representing Death. A man in the queue is reading a newspaper whose banner headlines proclaim a warning of U-boat danger ('U Boot Gefahr'). A bearded figure wearing a top hat raises a warning finger. This figure represents the German Ambassador to the USA, Count Johann-Heinrich von Bernstorff, warning Americans not to travel on a vessel sailing through the war zone. Above his head are the words 'Geschäft über Alles' ('Business First') – intended by the medallist as a satirical comment on Cunard's motto. The designer's initials, K.G., appear below.

There are three different versions of the medal. The first was the original medal with the incorrect date, 5 Mai 1915. The second is Goetz's corrected medal, reading 7 Mai 1915. The final version is the British copy with the date spelled in English, 'May 5, 1915'.

Goetz was a home-based one-man industry. He created his medals in his house, selling them as and when he could. Hence, the mintage figures varied widely; more popular medals would have greater sales, so Goetz produced them in greater numbers. Medals that proved to have less popular appeal would be melted down and the metal recast. Mintage figures for most of Goetz's pieces were lost during the bombing raids on Munich during the war.[4] However, in personal correspondence with the German Embassy in London via the State Department of Bavaria, Goetz stated how many *Lusitania* medals had been cast up to that time: as of September 1920, 430 pieces had been cast. It is not clear whether this number includes both the first and second versions of his medal or only the incorrectly dated original. Unconfirmed reports on the internet estimate the number of originals at forty-five. Certainly, the number cast was extremely small.

In a letter written in 1921 Goetz stated that the medal was cast for the first time in August 1915. Shortly afterwards an example fell into the hands of the British. Eager not to waste a perfect propaganda opportunity, it was copied and sold to the general public at a cost of a shilling apiece. The proceeds of the sale of the British medals went to the St Dunstan's Blinded Soldiers' and Sailors' Hostels and the Red Cross.

Under the directions of the flamboyant spy chief Captain 'Blinker' Hall, the British struck several hundred examples of the medal. The English version, which was cruder and less detailed, and made of white metal-plated iron rather than bronze or bronze-like material, came in an attractive presentation box with a picture on the top depicting the *Lusitania* and giving an account of her sinking. The inside of the lid bears the legend 'The Lusitania Medal. An exact replica of the medal which was designed in Germany and distributed to commemorate the sinking of the *Lusitania*. This indicates the true feeling the War Lords endeavour to stimulate, and is proof positive that such crimes are not merely regarded favourably, but are given every encouragement in the land of Kultur. The *Lusitania* was sunk by a German submarine on May 7th, 1915 . . . 1,198 perished.'

Also included in the box was a pamphlet in which the medal was described and the Germans were represented as evil incarnate. This view was supported by quotations from German official figures and media, such as 'With joyful pride we contemplate this latest deed of our Navy' (*Kölnische Volkszeitung*, 10 May 1915).

The pamphlet stated that the medallist depicts guns and aircraft on the liner's deck but neglects to show the women and children who were victims of the attack. Of the reverse, where passengers are shown purchasing tickets from Death, it stated that the medal 'seeks apparently to propound the theory that if a murderer warns his victim of his intention, the guilt of the crime will rest with the victim, not with the murderer'.

The medal sold very well and achieved the intended outpouring of revulsion. In response, on 18 January 1917 Baron von Speidel of the War Office of the Kingdom of Bavaria wrote a memo to the I, II and III Army Corps forbidding the further manufacture and sale of th German medal and announcing that any available pieces would be confiscated.[3] There is no record of how many examples were confiscated.

Why did Goetz put the wrong date on the medal to begin with? Kienast suggests that Goetz simply obtained his information about the sinking from a newspaper account that happened to report the wrong date. Goetz continued to make medals until he was stricken with paralysis and incapacitated. For the rest of his life he found himself in the position of having to defend his reasons for casting his *Lusitania* medal. Seventeen years later, in August 1932, in a letter to Rear Admiral Lutzow, he expressed regret that his medal had been exploited by the enemy for propaganda purposes.

Schwieger returned to a hero's welcome in Germany, but the tide of feeling began to change as Germany, and especially the Kaiser, became disturbed by international opprobrium, and things soon turned sour. Werner von Langsdorff, in his work on German submarines in the First World War, bitterly records:

> On 7 May 1915 *U-20* Kapitän-Leutnant Schwieger sank the English auxiliary cruiser *Lusitania*. Besides passengers, she was carrying munitions. America demanded compensation. Schwieger, who had only done his duty, was let down by those who should have supported him and fell into disfavour with the Kaiser. The German submarine captains and crew did their duty at risk of their lives; America protested, obviously in the interests of the Allies, and Bethmann-Hollweg's government crumbled; new restrictions were introduced, considerably increasing the risks for submariners and making it more difficult for them to succeed. Knowing that they lacked the backing of their government makes the extraordinary achievement of German submariners even more remarkable.[5]

Walther Schwieger would become known internationally as the man who sank the *Lusitania*. In the British press he was dubbed 'the Baby-Killer'. His name would appear on the Admiralty's 'Wanted' list of possible war criminals. This was by no means an unusual or unique distinction. Enemy submarine commanders who scored numerous successes against British shipping regularly featured on this list.

The Imperial German Navy needed commanders of Schwieger's calibre, and he was soon given another command, the newer *U-88*, and awarded many distinctions: the Iron Cross, both First and Second Class, the Order of the Crown, the Order of the Royal House of Hohenzollern and, in July 1917, the ultimate accolade, the prestigious 'Blue Max', the

Shwieger had sunk a total of between 183,883 and 190,00 tons of Allied shipping. His citation made no mention of the *Lusitania*.

Six weeks later he was killed when the *U-88* was blown up and sank with all hands, presumably having struck a mine while outbound from Germany for the French coast. He was thirty-two. After the war, his fiancée told an interviewer that when he visited her in the period following the *Lusitania*'s sinking he was much changed, taciturn and with a haggard look. He would write to a friend that he longed for the end of 'this very sad time'.

When he died Schwieger was the sixth most successful U-boat commander of his time and was officially accounted an 'ace'. In May 1918 the German Navy launched the first of its new large long-range U-139 submarine cruisers, originally designated 'Project 46' and designed for war service. The vessel was named *Kapitän-Leutnant Schwieger* in his memory.

Between 1924 and 1925 some of the wreckage from the *U-20* was recovered and exhibited in various international locations. Today her conning tower, one of her propellers and her deck gun are on display at Strandingsmuseet, Thorsminde, Denmark, just south of Vrist, where the *U-20* ran aground in November 1916 while attempting to assist another submarine and efforts to refloat her failed. The crew blew her up with one of her own torpedoes to prevent her falling into enemy hands. Her hull and her engines still repose in the shallows off the coast of Jutland where she stranded.

Controversy still rages over the putative culpability of Captain Turner, the actions of the British Admiralty and the cause of the second explosion. Turner survived the disaster and accounted for himself successfully in three subsequent inquiries. It is known that he received specific orders from the Admiralty, but to date the full extent of the information passed to him has not been made public. He had been accused of deliberately hazarding his ship and openly suspected by the authorities of being in the pay of the enemy, but he was cleared of all blame by Lord Mersey.

However, Turner remained embittered and aggrieved and paid a heavy personal price. After the inquiry his estranged wife Alice emigrated to Australia, taking his sons, Percy and Norman, with her. Turner was subsequently given command of the *Ultonia*, tasked with ferrying Canadian troops to France. His next command was the *Ivernia*, again on war service, but despite Turner's zigzagging the *Ivernia* was torpedoed and sunk off the coast of Greece on New Year's Day 1917 by Kapitän-Leutnant Steinbauer of the *U-47*. Once again Turner survived, but the *Ivernia* would be his last command.

In January 1918 Turner was awarded the OBE for his war service, at the behest of Cunard Chairman Alfred Booth. In 1919 Turner retired with Mabel Every, his long-time companion and housekeeper, to Yelverton, Devon, a village near Dartmoor, close to her birthplace. But in 1921, after the publication of Churchill's four-volume memoirs *The World Crisis*, in which the Admiralty's allegations against him were repeated, journalists hunted Turner down and so harassed him that he returned to Liverpool. After being diagnosed with stomach cancer he travelled to Australia, hoping to be reunited with his sons, but his quest was in vain. He had not seen his ex-wife and sons since Lord Mersey's inquiry in 1915, and he was never to see them again, perhaps because by the time he went to look for them they had moved on to Canada.

The shadow of the *Lusitania* lay over Turner's life. He felt people shunned him because they thought he should have gone down with the ship; his typical survivors' guilt was exacerbated by the master's sense of responsibility for his ship, her passengers and crew. Unsurprisingly, he found it painful to speak of the *Lusitania*.

In the autumn of 1932 Turner had an unexpected visitor at his home, now at 50 De Villiers Avenue, Crosby, which he also shared with Every. In the mess hall of the small steamer *Bluebell*, after the sinking of the *Lusitania*, Third Officer Bestic had seen the captain sitting alone and said to him that he was glad to see him alive. Turner asked why that should be. He did not think Bestic bore any affection for him. He had indeed done little to endear himself to Bestic. But Bestic replied that fondness did not enter into it. He said he was glad to see Turner alive because he respected him as his captain and admired him as a seaman.

Now Bestic had heard that his old captain was ill and had come to his house in Crosby to visit him. The story, which certainly seems in keeping with the captain's character, goes that when Every told Turner a man calling himself 'Bestic' was at the door Turner growled that he knew nobody by that name. Bestic was upset and about to leave when he remembered what Turner had always called him. 'Would you be kind enough to tell the Captain that my name is really Bisset.' Mystified, Every apparently went off to relay this to the captain. She returned smiling after delivering the message, saying, 'He said, "Why the hell didn't he say so in the first place?"'

Captain Turner, it is said, admitted to Bestic that he had been worried about the danger of submarines but had thought the *Lusitania* had a good chance of escaping. He remained embittered by what he regarded as the unfair treatment he had received. He had not been clearly instructed with regard to zigzagging, and it had been two years before specific orders were issued regarding distance from headlands and what course ships should follow. He felt that the fact that there had been no escort to meet him, despite the signals that revealed that the Admiralty was well aware of the lurking presence of enemy submarines, imbued him with a sense of false confidence. He assumed that if the Admiralty showed such a lack of concern for such a valuable ship and those aboard her, there could be no substantial danger. He had also been told he should have taken a 'mid-channel course' when his ship was in the middle of the Atlantic.

Captain Turner died on 23 June 1933 at home in Crosby. On the King's birthday and St George's Day he had always ensured that Mabel hoisted the Union Jack on the flagpole in the garden. He kept his sense of humour to the end, entertaining local children with sea-shanties and tunes he played on an old violin. Stricken with cancer, he would quip that he was all right fore and aft but his longitudinal bulkhead had given way. He nurtured resentment against Churchill to the end of his days for the blatant attempt to blame him for the loss of the *Lusitania.*

Mabel Every lived into her nineties, dying in 1978. She cherished a medal inscribed 'W.T. Turner, Fourth Officer, City of Chester, who jumped into the sea to rescue a drowning boy, April 1883.'

By an odd quirk of fate Captain Turner's son Percy, serving with Naval Intelligence, was killed during the Second World War when his ship was torpedoed just a mile from where the *Lusitania* sank.

The *Wanderer* and her small Manx crew continued to fish mackerel off the Cork coast or herring in Manx waters, according to the season, over the next couple of years. William Ball had been her skipper for twelve years as an employee of Charles Morrison. But he was soon to have a ship of his own. He received word that funds had been lodged with a lawyer in Peel on behalf of one of the American survivors that he and his crew had rescued. 'The money was to be used to underwrite the building of his own fishing boat, to be built in Peel to his personal specifications, and the result was his dream ship, the *Aigh Vie*, launched in 1916.'[6]

In January 1917 Ball and his son took delivery of a nobby built for them at the Peel shipyard of Neakle and Watterson, registered under the

Traditional Boats of Ireland as 'Nicholson & Watson'; the craft was first registered as *RY40* or *Ramsey 40*.

Patrick Murphy of County Galway, who later acquired the *Aigh Vie*, related a story that had been passed from one owner to the next. One of the female survivors rescued by the *Wanderer* was a wealthy heiress who was with child. She was so well treated by the Ball family while aboard that after her child was born, to express her gratitude, she gave them enough money to purchase their own boat and call it *Good Luck – Aigh Vie* in Manx Gaelic.

Emily Anderson and Jessie Marichal were both pregnant when the *Wanderer* picked them up, but it appears unlikely that either of these women were the Ball family's benefactress. They were not first-class passengers travelling in luxury. Neither Emily nor the son she bore later that year would long survive. (Her daughter Barbara always ascribed their deaths to the dreadful experience of the *Lusitania*.)

Meanwhile the destitute condition of the unfortunate Marichals is well documented. Jessie miscarried her child and was in poor health thereafter.

The *Wanderer* herself was sold to a man in Skibbereen by her owner, Charles Morrison. The new owner and his brother collected her from Peel to sail to Baltimore, the Cork port used by the Skibbereen fishing fleet. She was renamed *Erin's Hope*. 'Boy Dick' Costain was engaged as a pilot for the journey to Baltimore. The *Wanderer* left Peel for the last time on Saturday, 10 March 1918. The Irish Sea and St George's Channel were infested with German U-boats, so Costain set a course hugging the Irish coast, and they made good progress as far as the Saltee Islands. Here, with no warning, a marauding U-boat surfaced and shelled them. They hastily launched the yawl and scrambled into it, only to discover more problems – the yawl had suffered sprung planking and was rapidly taking on water. Despite furious bailing activity the yawl was on the point of sinking when the submarine stopped firing and dived. The jolly-boat remained afloat, her masts and spars smashed, her sails in shreds, until some three hours later when a British cruiser found her and towed her into Waterford. With the help of some local fishermen the crew managed to patch her up sufficiently to enable her to proceed to Baltimore, arriving on Sunday, 7 April 1918. Here permanent repairs were completed and an engine was installed.

For the next four years she worked the fishing grounds without incident, but her adventures were not over. In 1922, at the height of the

Irish Civil War, her propeller became fouled in the trawl net and warps. The crew were obliged to beach her on a strand in Baltimore Lough to await low water when it would be possible to clear the obstruction. At 2 p.m. the crew embarked on this operation but suddenly found themselves coming under heavy rifle fire; they had to scramble aboard and crouch in the bottom of the boat on top of the ballast. After about an hour the gunfire ceased, and the fishermen were approached by a sergeant of the Royal Irish Constabulary. After checking that nobody had been injured he explained that the British troops had taken them for illegal gun-runners. The misunderstanding cleared up, they were free to leave. The British government paid a large sum for repairs to the boat, and the crew were compensated for loss of earnings.

Four years later, when the former *Wanderer* was laid up in a cove near Skibbereen, a south-south-east hurricane smashed her legs and pounded her to pieces.

Thomas Woods, who had been at the helm and sounded the alarm when he saw the torpedo strike the *Lusitania*, spent many more years fishing for herring from Balbriggan. He is recorded as skippering a couple of Manx vessels from the harbour, including the *Wanderer*. He was well known in the town and well liked by the locals.

The sinking of the *Lusitania* would have a massive impact on the *Wanderer*'s original home port, Peel, in the Isle of Man. The island had long been recognized as the ideal location for enemy alien internment camps. The first suggestion came in 1797, during the French Revolutionary Wars, when one Captain Cable, a naval officer residing on the island, wrote to the 4th Duke of Atholl suggesting the Calf of Man as a suitable site. 'Should any of these prisoners by chance get over to the Island, such is the timidity of the Manx people, as Your Grace likewise knows, that they must be infallibly discovered immediately.' For logistical reasons this scheme was never implemented. The island was to wait over a hundred years for the arrival of its first internees.

In early September 1914 the huts of Joseph Cunningham's Douglas Holiday Camp, which had operated under the slogan 'Good clean fun for young men', were hastily fenced off with barbed wire. On 22 September some two hundred 'enemy alien' men of military age were brought there to be interned. By 24 October 1914 this number had increased to 2,600.

It soon became apparent that the explosive demand for accommodation meant that another larger camp would have to be established without delay. The chosen site was Knockaloe Mooar, near Peel, an area nearly three miles in circumference that had formerly been used as a camp and training ground for up to 1,600 Territorial Reserves during the summer. Eventually Knockaloe would house 24,500 men. The Isle of Man's principal source of income, the tourist trade, had been wiped out by the war, and times were hard. Now, in catering to the camps, fortunes were made on the island. Knockaloe grew into a town. The impact of the huge numbers of internees – 25,000 at times – on an island whose own population was only 52,000 with most able-bodied men of military age away at the front, was inestimable.

In 1915 the wave of hostility and outrage that swept through Britain in response to the sinking of the *Lusitania* pushed the Asquith government into a policy of mass internment of enemy aliens on an island already bearing a heavy burden as a result of the war.

The Isle of Man would send over 8,000 men to the war, representing 82.3 per cent of the male population of military age. Of these, 2,334 were casualties, 2,770 were killed, 395 died of wounds or disease or were reported missing. A further 182 became prisoners of war.

Before May 1915 the National Reservists (later the Royal Defence Corps), which had been sent to the island to guard the enemy aliens, often escorted groups of up to two hundred prisoners on exercise marches. In May 1915 these outings were brought to an abrupt close when a group of prisoners caused a riot in the little east-coast village of Laxey. Seeing outside a newsagent's a poster depicting the sinking of the *Lusitania*, the prisoners started cheering, jeering and dancing in gleeful triumph. The villagers were incensed. Recreational excursions for the internees were thereafter curtailed.

After their moment of glory the *Wanderer* and her heroic crew had returned to the fishing, the life they knew. When King George V and Queen Mary visited the *Wanderer*'s home port of Peel in July 1920 the nautically minded monarch expressed a wish to meet and personally congratulate the skipper and crew of the famous vessel. He was disappointed to be told that this would not be possible. Skipper William Ball had died. As for the rest of the crew, they were away at the fishing.

Notes

INTRODUCTION

1 Colin Simpson, *Lusitania*, Prentice Hall, Englewood Cliffs, New Jersey, 1972.
2 Winston S. Churchill, *The World Crisis*, Butterworth, London, 1927, Vol. 1, p. 323; National Archives blog: Dr Richard Dunley, 24 September 2014 (ADM 1/8396/356; ADM 137/47; ADM 178/13).
3 Michael Dow, 6 May 2009: Encyclopedia Titanica forum. www. encyclopedia-titancia.org/forums/forum.php.
4 Jim Kalafus, 6 May 2009, www. encyclopedia-titancia.org/forums/ forum.php.
5 Bertram E. Sargeaunt, *The Isle of Man and the Great War*, Brown and Sons, Douglas, Isle of Man, 1921.
6 Personal conversation by the author with members of the Ball family.

ONE

1 Eric Hobsbawm, *The Age of Empire: 1875–1914*, Weidenfeld, London, 1987, p. 312.
2 Daniel Allen Butler, *The Age of Cunard*, Lighthouse Press, Annapolis, Maryland, 2003.
3 Louis W. Collins, 'Samuel Cunard – Citizen of Halifax: A Sketch', paper presented at a meeting of the East Hampshire Historical Society in Maitland Elementary School, Maitland, September 1968.

TWO

1 *New York Times*, 21 November 1915.
2 Robert K. Massie, *Castles of Steel: Britain Germany, and the Winning of the Great War at Sea*, Ballantine Books, New York, 2003, p. 126.
3 Baron John Arbuthnot Fisher, *Memories and Records*, Vols 1 and 2, George H. Doran Company, New York, 1920, pp. 10, 24.
4 Fisher to unknown correspondent, 22 February 1905, in Arthur J. Marder, *From the Dreadnought to Scapa Flow: The Royal Navy in the Fisher Era, 1904–1919*, Oxford University Press, London, 1970, Vol. 2, p. 51; Shawn Grimes, *Strategy and War Planning in the British Navy 1887–1918*, Boydell Press, Woodbridge, Suffolk, 2012, p. 60, n. 64, surmises that the letter was to Fisher's journalist friend and ally W.T. Stead and refers the reader to

Ruddock F. Mackay, *Fisher of Kilverstone*, Clarendon Press, Oxford, 1973, pp. 222–3.

5 Selborne Papers, SP 1/1512, Bodleian Library.

6 Sir Julian S. Corbett, *Naval Operations: History of the Great War Based on Official Documents*, Vol. II, Naval and Military Press (IWM), Longmans, Green, London, 1920, pp. 260–61.

THREE

1 Vincent Fitzpatrick, *H.L. Mencken*, Mercer University Press, Macon, Georgia, 1989, p. 11; *H.L.* Mencken, *A Mencken Chrestomathy*, Alfred P. Knopf, New York, 1949, pp. 148–51; Guy J. Forgue (ed.). *Letters of H.L. Mencken*, Alfred P. Knopf, New York, 1961, letter to Burton Roscoe, summer 1920, p. 188.

2 Malcolm Magee, 'Review of Robert W. Tucker, *Woodrow Wilson and the Great War: Reconsidering America's Neutrality, 1914–1917*' [University Press of Virginia, Charlottesville, Virginia, 2007], http://www.amazon.com/exec/obidos/ASIN/0813926297.

3 Lawrence W. Levine, *Defender of the Faith: William Jennings Bryan, The Last Decade, 1915–1925*, Harvard University Press, Cambridge, Massachusetts, 1965, p. 8.

4 'Letter to Sir Arthur Nicolson Concerning William Jennings Bryan's Opinion of the Great War', 1 November 1914 (from Sir Cecil Spring-Rice, British Ambassador in Washington), WW1 Document Archive, 1914 Documents; http://wwi.lib.byu.edu.

5 Paxton Hibben, *The Peerless Leader, William Jennings Bryan*, Farrar and Rinehart, Inc., New York, 1929, p. 356.

6 E.M. House, *Diary*, 30 August 1914, Sterling Memorial Library, Yale University, New Haven, Connecticut.

7 Woodrow Wilson, 'Speech to Ohio Chamber of Commerce, December 10, 1915', *Papers of Woodrow Wilson*, Princeton University Press, Princeton, New Jersey, 1980, p. 327.

8 Charles Seymour (ed.), *The Intimate Papers of Colonel House*, Boston: Houghton Mifflin, 1926, Vol. 1, p. 249.

9 John H. Maurer, 'Averting the Great War?', *Naval War College Review*; Summer 2014, Vol. 67, No. 3, p. 24.

10 E.M. House, *Diary*, 23 May 1914, Sterling Memorial Library, Yale University, New Haven, Connecticut

11 Viscount Grey of Fallodon, *Twenty-Five Years 1892–1916*, Frederick A. Stokes Company, New York, 1925, p. 20.

12 Barbara W. Tuchman, *The Zimmermann Telegram*, Ballantine Books, New York, 1985, pp. 34–8.

13 Franz von Rintelen, *The Dark Invader: Wartime Reminiscences of a German Naval Intelligence Officer*, Routledge, London, 1998, p. 57.

14 Heribert von Feilitzsch, *In Plain Sight: Felix A. Sommerfeld, Spymaster in Mexico, 1908 to 1914*, Henselstone Verlag LLC, Amissville, Virginia, 2012,

p. 76; Horst von der Golst, *My Adventures as a German Secret Agent*, R.M. McBride and Co., New York, 1917.

15 Earl E. Sperry, assisted by M. Willis, *German Plots and Intrigues in the United States During the Period of Our Neutrality*, Red, White and Blue Series, No. 10, July, 1918, issued by the Committee on Public Information, Washington, DC.

16 Gilbert King, 'Sabotage in New York Harbor', www.smithsonian.com, 1 November, 2011.

17 James W. Gerard, 'American Leaders Speak: Recordings from First World War and the 1920 Election, 1918–1920', Library of Congress. 'The German Peril', speech to the Ladies Aid Society of St Mary's Hospital, New York City, 1917.

FOUR

1 John Drew, *My Years on the Stage*, Dutton, New York, 1922, p. 228.

2 Theodate Pope, letter to her mother, quoted in *Hartford Courant*, Hartford, Connecticut, 19 May 1996, p. 2.

3 A.A. Hoehling and Mary Hoehling, *The Last Voyage of the Lusitania*, Henry Holt and Company, London, 1956, p. 7.

4 Elbert Hubbard, *Who Lifted the Lid Off Hell?*, Western European Theater Political Pamphlet Collection, Box 3, Public Policy Papers, Department of Rare Books and Special Collections, Princeton University Library, New Jersey, 1914.

5 Elbert Hubbard and Felix Shay, 'The Titanic', *The Fra: For Philistines and Roycrofters*, East Aurora, New York, Vol. 9, 1912, p. 2.

FIVE

1 Bernd Langensiepen, 'Die Legende von Karl Vögeles "Meuterei" auf U20', in *Marine-Nachrichtenblatt. Das Veröffentlichungsblatt des Arbeitskreises Krieg zur See 1914–18*, Vol. 8, No. 3, 2012, pp. 55–60.

2 Ibid.

3 Ibid.

4 Walter Schwieger's diary is part of the collection of the National Archives: Record Group 45: Naval Records Collection of the Office of Naval Records and Library, 1691–1945; 'Kriegstagebuch S.M.U-Boote U20, Band 3, vom 30.IV bis13.V.15, Kapitänleutnant Schwieger', German Marine Archives.

5 Ibid.

6 Ibid.

7 Robert Lansing Papers at the Seeley G. Mudd Library, Princeton University, New Jersey, Vol. 1, p. 439.

8 Woodrow Wilson, 'Citizens of Foreign Birth. Address to Naturalized Citizens at Convention Hall, Philadelphia', *Selected Addresses and Public Papers of Woodrow Wilson*, ed. Albert Bushnell-Hart, University of the Pacific, Honolulu, 2002, pp. 85–9.

9 'President Wilson's Declaration of War Message to Congress', 2 April 1917, Records of the United States Senate, Record Group 46; National Archives.

SIX

1 Charles E. Lauriat, *The Lusitania's Last Voyage: Being a Narrative of the Torpedoing and Sinking of RMS Lusitania by a German Submarine off the Irish Coast, May 7, 1915, by Charles E. Lauriat Jr., One of the Survivors*, Houghton Mifflin Co., Boston, 1915.

2 Sir Archibald Hurd, *World War I at Sea: Contemporary Accounts, History of the Great War – The Merchant Navy, Vol. I, 1914–Spring 1915*, Part 2, John Murray, London, 1921.

3 Hoehling and Hoehling, *The Last Voyage of the Lusitania*, p. 102.

4 Walter Schwieger's diary is part of the collection of the National Archives: Record Group 45: Naval Records Collection of the Office of Naval Records and Library, 1691–1945; 'Kriegstagebuch S.M.U-Boote U20, Band 3, vom 30.IV bis13.V.15, Kapitänleutnant Schwieger', German Marine Archives.

5 British Wreck Commissioner's Inquiry, Day 2, 16 June 1915, testimony of Leslie Morton, examined by the Solicitor-General.

6 British Wreck Commissioner's Inquiry, Day 3, 17 June 1915, testimony of Albert Arthur Bestwick [*sic*].

7 British Wreck Commissioner's Inquiry, Day 2, 16 June 1915, testimony of Leslie Morton, examined by the Solicitor-General.

8 *The Last Voyage of the Lusitania,* ITV Network First Ltd, National Geographic, Carlton Television, 22 March 1994.

SEVEN

1 George Kessler, 'Looked at His Watch as Torpedo Flashed By', *Cleveland Plain Dealer,* 10 May 1915, p. 2.

2 George Slingbsy, letters to his mother, written from the Hotel Imperial, Cork, and published in *Retford, Gainsborough and Worksop Times, Newark and Mansfield Weekly News*, 28 May 1915 and 11 June 1915. His daughter Nina Slingsby-Smith later published a memoir of her father entitled *George: Memoirs of a Gentleman's Gentleman*, Jonathan Cape, London, 1984.

3 British Wreck Commissioner's Inquiry, Day 2, 16 June 1915, testimony of Arthur Roland [*sic*] Jones, examined by Mr Branson.

4 Charles Lauriat, *The Lusitania's Last Voyage*, p. 70.

5 'Survivors Tell Lurid Tales of Torpedoing and Escape', *The Daily Missoulian*, Missoula, Montana, Sunday, 9 May 1915, p. 1.

6 The Last Word, Letter to Elbert Hubbard II, From Ernest C. Cowper, A Surviving Passenger of the Lusitania', *The Vancouver Province*, Vancouver, BC, 12 March 1916.

7 Charles Lauriat, *The Lusitania's Last Voyage*, p. 71ff.

8 James Brooks, *New York Times*, 10 May 1915, p. 3.

9 *The Daily Missoulian*, Sunday, 9 May 1915.

10 Titanic International Society's *Voyage*, No. 46, Winter 2003–4.

11 Isaac Lehmann, 'My Experiences on the Steamship Lusitania, Friday, May 7, 1915', *New York Times*, 2 June 1915.

12 Hoehling and Hoehling, *The Last Voyage of the Lusitania*, p.116.

13 Ibid.
14 George Kessler, 'Looked at His Watch as Torpedo Flashed By,' *Cleveland Plain Dealer,* p. 2; *New York Times,* 10 May 1915, p. 7; Hoehling and Hoehling, *The Last Voyage of the Lusitania,* p. 114.
15 British Wreck Commissioner's Inquiry, Day 3, 17 June 1915, testimony of Robert J. Timmis.
16 Ibid.
17 Ian Stourton Holbourn, *The Isle of Foula,* Johnson and Greig, Lerwick, Shetland Isles, 1938, p. 248.
18 Ian Stourton Holbourn, *The Isle of Foula,* p. 249.
19 Hoehling and Hoehling, *The Last Voyage of the Lusitania,* p. 114.
20 *New York Times,* 10 May 1915, p. 2.
21 Hoehling and Hoehling, *The Last Voyage of the Lusitania,* p. 137.
22 Margaret Haig Thomas Mackworth, Viscountess Rhondda, *This Was My World,* Macmillan, London, 1933.
23 Ibid.
24 'The Unsinkable Theodate Pope', *Hartford Courant,* 19 May 1996, p. 3.
25 Dr Daniel V. Moore, 'Long Battle in the Water: Surgeon's Vivid Description of Death Cries of Drowning', *New York Times,* 10 May 1915; 'Submarines Seen Two Miles Away: American, With Glasses, Tells Story With Interesting Details
of Sinking', *The Daily Missoulian,* 9 May 1915.
26 Ibid.
27 Ibid.
28 'Joseph L. Myers Returns: New Yorker Was Badly Injured When Lusitania Was Blown Up', *New York Times,* 31 August 1915.
29 'A Manx Lady's Experiences', *Peel City Guardian,* 15 May 1915; *Mona's Herald,* 19 May 1915.
30 Ibid.
31 Item 232, Letter from W. Wilson Burns for Gladys Bilicke, dated 6 March 1916. The Prichard Letters, Imperial War Museum.
32 Extracts from Letters, *Mannin,* Vol. 6, Douglas, Isle of Man, 1915.
33 Ibid.
34 Ibid.
35 Ibid.
36 Charles E. Lauriat, *The Lusitania's Last Voyage,* p. 33ff.
37 Daniel Allen Butler quoted in *The Age of Cunard: A Transatlantic History 1839–2003,* Lighthouse Press, Annapolis, Maryland, 2003, p. 220.

EIGHT

1 Courtmacsherry Lifeboat Station log for 7 May 1915.
2 Ibid.
3 *Mannin,* Vol. 6, 1915.

4 Isaac Lehmann, 'My Experiences on the Steamship Lusitania, Friday, May 7, 1915', *New York Times*, 2 June 1915.
5 British Wreck Commissioner's Inquiry, Day 5, Testimony of Joseph Marichal.
6 Ibid.
7 Ibid.
8 Margaret Gwyer's oil-stained camisole was displayed in the Imperial War Museum's First World War ninetieth anniversary exhibition, September 2008–September 2009.
9 Charles Lauriat, *The Lusitania's Last Voyage*, pp. 40–50.
10 Lehmann, 'My Experiences on the Steamship Lusitania'.
11 Ibid.
12 British Wreck Commissioner's Inquiry, Day 5, testimony of Joseph Marichal.
13 Liam and John Nolan, *Secret Victory: Ireland and the War at Sea 1914–1918*, Mercier Press, Cork, 2009, p. 59ff.

NINE

1 British Wreck Commissioners' Report, Day 1.
2 *Associated Press*, Berlin, 14 May 1915 via Amsterdam to London, 15 May 1915.
3 *Glasgow Evening Citizen*, 17 July 1915, quoted in George Abel Schreiner, *The Iron Ration: Three Years in Warring Central Europe*, Harper and Brothers, New York, 1918, p. 314.
4 Preston, 2002, pp. 415–16.
5 Papers of Lord Mersey, Bignor Park, Sussex.
6 Nigel West, *Historical Dictionary of Naval Intelligence*, Rowman and Littlefield, Lanham, Maryland, 2010, p. 178.
7 Webb memoranda, Lord Mersey's papers, duplicated in P.R.O., ADM / 137 / 1058.
8 Walter Schwieger, 'Kapitänleutnant W., Kriegstagebuch S.M. U-Boote U20, Band 3, vom 30.IV bis13.V.15, Schwieger', German Marine Archives.
9 British Wreck Commissioner's Inquiry, Day 1, Captain William Thomas Turner – recalled, testimony taken *in camera*, further examined by the Attorney-General.
10 British Wreck Commissioner's Inquiry, Day 2, testimony of Hugh Robert Johnston.
11 British Wreck Commissioner's Inquiry, Day 1, testimony of William Thomas Turner, examined by the Attorney-General.
12 Ibid.
13 Ibid.
14 Ibid.
15 Mersey Report, *Loss of the Steamship Lusitania: Report of a Formal Investigation into the Circumstances Attending the Foundering on 7th May,*

1915, of the British Steamship Lusitania, of Liverpool, After Being Torpedoed Off the Old Head of Kinsale, Ireland; presented to both Houses of Parliament by Command of His Majesty, London, and printed under the authority of His Majesty's Stationery Office by Darling and Son Ltd, Bacon Street, London.

TEN

1 British Wreck Commissioner's Inquiry, Day 5, testimony of Joseph Marichal, examined by the Solicitor-General.
2 Ibid.
3 Ibid.
4 British Law Court Reports, *Lusitania Inquiry*, Lord Mersey.
5 Geoff Whitfield, www.encyclopedia-titanica.org, 'Lusitania Passengers and Crew', 27 September 2001.
6 'Sinking Justified, Says Dr Dernburg; Lusitania a "War Vessel," Known to Be Carrying Contraband, Hence Search Was Not Necessary', *New York Times*, 9 May 1915, p. 4.
7 Francis Whiting Halsey, *The Literary Digest History of the World War, Compiled from Original and Contemporary Sources: American, British, French, German, and Others* (10 volumes, 1919–20), Funk and Wagnalls, New York, 1919, p. 255.
8 *New York Times*, 10 May, 1915.
9 *Glasgow Evening Citizen*, 17 July 1915, quoted in Schreiner, 1918, p. 314.
10 Paddy O'Sullivan, *Lusitania: Unravelling the Mysteries*, Collins Press, Dublin, 1998.
11 Erin Mullally, '*Lusitania*'s secret cargo', *Archaeology Archive*, Vol. 62, No. 1, January/February 2009.
12 Hampton and Anne Goodwin Sides, 'Lusitania Rising', *Men's Vogue*, January 2009.
13 Ibid.
14 Steven Danver, *Popular Controversies in World History: Investigating History's Intriguing Questions*, 2010, ABC-Clio, Santa Barbara, California, p. 114.
15 *Associated Press*, San Francisco, 6 February 2014.
16 Ibid.
17 Ibid.
18 Winston Churchill to Walter Runciman, 12 February 1915.
19 Diana Preston, *Wilful Murder: The Sinking of the Lusitania*, Doubleday (reproduced by permission of the Random House Group), London, 2002.
20 David Kahn, *The Codebreakers*, Scribner, New York, 1996.
21 Alan Travis, *Guardian*, 1 May 2014.
22 Ibid.
23 Ibid.
24 Press Association, 1 May 2014.
25 John Arbuthnot Fisher, Admiral of the Fleet, *Memories*, Hodder and Stoughton, London, New York and Toronto, 1919, p. 30.

EPILOGUE

1 Ian Stoughton Holbourn, *The Child of the Moat: A Story for Girls, 1557 AD*, Arnold Shaw, New York, 1916.
2 Thomas A. Reppetto, *Battleground New York City: Countering Spies, Saboteurs, and Terrorists Since 1861*, Potomac Books, Inc., Sterling, Virginia, 2012. Douglas Waller, *Wild Bill Donovan: The Spymaster Who Created the OSS and Modern American Espionage*, Free Press, Simon and Schuster, New York, 2011.
3 Oliver Percy Bernard, *Cocksparrow*, Jonathan Cape, London, 1936.
4 G.W. Kienast, *The Medals of Karl Goetz*, Artus Company, Cleveland, 1967.
5 Werner von Langsdorff, *U-Boote am Feind*, C. Bertelsmann, Munich, 1937, p. 12f.
6 *New York Times*, 8 May 1915, p. 4.
7 'Ireland's West Coast: Special Boats and Big Hearted Sailors', *Afloat Magazine*, Baily Publications (Dun Laoghaire, Dublin), 29 March 2014.

Bibliography

Amory, Phoebe, *The Death of the Lusitania*, Thomas Briggs, Toronto, 1917
Bailey, Thomas A. and Paul B. Ryan, *The Lusitania Disaster: An Episode in Modern Warfare and Diplomacy*, Free Press/Collier Macmillan, New York/London, 1975
Ballard, Robert D., Rick Archold and Ken Marschall, *Lost Liners: From the Titanic to the Andrea Doria*, Hyperion, New York, 1997
Ballard, Robert D. and Spencer Dunmore, *Exploring the Lusitania: Probing the Mysteries of the Sinking That Changed History*, Warner Books/Weidenfeld and Nicolson, New York/London, 1995
Beesley, Patrick, *Room 40: British Naval Intelligence 1914–18*, Harcourt Brace Jovanovich, New York, 1982
Bernard, Oliver Percy, *Cocksparrow*, Jonathan Cape, London, 1936
Butler, Daniel Allen, *The Age of Cunard: A Transatlantic History 1839–2003*, Lighthouse Press, ProStar Publications, Culver City, California, 2003
Butler, Daniel Allen, *The Lusitania: The Life, Loss and Legacy of an Ocean Legend*, Stackpole Books, Mechanicsburg, Pennsylvania, 2000
Chidsey, Donald Barr, *The Day They Sank the Lusitania*, Award Books, New York, 1967
Churchill, Winston S., *The World Crisis*, Vol. 1, Butterworth, London, 1927
Cooper, John Milton, *Woodrow Wilson: A Biography*, Vintage Books, New York, 2009
Corbett, Sir Julian S., *Naval Operations: History of the Great War Based on Official Documents*, Vol. 2, Naval and Military Press, Longmans, Green, London, 1920
Droste, Christian Ludwig (Compiler), W.H. Tantum IV (Editor), *The Lusitania Case*, Documents on the War Series, 1916; Stephens, London, 1972
Ellis, Captain Frederick D., *The Tragedy of the Lusitania*, National Publishing Company, George W. Berton, Washington, DC, 1915
Fitzpatrick, Vincent, *H.L. Mencken*, Mercer University Press, Georgia, 1989
Forgue, Guy J. (Editor), *Letters of H.L. Mencken*, Alfred P. Knopf, New York, 1961
Gentile, Gary, *The Lusitania Controversies*, 2 vols; Vol. 1: *Atrocity of War and a Wreck-Diving History*; Vol. 2: *Dangerous Descents into Shipwrecks and Law*, Gary Gentile Productions, Philadelphia, 1998/9

Hickey, Des and Gus Smith, *Seven Days to Disaster: The Sinking of the Lusitania*, Collins, London, 1981
Hobsbawm, Eric, *The Age of Empire: 1875–1914*, Weidenfeld, London, 1987
Hoehling, Adolph A. and Mary Duprey Hoehling, *The Last Voyage of the Lusitania*, Henry Holt and Company, New York, 1956
Holbourn, Ian B. Stoughton, *The Isle of Foula* and *Memoir* by Marion C. Holbourn, Johnson and Greig, 1938 (reprinted by Birlinn Books, Edinburgh, 2001)
Holbourn, Ian Stoughton, *The Child of the Moat: A Story for Girls, 1557 AD*, Arnold Shaw, New York, 1916
Kahn, David, *The Codebreakers*, 2nd edn, Scribner, New York, 1996
Kienast, G.W., *The Medals of Karl Goetz*, Artus Company, Cleveland, 1967
Langensiepen, Bernd, 'Die Legende von Karl Vögeles "Meuterei" auf U 20', in *Marine-Nachrichtenblatt. Das Veröffentlichungsblatt des Arbeitskreises Krieg zur See 1914–18*, Vol. 8, No. 3, Stuttgart, 2012
Langsdorff, Werner von, *U-Boote am Feind*, C. Bertelsmann, Munich, 1937
Lauriat, Charles E., *The Lusitania's Last Voyage*, Houghton Mifflin and Company, Boston, 1915
Layton, J. Kent, *Lusitania: An Illustrated Biography of the Ship of Splendor.* Amberley Publishing, Stroud, 2010
Lehman, Isaac, 'My Experiences on the Steamship Lusitania, Friday, May 7, 1915', *New York Times*, 2 June 1915
Levine, Lawrence W., *Defender of the Faith: William Jennings Bryan, the Last Decade, 1915–1925*, Harvard University Press, Boston, 1965
Link, Arthur, *Woodrow Wilson and the Progressive Era 1910–1917*, New American Nation Series, Harper and Brothers, New York, 1954
Mackworth, Margaret Haig Thomas, *This Was My World*, Macmillan and Company, New York, 1933
Magee, Malcolm, 'Review of Robert W. Tucker, *Woodrow Wilson and the Great War: Reconsidering America's Neutrality, 1914–1917*' (University Press of Virginia, Charlottesville, 2007), http://www.amazon.com/exec/obidos/ASIN/0813926297.
Massie, Robert K., *Castles of Steel: Britain, Germany and the Winning of the Great War at Sea*, Cape, London, 2004
Mencken, H.L., *A Mencken Chrestomathy*, Alfred P. Knopf, New York, 1949
Moloney, Senan, *Lusitania: An Irish Tragedy*, Mercier Press, Cork, 2004
Morrison, Sophia, and William Cubbon (Editors), *Mannin: Journal of Matters Past and Present Relating to Man*, Manx Society, Yn Cheshaght Ghailckagh, Douglas, Isle of Man, 1913–17
Nolan, Liam, and John Nolan, *Secret Victory: Ireland and the War at Sea, 1914–1918*, Mercier Press, Cork, 2009
O'Sullivan, Patrick, *The Lusitania: Unravelling the Mysteries*, Collins Press, Cork, 1998
Peeke, Mitch, Kevin Walsh-Johnson and Steve Jones, *The Lusitania Story*, US Naval Institute Press, Annapolis, Maryland, 2003
Preston, Diana, *Lusitania: An Epic Tragedy*, Walker and Company, London, 2002

Preston, Diana, *Remember the Lusitania*, Raincoast Book Distribution, Vancouver, British Columbia, 2003

Preston, Diana, *Wilful Murder: The Sinking of the 'Lusitania'*, Doubleday, London, 2002

Ramsay, David, *Lusitania: Saga and Myth,* Chatham Publishing, London, 2001

Reppetto, Thomas A., *Battleground New York City: Countering Spies, Saboteurs, and Terrorists Since 1861*, Potomac Books, Inc., Sterling, Virginia, 2012

von Rintelen, Franz, *The Dark Invader: Wartime Reminiscences of a German Naval Intelligence Officer*, Routledge, New York, 1998

Sauder, Eric, *RMS Lusitania: the Ship and Her Record,* History Press, Stroud, 2009

Schmidt, Donald E., *The Folly of War: American Foreign Policy, 1898–2005*, Algora Publishing, New York, 2005

Schreiner, George Abel, *The Iron Ration: Three Years in Warring Central Europe*, Harper and Brothers, New York, 1918

Schwieger, Kapitänleutnant Walther von, *War Diary*, in National Archives: Record Group 45: Naval Records Collection of the Office of Naval Records and Library, 1691–1945; 'Kriegstagebuch S.M.U-boat U20, Band 3, vom 30. IV bis13.V.15, Kapitänleutnant Schwieger', German Marine Archives, 30 April–13 May 1915.

Simpson, Colin, *The Lusitania*, Longmans, London, 1972

Slingsby-Smith, Nina, *George, Memoirs of a Gentleman's Gentleman*, Jonathan Cape, London, 1984

Thompson, John, *Woodrow Wilson,* Longmans, London, 2002

Tuchman, Barbara, *The Zimmermann Telegram,* Ballantine Books, New York, 1958

Walker, Alistair, *Four Thousand Lives Lost: The Inquiries of Lord Mersey into the Sinkings of the Titanic, the Empress of Ireland, the Falaba and the Lusitania*, History Press, Stroud, 2012

Waller, Douglas, *Wild Bill Donovan: The Spymaster Who Created the OSS and Modern American Espionage*, Free Press, Simon and Schuster, New York, 2011

West, Nigel, *Historical Dictionary of Naval Intelligence,* Rowman and Littlefield, Lanham, Maryland, 2010

Yount, Lisa, *Robert Ballard: Explorer and Undersea Archaeologist,* Chelsea House, New York, 2009

Index

Aigh Vie, 214
Albert, Dr Heinrich, German spymaster in USA, 51, 53, 54, 55, 56, 57
Allan, Lady Marguerite (survivor), 123
Amory, Phoebe (survivor), 111
Anderson, Barbara (child survivor), 80, 124, 154, 207, 215
Anderson, Emily (survivor), 80, 124, 154, 215
Anderson, Captain James, Staff Captain, *Lusitania* (lost), 68, 71, 78, 79, 110, 112, 119, 128, 181
Aspinall, Butler, K.C., lawyer for Cunard, 172, 187
Austro-Hungary, 45, 47

Bailey, Frederick (survivor), 145, 207
Balfour, Arthur J., British politician, 31
Ball, Stanley, *Wanderer*, 11, 157
Ball, William, skipper, *Wanderer*, 11, 118, 157, 158, 162–3, 214, 215, 217
Ballard, Robert, former US naval officer and professor of oceanography, 192
Barnes, William, saloon cabin bed steward, *Lusitania* (survivor), 135
Bartzke, Ralf, expert on U-boats, 99, 101
Battenberg, Prince Louis, replaced as British First Sea Lord, 30
Behncke, Admiral Paul, Imperial German Navy, 173
Beesley, Patrick, author, 176
Belgium, 43, 47, 85
Bemis, Gregg, diver and owner of the wreck of *Lusitania*, 190–2
Beresford, Admiral Lord Charles, British Admiral, 28
Berlin, 177
Bernard, Clinton 'Bill' (survivor), 132
Bernard, Oliver (survivor), architect and designer, 82, 90, 111, 112, 131, 132, 133, 145, 208
Bernstorff, Count Johann Heinrich von, German Ambassador to the USA, 49, 50, 58, 61–2, 106, 209
Bestic, Albert, Third Officer, *Lusitania* (survivor), 71, 112, 116, 117, 119, 120, 177, 213, 214
Bethmann-Hollweg, Theobald von, Chancellor of Germany, 1909–17, 211
Bilborough, George (survivor), 84
Bilicke, Albert (lost), 90, 152, 153
Bilicke, Gladys (survivor), 90, 152, 153
Bird, Marion 'May' (survivor), 156, 206
Bismarck, Otto von, Minister-President of Prussia, 1862–90, 16, 17

Black Tom Island, munitions depot in New York Harbor, 58, 59, 62
Bloomfield, Thomas (lost), 132
Blue Riband, 15, 16, 67
Bluebell, 168, 174, 208, 213
Booth, Alfred, Chairman, Cunard, 114, 213
Boulton, Harold (survivor), 82, 85
Boy-Ed, Captain Karl, German Naval Attaché, USA, 50, 55, 57, 59, 60, 78
Braithwaite, Dorothy (lost), 86
Brandell, Josephine, opera star (survivor), 76, 77, 110, 111, 155, 207
Brierley, Captain Thomas, master of the *Flying Fish*, 162–4
Brock, patrol boat, 148
Brooks, James (survivor), 124, 128, 129, 157
Brown, John and Co., shipbuilders, 18, 19, 20, 80
Bryan, William Jennings, US Secretary of State, 40–3, 47, 48, 82, 104
Buchanan, Frank, US Congressman, 51
Burden, Ellen (survivor), 154
Burke, Frank, US agent, 54, 55, 56
Butler, George Ley Pearce (Vernon), singer (lost), 76
Butler, Inez, 76

Candidate, British vessel sunk by *U-20*, 95, 96, 114, 196
Carson, Sir Edward, Attorney-General, 172, 173, 174, 178, 179, 180, 181
Cayo Romano, vessel escaped *U-20,* 94, 196
Centurion, British vessel sunk by *U-20*, 96, 114, 196
Churchill, Sir Winston, First Lord of the Admiralty, 9, 10, 30, 31, 33, 46, 78, 112, 175, 180, 194, 195, 196, 197, 198, 199, 203, 213, 214
Cobb, Frank I., editor, *New York World*, 56
Cobh (Queenstown), Ireland, 96, 101, 102, 103, 110, 114, 116, 118, 130, 137, 148, 150, 153, 157–66, 168, 174–8, 182, 203, 207
Coke, Vice-Admiral Charles H., 96, 101, 114–16, 174, 175, 176, 178, 182, 195
Collins shipping line, 15
Conner, Dorothy (survivor), 72, 89, 117, 143, 146
Conners, Maurice, bomber, 52
Coombes, Jim, senior lawyer, Treasury, 202
Costain, Harry, *Wanderer*, 11, 157, 215
Courtmacsherry lifeboat, 161, 162
Cowper, Ernest (survivor), 88, 89, 125, 127, 133, 134
Cox, Desmond (infant survivor), 151, 152, 154
Cox, Margaret (survivor), 151, 152, 154
Crichton, Mabel (lost), 76
Crompton family (lost), 77
'Cruiser Rules', 32, 33, 34, 36, 104
Cunard, shipping line, 9, 13, 14, 15, 17, 18, 19, 20, 21, 22, 64, 65, 66, 67, 68, 72, 75, 80, 99, 103, 110, 114, 137, 156, 160, 164, 166, 167, 168, 169, 172, 174, 182, 185, 186, 187, 188, 189, 195, 200, 205, 206, 209, 213
Cunard, Samuel, shipping magnate, 13, 15, 17
Cunliffe, Sir Ellis, solicitor for the Board of Trade, 182

Danver, Steven, historian, 192
Dardanelles, 192
Davies, Captain D., merchant navy, assessor at the *Lusitania* inquiry, 172
Davies, John, bo'sun, *Lusitania* (survivor), 134
Davis, Emily (survivor), 86, 87, 123
Dearbergh, Robert (lost), 81, 82, 132
Depage, Marie (lost), 85, 89, 144, 145, 146, 147

Dernburg, Dr Bernhard, former German Colonial Secretary, 188
Docherty, Mabel (survivor), 208
Docherty, Thomas (child survivor), 208
Dolphin, Avis (child survivor), 81, 125, 139, 140, 167, 206
Donald, Archibald (survivor), 84, 125, 127, 143
Dow, Daniel, former Captain of *Lusitania*, 10
Dow, Michael, grandson of Daniel Dow, 10
Drew, John, friend of Charles Frohmann, 70
Duckworth, Elizabeth (survivor), 141, 156–7, 167, 207

Earl of Latham, British schooner sunk by *U-20*, 94, 169, 196
Edward VII, King of England, 1901–10, 27
Ehrhardt, Herbert (survivor), 126
Ellis, Hilda (lost), 139
Empress of India, sank in the St Lawrence River, 1914, 87
'Entente Powers', 60
Every, Mabel, companion of Captain William Turner, 68, 213, 214

Fish family (survivors), 142
Fisher, Admiral of the Fleet John 'Jackie' Arbuthnot, Baron F. of Kilverstone, 23, 24, 27, 28, 29, 30, 31, 33, 34, 89, 174, 175, 196, 198, 199, 204
Fisher, Dr Howard, physician, (survivor), 72, 117, 143
Flying Fish, paddle steamer, 137, 157, 158, 159, 162, 163, 165
Flynn, William J., Chief, American Secret Service, 54, 55, 56
Forde, Rev. William, Hon. Secretary, Courtmacsherry lifeboat, 161
Forman, Justus Miles, writer (lost), 70, 71, 76, 110
France, 42, 45, 49, 53, 59, 68, 72, 89, 197, 198, 205, 206, 207, 212
Franz Ferdinand, Archduke, 47
Freeman, Matthew (survivor), 146, 147, 146–9
Freeman, Richard, engineer (lost), 144–5
French, Grace (survivor), 84
French, Sir John, Field Marshal, Commander-in-Chief, British Expeditionary Force, 198
Friend, Edwin, professor (lost), 77, 109, 145, 146, 147
Frohman, Charles, impresario (lost), 69–71, 75, 76, 87, 110 123, 131, 138
Fuchs, George, German spy, 57

Gallipoli, 30, 175
Galt, Edith Bolling, second wife of President Woodrow Wilson, 48–9, 61
Gauntlett, Frederic, shipbuilder (survivor), 109, 124, 128, 129
Gell, William, *Wanderer*, 11
George V, King of England, 217
Georgic, 192
Gerard, James, US Ambassador to Germany, 60, 61
Germany, 15, 16, 17, 18, 20, 23-30, 32, 34, 35, 36, 37, 39, 42, 43, 44–50, 54, 54, 60–3, 92, 94, 104, 112, 126, 171, 183, 185, 188, 194, 195, 197, 200, 203, 204, 210, 211, 212
Goetz, Karl, Bavarian medallist, 208–11
Goltz, Horst von der (Franz Wachendorf), German counter-intelligence agent, 52, 53
Grab, Oscar (survivor), 124
Grant, Chastina (lost), 128
Grant, Montagu (lost), 128
Grasmere, wrecked off N. Ireland, 65
Grey, Sir Edward, British Foreign Secretary, 45, 46, 47, 48, 82
Gwyer, Rev. Herbert (survivor), 84, 125, 150, 154, 165, 205
Gwyer, Margaret (survivor), 84, 125, 150, 151–2, 154, 165, 205

Hall, Captain William Reginald 'Blinker', Director of British Naval Intelligence, 198, 199, 210
Hamburg-Amerika shipping line, 15, 16, 54, 56, 57
Hampshire, Elizabeth 'Nellie' (survivor), 133, 134
Harkness, William, Assistant Purser (survivor), 125, 134, 154, 155, 207
Hass, Rickey, Deputy Inspector General, US Energy Department, 193
HMS *Aboukir*, 'livebait' squadron, 9
HMS *Ajax*, 58
HMS *Cressy*, 'livebait' squadron, 9
HMS *Dreadnought*, 27
HMS *Duke of Edinburgh*, 176
HMS *Gloucester*, 176
HMS *Hogue*, 'livebait' squadron, 9
HMS *Juno*, *Lusitania*'s naval escort, 9, 68, 96, 97, 170, 171, 178
Hearn, Lieutenant-Commander H.J., assists at *Lusitania* inquiry, 172
Hefford, Percy, 2nd Officer, *Lusitania* (lost), 71, 130, 141
Held, Martha, kept a 'safe house' for German spies in Manhattan, 53
Hellespont, Merchant Fleet Auxiliary tug, 176
Henderson, George, observed the sinking from the coast, 121
Heron, 168
Hobsbawm, Eric, historian, 17
Hoehling, Adolph A., US judge and author, 207
Hoehling, Mary, author, 207
Hogg, Ellen (survivor), 142
Holbourn, Professor Ian, writer (survivor), 80, 81, 110, 125, 139, 140, 142, 167, 206
Holbourn, Marion, writer, 81, 206
Hollmann, Friedrich von, German State Secretary of the Navy, 25, 26
Hood, Rear Admiral Sir Horace, 178
Hook family (survivors), 113
Horgan, John J., Coroner, Co. Cork, Ireland, 168, 169, 170, 178
Houghton, Dr James (survivor), 85, 144, 145, 146, 147
House, 'Colonel' Edward, adviser of President Wilson, 44–8, 56
Hubbard, Alice (lost), 88, 126, 127
Hubbard, Elbert, writer, artist, philosopher, 72, 88, 89, 126, 127, 156
Huerta, Victoriano, President of Mexico, 52, 68
'Hunger Blockade', 34

Ignatieff, Count Alexis, Russian military attaché, Paris, 58
Inglefield, Admiral Sir F.S., member of the official inquiry into the disaster, 172, 181, 182, 184
Inverclyde, James Cleland Burns, 3rd Baron, Chairman of Cunard, 17, 18, 19
Inverclyde, Lady Mary, 19
Isle of Man, 10, 11, 152, 163, 216, 217

Jackson, Admiral Sir Henry B., succeeds Fisher as First Sea Lord, 31
Jackson, Thornton (lost), 84
James, Violet (survivor), 152, 153
Jenkins, Francis Bertram (survivor), 77
Johnston, Hugh, Quartermaster, *Lusitania* (survivor), 130, 174, 177
Jolivet, Rita, actress and film star (survivor), 71, 75, 76, 110, 111, 124, 144, 206, 207
Jones, Arthur Rowland, First Officer, *Lusitania* (survivor), 71, 91, 118, 124, 130, 137, 206

Kalafus, Jim, *Lusitania* researcher, 10
Kay, Marguerite (lost), 89, 131–2
Kay, Robert, young son of Marguerite Kay (survivor), 89, 131–32
Keller, Helen, author and political activist, 205
Kessler, George, 'champagne king', millionaire (survivor), 69, 90, 91, 109, 110, 123, 134, 137, 138, 205

Kienast, G.W., medals expert, 211
Kingston, Professor William, adjunct professor, Trinity College, Dublin, 190
Kinsale, Co. Cork, Ireland, 12, 36, 93, 103, 116, 118, 121, 128, 157, 162, 168, 172, 177, 180, 190, 199
Klein, Charles, playwright (lost), 76, 110
Kleist, Captain Charles von, German spy, 58, 59
Kludas, Arnold, maritime historian, museum director, 72
Knockaloe, Isle of Man, internment camp, 217
Knox, Samuel, arms dealer (survivor), 109, 128, 129
Koenig, Paul, head of US detective agency, 56, 57
Kristoff, Michael, suspected of sabotage, 59
Kueck, Otto, German consul in Mexico, 52

Lamar, David, 'the Wolf of Wall Street', conman, 51
Lane, Sir Hugh, art collector and philanthropist (lost), 85, 86
Langensiepen, Bernd, German author and marine historian, 99
Langsdorff, Werner von, German author and marine military historian, 204, 211
Lansing, Robert, US Under-Secretary of State, 48, 56
Lassetter, Elisabeth (survivor), 85
Lassetter, Frederic (survivor), 85
Lauriat, Charles (survivor), 91, 109, 114, 124, 126, 127, 128, 129, 136, 151, 158, 163, 166
Law, Andrew Bonar, British politician, 31
Lawrence Livermore National Laboratory, 193, 194
Lawrenny Castle SA-52, armed naval trawler, 95, 96
Leach, John Neil, waiter (lost), 78, 79
Lehmann, Isaac, export broker (survivor), 91, 109, 124, 134, 135, 136, 137, 154, 164, 166–7, 206
Lewis, John Idwal, Senior 3rd Officer, *Lusitania* (survivor), 72, 116, 118, 123, 124, 129, 156
Light, John, US diver, 190, 191
Lindsey, William, Boston millionaire, 82, 112, 159
'livebait' theory, 9, 10, 182, 194, 196, 197
Liverpool, 9, 10, 18, 37, 58, 64, 65, 67, 78, 91, 92, 94, 95, 104, 113, 114, 116, 117, 133, 138, 172, 177, 179, 180, 182, 183, 190, 195, 213
Liverpool Shipwreck and Humane Society, 65, 67
Lohmann, Johann, managing director at Norddeutscher Lloyd, 16
Luker, Francis, survivor, 140, 141, 206, 208
Lund, Sarah Mounsey, survivor, 87, 138, 139, 156
Lusitania
  Admiralty subsidy, 13, 15, 18, 21
  building and design of, 14, 18, 19, 21, 73, 74, 75, 79, 80, 100, 197
  captains, 10, 12, 64, 64, 68 *and see* Turner
  crew, 22, 68, 71, 7, 90, 91, 103, 109, 120, 121, 128, 134, 136, 139, 143, 150, 151, 154, 169, 173, 182, 183, 186, 192, 200, 213
  livery, 22, 69, 156
  lifeboats, 22, 69, 90, 103, 109, 111, 119, 120, 128, 136, 137, 138, 143, 144, 145, 146, 148, 149, 150, 151, 152, 157, 159, 162, 166, 168, 183, 200
  loss inquiry, 10, 116, 118, 119, 171, 172, 173, 175, 177, 179, 180, 181, 182, 183, 185, 186, 187, 200, 202, 212, 213
  medals, 208, 209, 210, 211

reaction to loss, 12, 37, 41, 47, 60, 79, 99, 103, 155, 160, 168, 179, 196, 202, 203, 204, 217
shakedown trials, 19
sinking, 41, 47, 60, 99, 105, 107, 138, 160, 162, 199, 202, 203, 206, 207, 210, 213, 216, 217

McAdoo, William G., US Secretary of the Treasury, 56
McCubbin, James, Chief Purser, *Lusitania* (lost), 83, 90, 91, 135
McDermott, Dr James, Ship's Surgeon, *Lusitania* (lost), 135
McDonald, John, *Wanderer*, 11, 118, 157
McGarry, Eoin, diver and maritime historian, 190
Mackworth, Lady Margaret, later Viscountess Rhondda (survivor), 77, 89, 117, 143, 146
Maienschien, Dr Jon, Livermore Laboratory, California, 194
Malone, Dudley Field, Collector of Customs for the Port of New York, 79, 188
Marichal, Jessie Emerson (survivor), 164, 168, 185, 215
Marichal, Joseph (survivor), 164, 165, 168, 185, 186, 187, 199, 205
Marshall, Noel, Foreign Office, North America Office, 201, 202, 203
Mason, Leslie Lindsey (lost), 82, 112, 160
Mason, Stewart (lost), 82, 112
Mayer, Judge Julius, American lawyer, politician and judge, 181, 189, 202
Medbury, Maurice Benjamin (lost), 134–5
Mencken, H.L., American journalist, scholar and satirist, 40
Mersey, John Bigham, 1st Viscount, QC, British jurist and politician in charge of inquiry, 10, 119, 172, 173, 174, 179, 181, 182, 183, 184, 185, 186, 187, 188–9, 200, 202, 212, 213
Mexican Civil War, 42
Mexico, 50, 52, 68
Middleton, Alice (survivor), 72, 84, 130, 131
Mitchell, Arthur Jackson (survivor), 110, 142
Moodie, Ralph (lost), 137
Moore, Dr Daniel (survivor), 148, 149, 180
Morecroft, Fannie (survivor), 156, 205, 206, 207,
Morgan, J. Pierpoint, tycoon, 17
Morrison, Charles, merchant, Peel, Isle of Man, 11, 158, 214
Morton, Leslie, A.B., 119, 121, 128, 129, 151
Mounsey, William (lost), 87, 138
Murphy, Patrick, Co. Galway, *Wanderer*, 215
Myers, Joseph, survivor, 150

Naish, Belle (survivor), 82
Naish, Theodore (lost), 82
Napier, Robert, marine engineer, 14
National Geographic, 193
Nelson, Admiral Lord Horatio, 27, 28
Neilson, Gerda (survivor), 113
Nicholson, Sir Arthur, British diplomat and politician, 42
Nicholson, Harry, British Min. of Defence, 203
Norddeutscher Lloyd shipping, 15, 16

O'Connell, John, fireman, *Lusitania*, (survivor), 179
O'Gorman, James A., US Senator, 79
Oliver, Admiral Henry, Director, British Naval Intelligence, 195
Ordiana, 192
Orr-Lewis, Frederick (survivor), 86, 87, 123
O'Sullivan, Paddy, diver, author and maritime historian, 189
Owens, Cecelia (survivor), 125

Page, Walter Hines, US Ambassador to Britain, 45, 198
Papen, Captain Franz von, German military attaché, 50, 53, 55, 56, 57, 59, 60
Pappadopolou, Angela (survivor), 160
Pappadopoulou, Michael (lost), 113
Partridge, patrol boarding vessel, 113
Pavey, Lorna (survivor), 84, 125, 126
Pearson, Sir Arthur, newspaper magnate, philanthropist, 205
Pearson, Dr Fred (lost), 86, 87, 88, 109
Pearson, Mabel (lost), 86, 87, 88, 109
Peel, Isle of Man, 11, 152, 157, 163, 214, 215, 216, 217
Peskett, Leonard, Senior Naval Architect, Cunard, 9
'Phenol Plot', 51, 56
Phillips, Wallace Banta (survivor), 76, 142, 206
Pierpoint, Inspector William, Liverpool City Police (survivor), 78, 151
Piper, John P., Chief Officer, *Lusitania* (lost), 116, 129, 141, 181
Plamondon, Charles (lost), 90, 111
Plamondon, Mary (lost), 90, 111
Pohl, Admiral Hugo von, Commander-in-Chief, German High Seas Fleet, 35
Poirier, Michael, maritime historian, 207
Pope, Theodate, US architect (survivor), 77, 109, 111, 145, 146
Poppe, Johannes, German architect and interior designer, 16
Preston, Diana, historian, 174, 198
Prichard, Richard Preston (lost), 84, 131
Princip, Gavrilo, Serbian assassin, 47
Prussia, 15, 17, 24, 53
Pye, Charlotte (survivor), 111, 131
Pye, Marjorie, infant (lost), 111, 131

Quigley, Des, technical diver, 190–1
Quinn, Thomas, A.B., *Lusitania* (survivor), 119

RMS *Aquitania*, 19, 68
RMS *Mauretania*, 18, 19, 20, 21, 67, 70, 100, 117
RMS *Titanic*, 70, 73, 76, 87, 89, 91, 137, 155, 172, 186
Raglan, George Fitzroy Somerset, 3rd Baron, Governor, Isle of Man, 163
Rankin, Robert (survivor), 208, 132, 133
Rhys-Evans, Arnold, Secretary to D.A. Thomas (survivor), 208
Ricklin, M.A., Professor, University of Strasbourg, 97
Rintelen, Captain Franz von, German spy, 50, 51, 52, 57–8, 59
Rittenberg, Henry R., American artist, 82
Robinson, Emily (lost), 77, 146
Roper, Jack, A.B., *Lusitania* (survivor), 174
Runciman, Walter, President British Board of Trade, 194
Russia, Russians, 25, 26, 45, 46, 47, 53, 58, 76, 138
Rutherford, Ernest, physicist, 29–30
Ryerson, Mary Amelia (lost), 86, 87

Salisbury, Robert Gascoyne-Cecil, 3rd Marquess, British statesman, 26
Sargeaunt, Bertram E., Government Secretary and Treasurer, Isle of Man, 10–11
Scadaun, yacht, 176
Scheele, Dr Walter, chemist and bomb-maker, 51, 57, 58, 59
Scott, Alice (lost), 141, 167
Scott, Arthur (child survivor), 141
Schwarcz, Max (lost), 77
Schwieger, Kapitänleutnant Walther, Commander, German U-boat *U-20*
- career, 93, 94, 211,
- operations, 95, 96, 97, 114, 115, 195
- death, 212
- war diary, 97, 99, 100, 101, 102, 103, 104, 177

mission, 92, 93,
attack on *Lusitania*, 97, 99, 100, 101, 102, 103, 107, 117, 160, 197, 211
Seaver, Lynda, spokesperson, Livermore Laboratory, California, 193
Selborne, William Palmer, 2nd Earl, British politician, 26, 31
Sellmer, Friedrich, Chief engine room artificer, *U-20*, 97, 117
Serbia, 47
Skibbereen, Co. Cork, Ireland, 215, 216
Slidell, Thomas, journalist (survivor), 69, 156
Slingsby, George (survivor), 86, 87, 123
Smith, Frederick E., 172, 182
Smith, Helen (child survivor), 125, 127, 133, 134
Smith, Sarah (lost), 139
Spedding, Captain J., merchant navy, assessor at *Lusitania* inquiry, 172
Speidel, Maximilian, Freiherr von, Bavarian General, Bavarian War Ministry, 210
Spring-Rice, Ambassador Sir Cecil, British Ambassador to the USA, 42
SS *Arabic*, 36, 47, 96, 192
SS *Cameronia*, 72, 84
SS *Cherbourg*, 65
SS *Friedrich der Grosse*, 16, 51
SS *Noordam*, 59
SS *Phoebus*, 58
SS *Sussex*, 60
Stahl, Gustav, 79
Star of the East, three-masted barque, Turner's first command, 66
Stackhouse, Commander J., explorer (lost), 81, 82
Stainton, William (lost), 87, 123
Steinmetz, Erich von, German spy, 57
Stephens, Frances (lost), 86
Stephens, John, infant (lost), 86
Stones, Hilda (lost), 113, 142
Stones, Norman (survivor), 142
Straus, Ida, lost on *Titanic*, 89
Straus, Isidor, tycoon, lost on *Titanic*, 89
Sullivan, Florence (survivor), 82, 83, 88
Sullivan, Julia (survivor), 82, 83, 88
Sumner, Charles, New York representative of Cunard, 64

Tauscher, Captain Hans, Krupp representative in New York, 53
Taylor, Harold (survivor), 151, 165, 166
Taylor, Lucy (survivor), 151, 165, 166
Terry, Ellen, actress, 71, 75
Thomas, David, Welsh industrialist and politician (survivor), 77, 89, 117, 143, 208
Thorsminde, Denmark, 212
Thummel, Kurt, German in employ of German military attaché to the USA, 79
Timmis, Robert (survivor), 113, 137, 138, 139
Tirpitz, Admiral Alfred von, Secretary of State, Imperial German Navy, 23, 24, 25, 26, 27, 28, 29, 31, 39, 46, 60, 62, 103, 204
'Treasure Quest', television programme, 191
Tunney, Thomas, Inspector, New York City Police Department, 58
Turner, Captain William, master of the *Lusitania*
youth, 64
career, 66, 67, 68, 212
heroism, 65, 67, 214
family, 64, 67, 68, 212, 213
in command of the *Lusitania*, 22, 64, 67–9, 71, 72, 90, 91, 97, 101, 110, 111, 113–20, 128, 159, 168, 176, 177, 178, 183, 213
scapegoated, 12, 168, 170, 171, 172–5, 179, 180, 181, 182, 198, 199, 200
visited by Bestic, 213, 214
Turner, Alice Hitching, wife of Captain William Turner, 67, 68, 212

Turner, Norman, son of Captain William Turner, 68, 212
Turner, Percy, son of Captain William Turner, 68, 212, 214

U-1, 20
U-9, 9
U-20
construction, 94
'kills', 95, 96, 114, 169, 176, 195, 196
mission, 93, 94
alleged insubordination, 97, 98
sinks *Lusitania*, 97, 99, 101, 103, 115, 117, 140, 175, 185, 211
destroyed, 212
U-24, 47
U-88, Schwieger's last command, 212
United States of America, 16, 18, 34, 35, 40, 42, 43, 44, 45, 48, 49, 50, 52, 54, 56, 60, 61, 82, 83, 85, 105, 106, 189, 192, 194, 197, 201, 202, 211

Vanderbilt, Alfred, tycoon (lost), 69, 70, 71, 111, 131, 138, 156
Veals, Agnes (survivor), 145, 147, 207
Veals, Albert (survivor), 145, 207
Victor-Emmanuel, King of Italy, 17
Victoria, Queen of England, 1837–1901, 24, 25, 27
Viereck, George Sylvester, Germanophile conspirator, 54, 56
Villa, Pancho, revolutionary Mexican general, 52, 142
Vögele, Carl-Alfons, stoker on German torpedo boat *S-142*, 98
Vögele, Charles, mythological mutineer on *U-20*, 97, 98

Walker, Annie (lost), 86, 87, 123
Wanderer, fishing vessel, 11, 104, 118, 121, 130, 137, 156–8, 162, 163, 164, 165, 167, 181, 186, 206–8, 214, 215, 216, 217
Watt, Captain Jim, master of the *Lusitania*, succeeded by Captain William Turner, 67
Watterson, Robert, the *Wanderer*, 11
Webb, Captain Richard, British Admiralty Trade Division, 170, 174, 175, 180, 199
Weisbach, Raimund, Oberleutnant, *U-20*, 97, 99
Welland Canal, attack on, 52, 56, 57
Welsh, John (survivor), 113
White Star Line, 17, 36, 57, 70, 73, 96, 162
Whitehead, Florence (survivor), 133
Whitfield, Geoff, British Titanic Society, 186
Wickings-Smith, Nancy (infant survivor), 140, 208
Wickings-Smith, Phyllis (survivor), 140, 208
Wilhelm II, Kaiser of Germany and King of Prussia 1888–1918, 16, 17, 23, 24, 25, 26, 31, 34, 36, 39, 44, 45, 46, 53, 54, 60, 61, 62, 72, 89, 103, 104, 126, 188, 204, 211
Williams, Annie (lost with four of her children), 85
Wilson, Ellen Axson, first wife of President Woodrow Wilson, 48
Wilson, John (survivor), 84, 126
Wilson, Thomas Woodrow, President of the USA, 1913–21, 39–49, 54, 56, 61, 79, 82, 88, 104–6, 194
Winter, Herman, Assistant Manager, Cunard, 189
Withington, Lothrop, geologist (lost), 91, 166
Wolfenden, Dora (survivor),147
Wolfenden, John (lost), 147
Woods, Thomas, the *Wanderer*, 11, 118, 158, 216
Wynne, Harry, Crown Solicitor for Co. Cork, 170

Zimmermann, Robert, German naval architect, 15

SOME AUTHORS WE HAVE PUBLISHED

James Agee • Bella Akhmadulina • Tariq Ali • Kenneth Allsop • Alfred Andersch
Guillaume Apollinaire • Machado de Assis • Miguel Angel Asturias • Duke of Bedford
Oliver Bernard • Thomas Blackburn • Jane Bowles • Paul Bowles • Richard Bradford
Ilse, Countess von Bredow • Lenny Bruce • Finn Carling • Blaise Cendrars • Marc Chagall
Giorgio de Chirico • Uno Chiyo • Hugo Claus • Jean Cocteau • Albert Cohen
Colette • Ithell Colquhoun • Richard Corson • Benedetto Croce • Margaret Crosland
e.e. cummings • Stig Dalager • Salvador Dalí • Osamu Dazai • Anita Desai
Charles Dickens • Bernard Diederich • Fabián Dobles • William Donaldson
Autran Dourado • Yuri Druzhnikov • Lawrence Durrell • Isabelle Eberhardt
Sergei Eisenstein • Shusaku Endo • Erté • Knut Faldbakken • Ida Fink
Wolfgang George Fischer • Nicholas Freeling • Philip Freund • Carlo Emilio Gadda
Rhea Galanaki • Salvador Garmendia • Michel Gauquelin • André Gide
Natalia Ginzburg • Jean Giono • Geoffrey Gorer • William Goyen • Julien Gracq
Sue Grafton • Robert Graves • Angela Green • Julien Green • George Grosz
Barbara Hardy • H.D. • Rayner Heppenstall • David Herbert • Gustaw Herling
Hermann Hesse • Shere Hite • Stewart Home • Abdullah Hussein • King Hussein of Jordan
Ruth Inglis • Grace Ingoldby • Yasushi Inoue • Hans Henny Jahnn • Karl Jaspers
Takeshi Kaiko • Jaan Kaplinski • Anna Kavan • Yasunuri Kawabata • Nikos Kazantzakis
Orhan Kemal • Christer Kihlman • James Kirkup • Paul Klee • James Laughlin
Patricia Laurent • Violette Leduc • Lee Seung-U • Vernon Lee • József Lengyel
Robert Liddell • Francisco García Lorca • Moura Lympany • Thomas Mann
Dacia Maraini • Marcel Marceau • André Maurois • Henri Michaux • Henry Miller
Miranda Miller • Marga Minco • Yukio Mishima • Quim Monzó • Margaret Morris
Angus Wolfe Murray • Atle Næss • Gérard de Nerval • Anaïs Nin • Yoko Ono
Uri Orlev • Wendy Owen • Arto Paasilinna • Marco Pallis • Oscar Parland
Boris Pasternak • Cesare Pavese • Milorad Pavic • Octavio Paz • Mervyn Peake
Carlos Pedretti • Dame Margery Perham • Graciliano Ramos • Jeremy Reed
Rodrigo Rey Rosa • Joseph Roth • Ken Russell • Marquis de Sade • Cora Sandel
Iván Sándor • George Santayana • May Sarton • Jean-Paul Sartre
Ferdinand de Saussure • Gerald Scarfe • Albert Schweitzer
George Bernard Shaw • Isaac Bashevis Singer • Patwant Singh • Edith Sitwell
Suzanne St Albans • Stevie Smith • C.P. Snow • Bengt Söderbergh
Vladimir Soloukhin • Natsume Soseki • Muriel Spark • Gertrude Stein • Bram Stoker
August Strindberg • Rabindranath Tagore • Tambimuttu • Elisabeth Russell Taylor
Emma Tennant • Anne Tibble • Roland Topor • Miloš Urban • Anne Valery
Peter Vansittart • José J. Veiga • Tarjei Vesaas • Noel Virtue • Max Weber
Edith Wharton • William Carlos Williams • Phyllis Willmott
G. Peter Winnington • Monique Wittig • A.B. Yehoshua • Marguerite Young
Fakhar Zaman • Alexander Zinoviev • Emile Zola

Peter Owen Publishers, 81 Ridge Road, London N8 9NP, UK
T + 44 (0)20 8350 1775 / F + 44 (0)20 8340 9488 / E info@peterowen.com
www.peterowen.com / @PeterOwenPubs
Independent publishers since 1951